THE IRISH TIMES

BOOK OF THE YEAR

2015

Edited by

Peter Murtagh

IRISH TIMES BOOKS

IRISH TIMES BOOKS
24-28 Tara Street, Dublin 2

First published by Irish Times Books 2015
© Irish Times Books
978 0 9070 1151 4

Cover design: Angelo McGrath. Layout: John Cassidy.
Irish Times Premedia.

Set in Adobe Caslon Pro
5 4 3 2 1
A CIP catalogue for this book is available from the British Library

Contents

Introduction

This year's Irish Times Book of The Year ends, as has become traditional, with Sean Moran's report of the All-Ireland Senior Football final, which was won by Dublin, something the Dubs hope no doubt will also become a tradition. However, two lengthy report preceding that, written by Michael Jansen, seek to capture some of the drama, struggle and heartbreak of the refugee migrants who left the Middle East en masse and struck out for a better life in central Europe.

The images that emerged from this extraordinary movement of people, Biblical in scale and still continuing at the time of going to press, were themselves also extraordinary, which is why several of them accompany Michael's fine writing. One in particular, that showing the body of three-year-old Aylan Kurdi washed up on Ali Hoca Point beach near Bodrum in Turkey, stopped people in their tracks, evoking in them a sense of sorrow and shame. The questions this drama asks of Europe have still not been answered, as the exodus continues and the cruel Balkan winter beckons. . .

In Ireland, a Spring general election beckons. The past 12 months have shown the degree to which a section of the electorate is giving vent to anger, a phenomenon that has done little to diminish the cynicism that some politicians, from across the whole political spectrum, bring to public affairs. It will be for another Book of the Year to record how this plays out.

The outstanding public affairs event in Ireland this year must surely have been the referendum giving popular approval to same sex marriage. Several writers who contributed to the Irish Times discussion on the issues raised grace these pages also, the most memorable, in my view, being the compelling personal story told by Ursula Halligan of TV3.

No anthology of reportage can capture all that has happened in the past 12 months but I hope that the writing of some, notably Roisin Ingle, Miriam Lord, Frank McNally, Paul Howard, Patrick Freyne and Conor Pope manage to amuse and entertain, amid all the other material drawn from colleagues writing about sport, politics, business and the arts.

This volume is the first yearbook to be produced in-house, as it were, and many thanks go to Michael Ruane and John Cassidy, and to Fergal Tobin also, for helping bring it all together.

Peter Murtagh
October 2015

Contributors

Paddy Agnew is Rome Correspondent

Dick Ahlstrom is Science Editor

Arthur Beesley is Economics Editor

Mary Boland is a freelance journalist specialising in foreign reporting

Brian Boyd is a freelance writer specialising in music and comedy

Tara Brady is a feature writer

Simon Carswell is Washington Correspondent

Peter Carvosso was a sub-editor with Independent newspapers

Donald Clarke is Irish Times Film Critic and a columnist

Tony Clayton-Lea is an arts and entertainment journalist, specialising in pop culture

Malachy Clerkin is a sports journalist

Stephen Collins is Political Editor

Clifford Coonan is Beijing Correspondent

Paul Cullen is Health Correspondent

Keith Duggan is a sports features writer

Paul Dunne is an amateur Irish golfer

Hilary Fannin is an Irish Times columnist

Diarmaid Ferriter is a historian and Irish Times columnist

Patrick Freyne is a feature writer

Fiona Gartland is a news reporter

Ciaran Hancock is Finance Correspondent

Mary Hannigan is a sports writer

Ursula Halligan is Political Editor at TV3

Michael Harding is an actor and Irish Times columnist

Mick Heaney is Irish Times radio critic and a general freelance writer

Mark Hennessy was until recently London Correspondent but is now News Editor

Kate Holmquist is an Irish Times features writer

Paul Howard is Frankenstein to the monster that is Ross O'Carroll-Kelly (qv)

Róisín Ingle is a columnist and features editor

Michael Jansen is a foreign correspondent and Middle East expert

Colm Keena is Public Affairs Correspondent

Fiach Kelly is a Political Correspondent

Karlin Lillington is a technology journalist and Irish Times columnist

Patrick Logue is Digital Editor and an Irish Times columnist

Miriam Lord is Irish Times parliamentary sketch writer

Suzanne Lynch is Brussels Correspondent

Ruadhan Mac Cormaic is Legal Affairs Correspondent

Una McCaffrey is a business and finance journalist

Patsy McGarry is Religious Affairs Correspondent

Ronan McGreevy is an Irish Times reporter

Frank McNally writes An Irishman's Diary

Deirdre McQuillan is Fashion Editor

Anthea McTiernan is an Irish Times reporter

Lara Marlowe is Paris Correspondent

Sean Moran is GAA Correspondent

Una Mullally is an Irish Times columnist

Carl O'Brien is Chief Reporter

Jennifer O'Connell retired this year as an Irish Times columnist

Brian O'Connor is Racing Correspondent

Ross O'Carroll-Kelly is the alter ego of Paul Howard (qv)

Barry O'Halloran is a business journalist

Fintan O'Toole is Literary Editor and an Irish Times columnist

Conor Pope is Consumer Affairs correspondent

Philip Reid is Golf Correspondent

Kathy Sheridan is a feature writer and an Irish Times columnist

Lorna Siggins is Marine Correspondent and Western Correspondent

Laura Slattery is a business journalist specialising in media and marketing

Denis Staunton is London Editor, having been Deputy Editor until recently

Gerry Thornley is Rugby Correspondent

Michael Viney writes Another Life, his observations of the natural world, as seen from his and his wife, Ethna's, home in western Mayo

Arminta Wallace is a feature writer

Noel Whelan is a barrister and Irish Times columnist

Paddy Woodworth is a freelance journalist specialising in ecology and the Basque country of northern Spain.

Photographers from the Irish Times: **Alan Betson, Cyril Byrne, Brenda Fitzsimons, Eric Luke, Dara Mac Donaill, Bryan O'Brien,** and Irish Times cartoonist **Martyn Turner,** and natural world writer and painter **Michael Viney**.

From other newspapers, agencies or freelance: Laszlo Balogh, Julien Behal, Chris Bellew, Allesandro Bianchi, Sam Boal, Abdeljalil Bounhar, Nick Bradshaw, Jonathan Brady, Patrick Browne, Ryan Byrne, Thubault Camus, Niall Carson, Gareth Chaney, Navesh Chitrakar, Felix Clay, James Connolly, Jemal Countess, Aidan Crawley, Eoghan Culligan, Nilufer Demir, Adrian Dennis, Veleriano di Domenico, Marko Djurica, Ivan Donoghue, Alexei Druzhinin, Laurent Dubrule, John Edelson, Donall Farmer, Leon Farrell, James Flynn, Leonhard Foeger, Emmanuel Foudrot, Brian Gallagher (artist), Sean Gallup, Nikolas Georgiou, Joe Giddens, Tommy Grealy, Sam Greenwood, Alexander Hassenstein, Sahlan Hayes, Lucas Jackson, Emma Jervis, Colin Keegan, Justin Kernoghan, Allen Kiely, Carsten Koall, Alan Landers, Francois Lenoir, Georgi Licovski, Peter Macdiarmid, Conor McCabe, Margaret McLaughlin, Stuart McNamara, Charles McQuillan, Guglielmo Mangiapane, Yui Mok, Brendan Moran, Cathal Noonan, Lexi Novitske, Jose Palazon, David Phillip, Charles Platiau, Sergey Ponomarev, Josh Reynolds, Crispin Rodwell, Gokhan Sahin, David Sexton, Michael Sheehan, Dan Sheridan, Bernadett Szabo, Morgan Treacy, Dylan Vaughan.

OCTOBER 2 2014

Taoiseach's contempt for the Seanad clear

Kathy Sheridan

There are times when Prof Morgan Kelly's dismissive description of this State as "tiny and boring" is annoyingly apt. Our political dramas are small and boring probably because they are so stupidly, self-destructively transparent. Like Coronation Street's stupid Jim McDonald robbing a bank without a balaclava.

So while endless airtime is sacrificed to fulminations over the McNulty fiasco, the would-be stroke that has reduced the Oireachtas to an orgiastic lather can be reduced to one small and boring fact: Enda Kenny's contempt for the Seanad. And what is more boringly predictable than that? He tried to abolish it a year ago. Could anyone be more transparent? The genie was well out of the bottle before yesterday's concession by Kenny that the Seanad seat targeted for a thoroughly humiliated John McNulty "should not be accepted in those circumstances", and no amount of breast-beating will squeeze it back inside. If Kenny had an atom of respect for the Seanad, McNulty would still be a fairly anonymous county council aspirant, running a store and dedicating himself to the pitiless regime endured by most prospective national election candidates. First, by serving as a community activist, schmoozing through selection meetings and on to the county council, before getting a party nomination for a general election.

But the Seanad precludes the need for all that. An important-sounding title, an office in Leinster House with "access", a pensionable salary well above the average industrial wage (for a part-time job) and – be still, my beating heart – free and safe parking in the heart of the capital. For life. Plus, they become media

catnip, a vital tool in the scheme to move to the big house next door. The assumption that none of the electors would look any deeper for McNulty's cultural credentials than a suspiciously recent elevation to the board of Imma says all we need to know about everyone involved.

On Monday's Morning Ireland, an academic who had campaigned for the Seanad's retention said the election system was "the elephant in the room". Really? In public, everyone murmurs that the system is insufferably elitist, and there is much talk of universal suffrage and votes for emigrants. It's worth recalling that just six of the 60 Seanad members are from the insufferably elite universities panels. The others are elected mainly by the lowly representatives of the plain people. It's also worth recalling that exactly a year ago this week, the plain people voted to retain the Seanad. Now, after all that Sturm und Drang, try this little experiment. Ask a few relatively informed people around you to name some Seanad members who have managed to penetrate their indifference. David Norris? Tick. Feargal Quinn? Tick. John Crown? Tick. Rónán Mullen? Tick. Ummm, getting harder now. Shane Ross? Nope. He made it into the big house next door. Katherine Zappone? Tick. Marie-Louise O'Donnell? Tick. The same names crop up repeatedly, and they all happen to hail from the universities panels and/or had public platforms anyway.

Of course there are thoughtful, patriotic people in the Seanad who value their own and the public's time and brain cells. The question is, looking at the overall calibre, how will universal suffrage solve that problem, to put it nicely? Michael D Higgins, for example, is now seen as the discerning choice of a national electorate of poets and visionaries. Frontline's role in his victory is conveniently forgotten.

So what kind of selection system will banish the layers of joy in this Seanad exchange from last January?

Jim D'Arcy (FG) : "I agree with the Minister that most parents and teachers are supportive of the need to overhaul the junior cycle for the good of students, but teachers have legitimate concerns. You cannot fly an aeroplane without a pilot."

1

David Norris (Ind): "You can with drones, and there are plenty of them in government."

D'Arcy: "That would be a bit of an omelette all right."

Norris: "A flying omelette."

Mary White (FF): "Drones are seriously destructive." What kind of magical reforms could produce a depoliticised upper house filled with patriotic people of ideas and relevance, wisdom and gravitas? People, crucially, with little or no regard for the perks of office or with a gimlet eye on the house next door?

Above all, why would such a distinguished individual propel herself into a type of Seanad X-Factor contest? The Fiscal Advisory Council might be a template of what the Seanad could be: a truly independent body with a brief, say, to assess how and whether the EU and Government are meeting certain objectives and to communicate that reality, honestly and accessibly, to the people. At least we could never again say we did not know.

A diver at Ballindinas, Barnstown, off the Wexford coast. One of the winning shots in the Love Your Coast photographic competition. Photograph: Ivan Donoghue

OCTOBER 15 2014

O'Shea a saviour of the century

Keith Duggan in Gelsenkirchen

Football is not immune to fairytales but even the Brothers Grimm might have raised eyebrows at the manner in which Ireland concocted one of those fables of defiance and last gasp heroics in Gelsenkirchen.

John O'Shea's name can be added to the roll call including Aldridge and Sheedy and Houghton and Keane, all scorers of Irish goals which tend to define entire epochs of Irish life. Maybe this was the night the recession finally died.

For on Budget night, on the night of his 100th cap, the popular Waterford veteran fired his third goal for Ireland. It came in the 94th minute, against the world champions and just when the German citizens watching on television across the nation had presumed it was business as usual from their cast of glittering stars. No. Not tonight. O'Shea stole the show in a manner that was truly fabulous.

"Ah, it was everything," beamed the Irish manager after leaving an exhilarated team in the dressing room. "He even had the captain's armband on at the time. Jeff Hendrick did really, really well to get the ball across. And we had a chance, funny enough, just before that with Wes. We just never gave up. We kept going. And I never felt we were out of the game."

That was the thing. This was a dauntless performance from the Irish team, who made good on their promise to ignore the memories of their last two previous, lacerating experiences at the hands of Germany. The statistics will show that the world champions lorded it on the football here. And they did. But they also struggled to break down a fiercely well organised and willing Irish collective.

For seventy minutes, Ireland had rigorously adhered to a plan which revolved around showing the Ruhr

John O'Shea (left) celebrates scoring Ireland's late equaliser against Germany. Photograph: Joe Giddens/Press Association

a thing or two about industriousness. Attitude was everything and from the first whistle James McClean, above all the Irishmen, signalled a flinty refusal to be intimidated by pre-match show of German superiority or by the company of Antonio Rüdiger. For most of the night, he had to scamper after lost causes but given half a chance to get his head to one of David Forde's many long clearances or to get up close and personal with the German back four, McClean was happy to take it. He clattered into the Toni Kroos late in the first half and shrugged at the Bayern man's protests. That spirit was evident throughout the field and rather than fade after Germany finally concocted a goal through an ambitious strike by Kroos, the Irish became emboldened.

"Well, it was a great point for us to come to the home of the world champions and get something out of the game," O'Neill said. "Obviously we had to stand a bit of pressure. The idea was to use the ball a bit when we had it in the first half. That was still very difficult. At half time we were okay. What is the point of losing the game if you can't go for it? That is what we did and there was always a chance that they would score a second goal. But they were fantastic."

Perhaps they did catch the Germans at a good time. There is no question that Jogi Löw's squad seem to be lukewarm about the prosaic business of qualifying for Europe after their transcendent heroics in Brazil last summer. Pockets of empty seats were notable in the stadium and just 51,204 fans showed up, almost 3,000 short of a full house. The old coal mining town is not one of the Ruhr's more prosperous enclaves but it was surprising that the world champions did not fill the theatre. And for all the sharp footwork and intricate passing movements, they weren't quite as crisp or dangerous as the visiting fans might have feared.

The preamble was an impressive and intimidating pageant of German football lore: the four huge gold stars bearing the gilded World Cup winning years of 1954, 1974, 1990 and 2014 on display as a reminder of the country's sustained tradition of excellence.

The home crowd came in the expectation of a show and the Germans were keen to provide it, seeking to unlock O'Neill's well-drilled defensive unit with a quick flick and run for Julian Draxler or Mario Götze or Thomas Müller to work magic with. But after half an hour, Erik Durm's instinctive thumped shot against Ireland's crossbar was all they really had to show for the patient approach work and complex attacks. And after half an hour, the German fans were silent, listening to the Irish corner of the ground belt out a raucous chorus of a Depeche Mode classic.

"Generally speaking it was to be expected that we would fall into this post World Cup hole," said Löw as the Irish sang on in the stadium.

" If you look at the players you can see in their eyes that they are a little bit knocked after the World Cup and then a short break and a short pre-season and some players need longer to get back to themselves. So there is a little bit missing still."

But as O'Neill respectfully pointed out, Ireland were missing regular starters too, including Séamus Coleman, "the best defender in Britain." This is a huge night in O'Neill's first campaign and leaves Ireland well placed after the first series of exchanges in Group D. They lived dangerously at times and relied on two excellent saves from David Forde, controlled and assured all night. Germany's goal came from a familiar source, a deftly driven strike from just outside the box by Toni Kroos but for whatever reason, the Irish defenders chose to back off the Bayern player as he looked for a gap. It was a rare moment of looseness and they paid dearly for it. All of Europe must have assumed it would be the usual story then; a plucky Irish loss in one of the great mansions of the continental game. Still, the visiting fans kept singing and O'Neill urged the players to press, to chase, to gamble. And then Hoolahan launched a ball from deep on the right wing and whoever Mats Hummel was expecting to materialise to meet Hendrick's returned cross, it definitely wasn't John O'Shea, who had made a rare venture into the enemy goal mouth. And it all ended happily . . .

A day rehearsing an opera for farters and drunks

Patrick Freyne

Rory Musgrave is making me yawn. He says that when you yawn, "the air goes in completely unimpeded and goes out completely unimpeded. That opens up everything, so you're getting the maximum capacity of your lungs and oxygen in your blood."

Musgrave is not a quack doctor, but a very fine opera singer. He recently featured in the Rape of Lucrece and is currently in the chorus of Silent Night, Kevin Puts's operatic take on the first World War Christmas armistice in which British and German soldiers played a game of football. "Like Paul McCartney's Pipes of Peace video," I say with excitement.

My tastes are significantly more lowbrow than Musgrave's, so I'm pleased that he, along with piano-playing répétiteur (director of rehearsals) Eithne Corrigan, have agreed to teach me how to sing an operatic aria in the lovely Wexford Opera House.

I love to sing. I was in a touring band and I studied music, but I know nothing about opera. Opera singing can seem strange to fans of contemporary pop or rock, but it evolved for a reason. Before PA systems, concert performers had to hold their own against musical ensembles. Musical combos were small in the days of Mozart, says Musgrave, but during the Romantic era they expanded "and the voices got bigger as the orchestras got bigger. [The style] developed to compete with the sound of an orchestra."

Opera singers have to be in complete control of their whole bodies, says Musgrave. "You're using your body, your head, all of the cavities, your breath control, everything; you're using that to resonate the song to create a performance and harmonics that just ping.

Baritone Rory Musgrave (right) does his best to tutor Patrick Freyne. Photograph: Patrick Browne.

We are our own amplifiers. That's fundamentally what it comes down to."

He likens opera performers to athletes. Not only do they have to sing pitch- perfectly, they also have to act and move at the same time. "You're expected to sing while fighting and crawling over rubble," he says. He mentions a scene from a production of Billy Budd in which opera star Simon Keenlyside sang while hanging with one arm from the stage rigging.

"I won't be doing that," I tell him firmly.

The song Musgrave and Corrigan are going to teach me is Der Vogelfänger bin ich Ja from Mozart's The Magic Flute. I will be singing the part of Papageno. After a scene in which a prince is saved from a serpent by the Queen of the Night's attendants, the stage directions introduce the character: "Papageno enters dressed as a bird. He describes his life as a bird-catcher, complaining he has no wife or girlfriend."

"The Magic Flute is about as lowbrow as opera gets," says Musgrave.

"Thanks for that," I say.

"I mean that in the best way," he says. "It's not grand opera quite in the same way as Giovanni or Figaro. People were paying their penny to see this and they were getting drunk and farting and chatting among each other as people were acting their heart out. This was vaudeville, circus clowning with singers."

It does sound right for me when he puts like that.

First we go through the verse line by line, ensuring I get the German pronunciation right. Then, we go through the melody. Eithne and Musgrave carefully correct my mistakes as we go.

It's good fun, but I don't sound remotely as sonorous as Musgrave. It's all to do with breathing and relaxation, he says, and that big, powerful sound only comes with practice and time. He gets me to do a big yawn and a stretch. It hurts. "It's probably not good that that hurts," I say. He laughs.

We do more stretching. He gets me to stand more imposingly with my legs apart. "That's the 'noble posture'," he says. "This way you can be relaxed and the weight can balance over both legs."

He gets me to stand behind him holding his ribs so I can feel how it expands as he breathes. Later he does the same to me. "It's a bit like in the film Titanic," I say, and put my arms out like Kate Winslet.

"It's a very intensely focused relaxation," he says of opera singing. Then he laughs. "Singing is riddled with contradiction."

We chat about how classic rock singers aren't intensely relaxed but coiled and tense. "That's part of the aesthetic of rock singing," says Musgrave. "The charm is that raw, untempered energy and sometimes aggression, that very visceral thing that training would perhaps stifle."

Singers of popular music, he says, tend to sing like they speak. In contrast, "nobody goes around talking like this all the time". He does what sounds like an impression of Brian Blessed.

To help my breathing and projection, he gets me to sing the first few syllables of the song while simultaneously conjuring up a yawn. "Der Vogel," I say, sounding like a man yawning ("Der Vogel" means "the bird").

"Der Vogel," he repeats operatically.

"Der Vogel," I say again, still sounding like a man yawn-talking.

Then I repeatedly sing the verse, and Corrigan and Musgrave chip in with adjustments and observations. They're very patient and sweet. Corrigan asks me if I'm nervous about singing opera in front of opera professionals. I don't tell her that in the past year I've learned the harp, dressed as a clown and walked down O'Connell Street dressed as St Patrick. I no longer have any shame.

Their advice is really good. Musgrave tells me to hold the score up in front of me because "it will make you stand straighter". Corrigan tells me to pick a point on the wall and focus on it. At one point she gets out the English translation because I'm singing what should be an upbeat song rather mournfully.

I read the text. It turns out that Papageno really, really wants a girlfriend. In the second verse he says he wants a net for catching girls. Then "all the girls would be mine", he declares.

"He's basically a sex pest," I say.

Musgrave points out that Papageno would trade all these hypothetical imprisoned women for the one woman who loves him.

I suppose they were different times, I think.

It's now nearly time for a performance. An audience of eight theatre professionals are ready to come in and see my progress.

"Don't look down until I've finished playing," says Corrigan. "And don't move a muscle until they applaud."

I introduce myself, sing my song and enjoy myself. I am not run out of town.

"So, could I be an opera singer?" I ask Musgrave after the audience leaves.

"With another 10, 15 years of solid investment, definitely," says Musgrave. I'm a bit disappointed by this timescale. "It [takes] years of dedication to really understand and build in all the elements that make an opera singer," he explains.

On the other hand, he observes that "big beardy baritones" often find career success late in life thanks to a surfeit of roles for kings, priests and fathers. "But if they think they'll take up opera singing at 39-40 and become the next Pavarotti, it's very unlikely."

"Challenge accepted," I say, and vow to quit my job.

"We'll meet up in 10 years' time and see how you're doing," says Musgrave.

Patrick Freyne on video: http://bcove.me/uvcwjnnd

Russian President Vladimir Putin (left) and Serbian President Tomislav Nikolic at a military parade in Belgrade to mark 70 years since the city's liberation by the Red Army in October 16, 2014.
Photograph: Marko Djurica/Reuters

OCTOBER 20TH 2014

'I'm not the world's most perfect person'

Tony Clayton-Lea

He could talk the hind legs off a herd of donkeys. Verbose, opinionated, defensive, outspoken, amusing, smart, allergic to humility, a man as eager to play to the gallery as to bow to no one, John Lydon is the owner of one huge ego and an occasionally impressive reputation.

You know the backstory by now, of course, but a concise refresher is no harm: in 1976/77, under the soubriquet of Johnny Rotten, Lydon fronted the Sex Pistols. The band's debut (and only studio) album, Never Mind the Bollocks, Here's the Sex Pistols, has never, since 1978, been out of the Best Albums of All Time lists, while their first four singles (Anarchy in the UK, God Save the Queen, Pretty Vacant, Holidays in the Sun) are regarded by some as the best sequential quartet of singles ever released.

Over the years, Lydon has done his best to stick to punk rock's early principles of integrity and individualism. For some years, however – particularly when seen on television, either being interviewed or during his time on reality-based programmes – there has been a creeping sense of caricature undermining the honesty. For every passionate putdown ("religion is the last gasp of the stupid person"), there is a gurning face; for every strongly held belief ("when I was a child I was determined to think for myself – that was considered a flaw by people in authority"), there is a vowel-curdling retort worthy of Kenneth Williams. Oh, what a carry-on.

Plugging a new autobiography (Anger Is an Energy: My Life Uncensored), Lydon is full of the joys, greeting me in a cod-Irish accent. The book fills in the gaps that his previous autobiography, Rotten: No Irish, No Blacks, No Dogs (Hodder & Stoughton, 1993), left wide open, notably his pre-Sex Pistols days, while also going over old ground with a fully-toothed rake. From the get-go, Lydon wants to

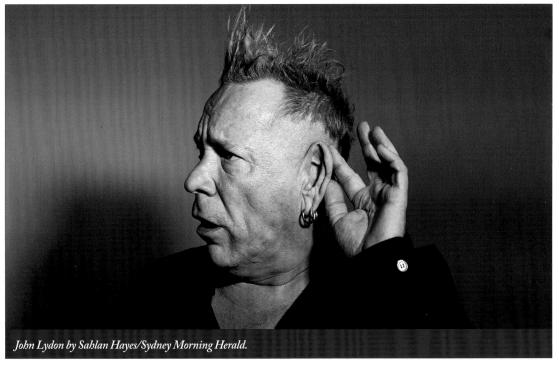

John Lydon by Sahlan Hayes/Sydney Morning Herald.

Dominic Ryan of Leinster evades Wasps defenders to score a try in the European Rugby Champions Cup, round 1, at the RDS Arena in Dublin. Photograph: Morgan Treacy/Inpho

forcefully stamp his credentials. The book has a pithy, almost declamatory dedication – "integrity" – a word that has been a credo for him across the decades.

"It's something I strive towards," he says. "I'm not the world's most perfect person – far from it – but it's a work in progress."

But there have been times, surely, when he has lacked the kind of integrity he espouses for himself and expects from others? "There probably have been, but none come to mind." Cue vowel strangulation, stage left. "Isn't that strange?"

The chapters on his early life in London, as the son of John Christopher Lydon, from Galway, and Eileen Barry, from Carrigrohane, Co Cork, are fascinating glimpses into the formation of a troublesome persona, and Lydon doesn't necessarily thank his parents for it. "I was raised by my parents to go through the school of hard knocks without self-pity," he admits. In the book's opening pages he writes, "I can't thank my family for giving me a career, because I did that to myself, but I can thank them for standing by me".

It helps the flow of conversation that Lydon has a refreshingly brusque sense of self, yet when he says things such as "no religion will tolerate opinion"; "collecting money just for the sake of it has never appealed to me"; and "I've made my own place by not pretending to be anything other than what I am", he teeters precariously on a thin line between cliche and truth.

Further doubt arrives when we bring up the topic of Lydon being offered the part of King Herod in Andrew Lloyd Webber and Tim Rice's Jesus Christ Superstar. He accepted the role, and the production was due to tour North America several months ago but was cancelled only days prior to the start date. "That would have been a terrific challenge," says Lydon, not altogether convincingly.

I ask what he thinks the 18-year-old John Lydon would say about his 58-year-old self appearing in an Andrew Lloyd Webber musical. "I would have sneered at the idea, but, you know, if somebody had challenged me to do it, I would have done it."

Really? A trace of annoyance raises its carrot-topped head. "Yes, really. Me tra-la-la-ing in a musical would have been great. I had to leave the Johnny Rotten ego, and everything I thought I knew about performing, at the stage door every morning. Learning dance steps; I've always liked to be challenged like that."

Even within the remit of a Lloyd Webber musical? "I'm very much into taking myself into areas I'm uncomfortable with." This is said quite defensively. "I'm constantly attacking my ego in that way."

Some musicians of a certain age lose sight of what inspired them to be great in the first place, don't they? More defensiveness. "The problem is that many people are surrounded by sycophants, and they grow accustomed to nobody saying no to them."

Do you surround yourself with people who say no when they need to? "All of my life, starting with my family, and that wasn't through choice. I have a handful of friends that will not allow me to run away with my big, bad self."

Lydon talks a sturdy talk, let it be said, but there's an undeniable swish of whitewashing when I ask what he makes of the U2/Apple business. "I don't know what to make of it. I don't know what that's all about."

What, then, does he think about Apple giving away the U2 album for nothing, and U2 being part of the company's $100 million marketing spend? If a telephone line can fume, then it is indeed fuming. "Fine. They can afford it. Well done." Does he think it's a compromise too far for U2? Cue a further series of clipped sentences. "I don't know what it is. I have no idea. I haven't really thought about it. It doesn't interest me."

This is nonsense. Not having an opinion on an issue such as this is one thing, but Lydon claiming that he, a veteran working musician, hasn't thought about it, and that it doesn't interest him, is ridiculous. Ever get the feeling you've been cheated? Well, perhaps not that, but certainly disheartened that he chooses not to engage with certain topics for no apparent reason. What does he think he'd have ended up as if he hadn't gone into music? This answer, at least, is impossible to argue with. "A huge bag of trouble for someone, but mostly myself."

OCTOBER 23RD 2014

This was not Leaders' Questions as we know it

Miriam Lord

Not so long ago, in a troubled place they called the Six County Statelet, decent IRA volunteers indiscriminately murdered in a futile attempt to unite the country they love. But their hearts were in the right place. And that's good enough for Gerry Adams, who is sad to see their revered names being sullied now by people who don't understand.

These IRA volunteers had so much love for Ireland they shunted their favoured perverts and paedophiles across the North's border to the rest of the country they claim to love. Oh, and they shot the ones they didn't need to protect.

Decent people. Adams – the IRA's Boswell – says he wasn't a member, yet is remarkably intimate with the organisation's inner workings; he won't hear a bad word uttered against them. As he said yesterday, these volunteers "were acting, in my opinion, in good faith" when seeking "to deal with some cases of abuse when asked to do so by families and victims".

Good faith is not how Maíria Cahill would see it. Yesterday's extraordinary session of Leaders' Questions took place right after the Taoiseach met the Belfast woman who says she was raped by an IRA man and then sworn to secrecy by senior members of that organisation who took it upon themselves to "interrogate" her over a number of months to test the validity of her claims. At one point, three of them also forced her to meet her rapist during a "kangaroo court". She says she met Gerry Adams in his office in west Belfast and told him her story. Adams, his deputy leader Mary Lou McDonald and the rest of the Sinn Féin parliamentary party accept that she was raped, but not the rest of her testimony.

Maíria Cahill hasn't deviated one bit from her version of events. The Gerry Adams/Sinn Féin version has subtly shifted from almost blanket denial to a revised state of knowledge.

Both Enda Kenny and Micheál Martin wanted to hear specific answers from Gerry Adams yesterday to questions posed by Cahill. What they got was generalised remorse and a scripted reply on doing the right thing by abused women and children, interspersed with pinpoint indignation over the wrongs being done to decent members of Sinn Féin.

When you read back over the short transcript of yesterday's extraordinary Dáil exchanges involving Enda Kenny, Micheál Martin and Gerry Adams, the words on their own go nowhere near conveying the electrifying atmosphere in the chamber.

The Taoiseach and the Fianna Fáil leader were in agreement over the need to investigate how, as Micheál Martin put it, "the most powerful men within the IRA interrogated victims of abuse at the hands of leading members of the IRA".

The Dáil did not accept the excuses of leading churchmen over their handling of abuse cases, he said, pointing out that Sinn Féin politicians were to the fore in condemning the Catholic Church when stories emerged of cover-ups over child sex abuse.

He read some of the trenchant comments made at the time by the likes of Martin McGuinness and Mary Lou McDonald.

The Taoiseach described Maíria Cahill as "a courageous, confident, brave young woman" who "overcame the horror of being raped to face down the IRA and its generals, secret or otherwise".

This was not Leaders' Questions as we know it. It was an unprecedented situation in the Dáil chamber, with the leaders of the two main parties challenging the leader of one of the biggest parties on the Irish political scene.

And they wanted to know why Gerry Adams and Sinn Féin should feel entitled not to be examined in the same way that the Church and other bodies were investigated when it emerged they ignored cases of abuse to protect their institutional reputations.

Gerry Adams was surrounded by his colleagues , with

IRA sexual abuse survivor Mairia Cahill at Leinster House where on October 22nd the Dail debated her treatment and Sinn Fein's response. Photograph: Gareth Chaney/Collins

Martyn Turner's take on Gerry Adams' response to Maíria Cahill's allegations about Sinn Fein and the IRA

Mary Lou McDonald to his left. And they looked rattled.

When Enda Kenny questioned her "blind allegiance" to her leader, she slowly shook her head. As the session unwound and Adams rose to defend himself, his party, the IRA and "republicans" in general, you could almost feel the anger and resentment radiating from their ranks.

Adams sounded hurt and outraged almost to the point of becoming emotional.

To shouts of "shame" from around the chamber, he said the Taoiseach had "cast a slur on thousands of decent Irish republicans". "Republicans are no different to any other Irish citizens," he added

But as he read his script and issued an all-encompassing apology for any wrongs that might have been done by IRA members (who apparently were only trying to do the decent thing by responding to requests for help from ordinary people), the look

of silent disgust on the faces of most of the non-Sinn Féin TDs told its own story.

And, of course, times were different during the war. (Maíria Cahill's ordeal happened in 1997.)

"I have set out the circumstances in the North when there was no democratic civic policing service" explained Adams. What is needed now is a "victim-centred approach."

Some of comments were treated with outright derision, like when he declared: "I refute the allegations that have been made about me and about other Sinn Féin members who assure me that all they did in their engagements, conversations and work with Maíria Cahill . . ."

"Work? Ha!" snorted Fianna Fáil's Michael McGrath. But Sinn Féin – including their young political stars who are too young to know – were fuming, in full post-Vietnam vet mode. They just stopped short of shouting . "It was a war, man! You weren't there!"

11

Most of the TDs in the chamber had read of Gerry's blog – in between teddy bear tweets and the like – at the weekend.

Here's a sample: "But these actions were of their time and reflected not only a community at war but also an attitude within Ireland which did not then understand or know as we now do, how deeply embedded abuse is in our society . . . as society became better informed as to the issue and handling of abuse, republicans began to develop victim-centred approaches."

And we were transported back to other difficult days, in wood-panelled rooms in big parochial houses, when troubleshooting bishops spoke of different times and how nobody really knew about abuse and now that they do, they are really, really sorry.

As for those simple questions for Adams, put to him by the Taoiseach in the Dáil, there were no straight answers. In fact, the Sinn Féin leader insisted he had already "refuted" them. Refute means to prove – he offered little proof.

And what about the alleged abusers moved south of the Border, or "sent to another parish", as Micheál Martin observed? "I don't know" he said. All he knows is that decent volunteers have been done down by "sleeveen" Enda Kenny and Micheál Martin.

And them pure as the driven truck . . . laden with explosives with an innocent man chained to the steering wheel.

OCTOBER 25TH 2014

I'm pretty content with nothing going on in my brain'

Mick Heaney

Richard Ford by Dara MacDonaill.

As with all good comebacks, Frank Bascombe was never supposed to return. Since his first appearance, in The Sportswriter, Richard Ford's 1986 novel, the laconic Everyman had been the American writer's most memorable fictional creation. But such was the strain of completing The Lay of the Land, the third volume chronicling the tribulations of his character, that in 2006 Ford decided he was done with Frank.

"It made me sick," Ford says. "I had all kinds of somatic and psychosomatic maladies, so I thought, I just don't want to do this anymore." And so it came to pass. Ford recharged his batteries and wrote another novel, Canada, far removed in tone and content from the Bascombe trilogy.

But Frank wouldn't go away. As Ford toured the US to promote Canada, readers constantly asked him to reconsider his decision not to write about the character again, requests that "struck a tender note" with the writer. The clincher came not long afterwards, when, in the devastating aftermath of Hurricane Sandy, Ford visited the New Jersey Shore area, site of the Bascombe books.

"Driving back, I was full of lines, and the lines were all in Frank Bascombe's voice," Ford says. "And I thought, Oh shit, I don't know what to do about this, because I don't want to write another long novel. So I had this idea of writing novellas. Because to be given a voice that is already plausible, and supple enough to hold all the things that you're capable of putting into a book, is such a plus. It's what people like me are all about. So I thought, Don't run away from what seems to be your destiny."

So, eight years after Ford retired Bascombe, he has brought him back for a new volume, Let Me Be Frank With You. A collection of four linked stories, it follows the now retired realtor as he deals with prosaic events in the weeks after Hurricane Sandy has demolished much of his home state. Along the way he encounters his terminally ill ex-wife, a dying friend and a genial visitor with a terrible past, all the while trying to avoid any more emotional entanglement than is necessary.

As the studiously flippant title suggests, it is not a work that groans under a sense of its own earnestness. "Most of the things in the book I play for some kind of joke," the 70-year-old author says, as he sips coffee in his rooms at Trinity College Dublin, where he regularly stays in his capacity as a professor of creative writing. Sure enough, the book is very funny, full of drily barbed observations on contemporary life and mores. For all the recurrent themes of mortality and the general fragility of life, the stories have none

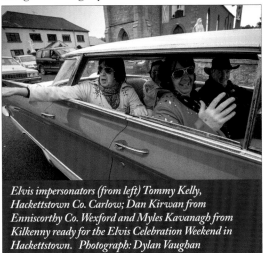

Elvis impersonators (from left) Tommy Kelly, Hackettstown Co. Carlow; Dan Kirwan from Enniscorthy Co. Wexford and Myles Kavanagh from Kilkenny ready for the Elvis Celebration Weekend in Hackettstown. Photograph: Dylan Vaughan

of the fulminating rage at the notion of dying that marks, say, the similarly premised work of Philip Roth. "It's something to be made fun of, at best, and to have a yuck with," he says. "I mean, Roth is entitled to his view, and he makes a lot of it, but I don't look at death that way."

Ford seems to approach most aspects of his work with this determinedly untortured attitude. Taken together, the four Bascombe books constitute a contemporaneous chronicle of US life over the past 30 years, at once intimate and epic, à la John Updike's Rabbit novels. But Ford downplays this element. Aside from The Lay of the Land, which sought to mirror the complacency of the United States before 9/11, "they're about this guy who does these things." He portrays writing the new stories as a comparative doddle. "I was happy to have something to do, because I hadn't really thought of anything else."

On the face of things, Ford has lived his life with a similarly pared-down lack of dramatics, characterising himself as "a little middle-class kid from Mississippi". He has always sought a settled existence with his wife, Kristina, whom he met when he was 19. "I've structured my life to avoid certain kinds of things that I saw happening around me when we were kids, children being one, alcoholism being another, poverty another. We've been very compact in how we've conducted life."

It all sounds very ordered. But at the heart of this streamlined self-sufficiency lies a life-wrenching event: the death of his father, from a heart attack, when Ford was still a teenager. "It certainly informed my belief that around 16 years old something flips," he says. "There's a way in which I think about myself, that I probably wrote books into the vacuum that my father's death created. Somewhat compensatory. It certainly made me understand that something can happen and everything changes, you never see the world the same way again."

One thing that Ford soon viewed differently was the racially segregated society of his youth. He grew up accepting the institutionalised racism of the American South – "I was a go-along person, in a bad way" – but that changed in the early 1960s. "By the time I was 17 I realised that what I had been trying to matriculate into was a morally corrupted system, and I tried to extricate myself from that. And I did, because I knew race inequality was wrong. I came to it really slowly. There was nothing heroic about it. I just figured it out and left."

The underlying notion of a life shaped by circumstances is a common thread whenever Ford talks about his past. He portrays even his decision to become a writer in a reactive frame, as a consequence of his having "failed" at his original career goals: to be a US marine officer and an attorney.

"I was 23 when I sat down in my mother's house, in January 1968, and for the first time I probably did something independent. I thought, What have I ever done that I enjoyed doing and that I haven't failed at already? It wasn't that I really enjoyed writing that much, but it felt like a little free zone that I could maybe wander into."

Success did not readily follow. It was the 1980s before he found his readership, first through his association with the "dirty realist" school of American writers, such as his close friend the late Raymond Carver, then with the publication of The Sportswriter. Even now Ford can sound almost suspicious of the path he took: "I'm unwilling to say any books are hard to write, because there are so many people in the world who do things that are useful and really hard."

Even still, he knows the value of his vocation, approaching his work with serious intent. The new book may have a humorous surface, but it is suffused with awareness of the United States' racial fault lines. "I want to be a white guy who writes about race – though it doesn't get me anywhere, it has to be said." Does he think this is because, as a white male of a certain age, he is seen to be unqualified to talk on such issues? "That's exactly why I would do it. To jangle the

People silhouetted on the top of a hill close to the border line between Turkey and Syria near the Mursitpinar crossing as they watch the US led airstrikes against ISIS positions in on the Syrian town of Kobani. Photograph: Gokhan Sahin/Getty Images

Would-be migrants sit atop a frontier fence dividing Morocco from the Spanish enclave of Melilla where golfers play.
Photograph: Jose Palazon/Reuters

bars on my cage a little bit. But it doesn't work."

It remains tempting to draw parallels between Ford and his most famous character. In the new book Frank muses on his "default self", the idea that we are shaped by what happens to us rather than by any inner core. Ford resists the idea that his writing yields greater self-consciousness. "I've given up on that. Perhaps it's that my own 'is', if I could be said to have one, is so unsatisfactory that I just gave up on the whole notion of it. I was brought up a Christian and steeped in the kind of American literature that says that human beings have what Emerson calls a mass. I never found it.

"So I've come to the conclusion that I'm just a composition of stuff put together, and it never completely makes a whole middle that you'd call a mass or a soul. It doesn't make me pessimistic about human beings or mean I don't hold people accountable, because I do. But I grew up around people who were always talking about other people's character. But it was a racist environment, so it was corrupted right from the start. If we have good character, why are we excluding all these other human beings? All of those things you get taught about people's interiority, they were all compromised for me at a very early date."

Ford, again like Frank, has little time for the idea that life has some kind of inherent trajectory. "In my case what's made it cohesive is my wife; that's what really has made life be life." But he is cheery in his slightly fatalistic outlook. He may be conscious of having a finite amount of time left – "My high-school friends are dying right and left" – but feels little pressing need to write furiously, with no plans for new novels in the offing. "I'm pretty content with nothing going on in my brain."

Of course, as the deceptively funny, magnificently realised latest chapter in the Frank Bascombe saga proves, Ford's commitment to writing is profound.

15

"If you take writing seriously, it's a very high calling. There's never any doubt about the fact that you're doing something that Chekhov did. All you have to do is work at it really hard." He is, in the end, a writer, not a tortured artist.

"I'm real good at going on, at putting both good and bad things behind me. My mother said to me on her deathbed – and I was fortunate enough to have this conversation – she said, 'Richard, of all the things in the world you must do, you must be happy.' And I took her seriously. All the things that have threatened to make me critically unhappy, I'd get away from them."

OCTOBER 28TH 2014

For the most part of any day I live a bewildered life

Michael Harding

I asked a monk one time what his best advice was for a happy life. He looked me in the eye and said, "Be here now".

He didn't have much English, so I went to a philosopher and asked him what it means to be or not to be. The philosopher said that the crucial point to understand is that existence is not a private matter. It's an attempt at conversation with "the other". But I didn't understand what he meant by "the other". So I went to a musician. And the musician couldn't tell me anything. All the musician could do was play music. And thus for the most part of any day I live a bewildered life.

Despite rumours to the contrary, I'm useless on the flute. It's something I do alone, and it's cheaper than therapy, but at least it's a way of being in the present moment. I send jigs and reels out like signals into the empty universe. Sometimes the tunes I play feel like they were always there in the emptiness.

I have a friend with long, black hair and a precious fiddle, and he comes to the house occasionally, up through the fog. He steps into the room and opens up the fiddle case and takes the instrument from the blue silk scarf he always wraps around it. He leans his chin on the fiddle so that his long hair falls over his cheeks, and then he pulls the bow across the low strings, bleeding a deep sound out of them, like a shaman opening a door to the other world. Between tunes he sits lazily waiting for more tunes to come in. Each time a tune lands on his fingertips, I realise that music induces in me a clarity of thought far beyond the fog of religion or philosophy.

One night during the summer I was at a concert in Tyrone. There were men on the stage with banjos, accordions and guitars, and then a woman came on stage, like a lamb, and folded herself around a bodhrán. I thought for a moment she was going to fall asleep. But all of a sudden it was as if someone had plugged her in; as if electricity was running through her body. The song possessed her. It was her toes, curled up under the chair, that caught my attention, however.

In the old days, when I was eating chicken soup at the kitchen table in Cavan my mother would sometimes look at her bowl of broth and say, "This soup will go down to your toes".

It was a way of describing the effects of good soup. And I was thinking that maybe the songs were having the same effect on the singer, because as she sang her toes curled up and tapped the floor with a dainty but intense energy.

My mother never sang, but she danced well. She squeezed her exuberance for life out through her toes on to the floor of the town hall in Cavan, dancing with men who reminded her of Fred Astair; that was until my father came along and seduced her with so much romantic blather that she was blinded to the fact that he danced like a donkey.

Perhaps she still dances in some ballroom of bliss or whatever heavenly realm she was dissolved into. I know it's not fashionable to believe in heaven any more, but I could no more accept the dogmas of

Emma Chambers (left) and Ella McCarthy from London practicing for the Rince na hEireann All-Ireland Dancing Championships 2014 in City West, Dublin.   Photograph: Alan Betson

modernity than I could accept a life without music.
I was at her grave recently. I wanted to examine the headstone because I was thinking that it's about time I got her name engraved on the black marble. It's not easy to chisel out the hard facts of a death in stone; it seems too final.

But there's nothing like a graveyard for giving a man an appetite, and so on the way home I stopped for a roast beef dinner in a local hotel where the shambles of a wedding party was strewn all around the lobby, with young men in morning suits slumped on sofas, and girls in pink dresses smoking at the door. And in the corner of the lounge, my old friend with the precious fiddle was providing the music.

"So this is where you are today," I said, as he played a hornpipe.

"I'll come visit you soon," he promised, and I gazed at the blue silk scarf lying in the fiddle case on the floor, as if it were a cloth that had come down from heaven.

Michael Harding on video: http://bcove.me/muls1xal

OCTOBER 30TH 2014

Ireland's rich history in science deserves acclaim

Karlin Lillington

The island of Ireland might be known, to those wearing emerald-tinted glasses, as the land of saints and scholars, but isn't it curious that in the popular mind, the cultural achievements to which the phrase implies always seems to refer to writers?

I'm the last person who is going to argue against the significance of writers in Ireland. Though I started my own university studies in the United States intending to take a science degree, I ended up completing them in Dublin, with graduate degrees in Anglo-Irish literature.

But as I quickly learned when I first came here years ago, this is rich soil for producing extraordinary scientists over the centuries. Some have gradually grown in public visibility, such as deeply important figures such as Waterford's Robert Boyle, the 17th-century chemist sometimes termed the "Father of Chemistry".

A number are the names connected with some of the best-known scientific laws, constants and scientific scales – the ones dutifully memorised by generations of students. Boyle's Law, of course, and then there's Belfast's William Thomson, also known as Lord Kelvin, as in the temperature scale.

There are those who have been pivotal in the development of computing, such as 19th-century Trinity College professor of astronomy William Rowan Hamilton, whose discovery of quaternion equations underlie the special effects you see in film, television and computer games.

Or Donegal's Kay McNulty Mauchly Antonelli, one of the first computer programmers, who, along with five other women, did the top-secret programming in the US for ENIAC, the first general-purpose electronic digital computer used at the tail end of the second World War.

Ireland seems to have a particular affinity for producing or giving a home to people who go on to have a major impact in astronomy. Alongside Hamilton, Ireland can claim people such as William Parsons, the Third Earl of Rosse, who grew up at Birr Castle and in 1845 built the largest telescope in the world at the time in the grounds of the castle.

And more recently, Jocelyn Bell Burnell, from Lurgan, Co Armagh, who discovered pulsars.

A number of books, essays and exhibits have emerged over the past decade to broaden awareness of these Irish-born and Irish-based scientists.

But one who, for some reason, has remained relatively unknown in Ireland, North and South, is Belfast man John Bell. Born in 1928, and from a modest family background that would not have indicated his future scientific fame, Bell went to Belfast Technical High School because his family could not afford to send him to more prestigious schools.

But that was probably a good thing. A technical school and its practical focus likely suited him, and when he finished school he went to Queens University at 15 –not as a student, but a lab technician. However, his abilities there impressed lecturers, who loaned him books, and using his savings from his year of work, Bell entered Queens as a student the following year, graduating with highest honours in experimental physics three years later.

He went on to a stellar physics career at CERN, the physics research centre and laboratory in Geneva, where he was officially focused on particle physics but became one of the most important figures associated with quantum theory, along with well-known names such as Heisenberg, Schrödinger, Einstein and Bohr. But Bell has been credited with exploring quantum theory in the greatest depth. He is especially recognised for demonstrating that the abstract ideas put forward by people such as Einstein could actually be demonstrated by real-world experiments and understood in the physical world as we experience it. In particular, a famous paper he published in 1964 established ideas now known as Bell's Theorem, and equations known as Bell's Inequalities, which underlie quantum physics. Bell died in 1990, a major figure in physics but mostly unknown to the wider public.

The Royal Irish Academy, in partnership with a range of organisations – Queen's University of Belfast, Northern Ireland Science Park, W5, the Institute of Physics, the Titanic Quarter, Belfast City Hall, the Northern Ireland Assembly and the owners of old Belfast Met College – hope to change that and make Bell better known as a prominent name in Irish science, especially in Northern Ireland.

To that end, they would like to see November 4th of this year celebrated as John Bell Day. That date marks the 50th anniversary of the publication of his paper articulating Bell's Theorem. And a range of activities will take place starting from the fourth, to mark Bells' significance to physics, computing and research.

These include a lecture series at Queens, with far more to be announced on November 4th.

It's certainly time to give Bell the recognition he deserves.

NOVEMBER 1ST 2014

Badly behaved children don't deserve a place at the cafe table

Donald Clarke

Allow me to paraphrase Lionel Hutz in The Simpsons. I don't use the word "hero" lightly, but you, Jodie Morris, are the greatest hero in world history.

Morris, proprietor of the Little French Cafe in Broadmeadow, New South Wales, attracted headlines last week after posting a Facebook message warning parents of badly behaved children to stay away.

Oh dear. Furious opponents began blathering about an "attack on parents" as Morris found herself embroiled in a cause célèbre. She eventually took the post down, but claims the publicity caused a surge in trade. "Everyone's said: 'Oh you're going to lose so much business.' But we're the busiest we've ever been," she said.

Let us take a deep breath here. Morris was not banning all children from her café. She was merely banning those who run madly between tables, ram breadsticks up their noses and otherwise behave like miniature Visigoths at the first sacking of Rome. Of course, such people should be banned from restaurants.

Were I to smear tomato ketchup on my face while wailing in teary despair I would fully expect to be escorted to the door and forbidden from ever returning.

Children have enough advantages. They don't have to go to work. They are allowed to eat delicious liquidised fruit pulp. They are, on average, significantly further from death than the rest of us.

I suppose the bleeding-heart, PC mob won't allow us to forbid them from entering all eating establishments and places of entertainment. But it is, surely, not asking too much that they observe decorum in such spots.

This is how things used to be. On the rare occasions the young Donald was brought to restaurants he was expected to sit calmly and eat his chips in relative quiet. This did me no harm. Indeed, it helped form the reasonable human being who sits figuratively before you now.

It has become an accepted truth that the continuance of the human species is preferable to the apocalyptic alternative. Those of us who think otherwise remain in a fairly cosy minority. Therefore we must (I suppose) allow people to have children if they really insist. Nobody wants a repeat of that King Herod misunderstanding.

Does this mean that we are required to endure endless irritation in planes, trains and Antipodean French-themed cafés? As I understand it, no airline allows its passengers to operate cement mixers from their seats. Yet restless babies – somewhat messier and occasionally louder – are permitted on all flights and, it seems, must be placed next to the childless man with the least patience for infantile regurgitation.

Perhaps the best plan would be to institute a sort of benign apartheid. All couples with children could be confined . . . Sorry, no I don't mean "confined". Let me start again.

All couples with children could be, erm, housed in

securely constructed camps some distance from civilisation. Such facilities, profiting from economies of scale, could provide daytime childcare much more efficiently than is the case under the current regime.

Every day, both parents – or one – could journey from the stockade to the city beyond, carry out their work duties and, refreshed from eight hours in adult company, return home to their developing brood.

After 18 years in Happy Acres, the young people could be released . . . No, not "released". After 18 years in Happy Acres, the young people could be, erm, transported to a happier, quieter, less Fanta-soaked society than we currently endure.

The English upper classes have already experimented with a successful variation on this system.

Lord Bucket-Tucket is shown his son a few minutes after birth. Some four years later, he sees him again, just before the heir is dispatched to a windswept pile staffed by caring lunatics. From that point until the day he sets off to be decapitated in the Orange Free State there is no need for the future Lieutenant Bucket-Tucket to meet any adult outside the teaching profession.

What's wrong with that?

It won't wash, of course. There are downsides to our current indulgence of children.

Restaurants are a little noisier. Aeroplanes seem a little more like afternoon screenings of Harry Potter. Teenagers dare to call adults by their first name.

The upside to the decline in decorum is a greater confidence to question authority when it really needs to be questioned. Without wishing to deflate the facetious tone, we have, in recent years, all seen what happens when children feel unable to speak out about outrages perpetrated by priests, teachers and television personalities.

So, we'll ditch the otherwise impeccably thought-through scheme for generational apartheid. Life is, on average, better for kids than it ever was. It's probably better for adults too. But I'm still going to scowl whenever a highchair arrives at the neighbouring table.

NOVEMBER 3RD 2014

Saturday's water protest was like St Patrick's Day but minus the drink

Miriam Lord

There was a touch of St Patrick's Day about Saturday.

With the rain and parades and the fancy dress, but without the drink.

The bus was crowded going into town. People seemed in unusually high spirits for a damp and dull Saturday. Two women boarded wearing fluffy pink head-boppers.

Nobody seemed too bothered when the driver announced he was going to have to take a detour because of the protests.

Up ahead, the last few flags from a demo that started from the Five Lamps in Dublin's North Strand were up the road opposite Connolly Station.

There was a gallop for the doors.

"I hope yis'll all be going on the march now," laughed the driver to the departing passengers. "No to the water charges!"

And with that, they gave him a little cheer.

As it turned out, the Five Lamps protest wasn't up to much. There were, at most, a few dozen people taking part, most of them with Sinn Féin banners and posters.

Nonetheless, it attracted a good deal of media attention because it marked the return to the spotlight of the party's deputy leader. Mary Lou McDonald went uncharacteristically quiet in the embarrassing aftermath of the Maíria Cahill revelations.

But she gave a rousing address in Talbot Street outside the anonymous-looking offices of Irish Water, calling for the immediate abolition of charges.

"It's the right thing to do. It's the decent thing to do.

1. **de·cent** *adj.*
conforming with generally accepted standards of
respectable or moral behaviour

2. **in·de·cent** *adj.*
obscene. not conforming with general standards
of behaviour or propriety

Martyn Turner's take on Sinn Fein and the water protests.

Let us say with our voices that we're not having it."
Among the group were a number of men in hi-vis
jackets with "Vote Mary Lou McDonald" across the
back of them.

Also there was Peter Wall (70) from Summerhill in
the north inner city, with his homemade coffin and
resident skeleton. Peter is a paid-up member of the
Labour Party, but it doesn't stop him from wheeling
out his "RIP Fine Gael and Labour" corpse when he
feels the occasion demands it.

"He was outside Leinster House for the budget the
year before last. I'm just out of the hospital after
taking a stroke, but I don't agree with this tax."

Does the skeleton have a name?

"Yeah, Eamon Gilmore."

Back at Connolly Station, a much larger group was
massing. They intended marching up and down
Dublin's quays, finishing outside the GPO. A second
march from Heuston Station was also due to converge
on the rally in O'Connell Street.

Brenda Murtagh and Rona Pears travelled in on the
train from Leixlip to join the Connolly crowd. Rona
was dressed as a winged "water meter fairy" while
Brenda, gussied up as a giant leek, offered a play on
words with her "Irish Water leek".

"I have four children and these charges will be too
much. It's not like we don't pay enough already" said
Brenda. "It's getting to the stage that people won't be
able to afford to feed their children. I'm not paying."

Rona, who has two children and one grandchild, fears
that once the charges come in, they will continue to
rise.

She also has a worry about the security of individual
meters. "Anyone can open your meter if they want
and tamper with your water supply. They can put
poison in and it could be in your tap 30 seconds later.
It's on YouTube – have a look at it."

The two women said they had never been on a protest
march until the water charges arrived – Saturday was
their second. They were joined by a friend and her

homemade placard: "Off to jail I will go/before I pay for my H20."

It was difficult to gauge the number of people who turned out in Dublin. The crowd filing along the quays looked very impressive, but it seemed to have dwindled considerably by O'Connell Street.

The gathering was contained in the block between Henry Street and Abbey Street and it was relatively easy to walk around through the protesters.

But then, not everyone who attended a neighbourhood protest will have continued on into town. Government TDs will be well aware of this. The Right2Water umbrella group organised the local protests, while a different grouping that included Dublin Says No and The New Land League was behind the two city centre marches.

There was musical entertainment from a platform in front of the GPO. Two of the bands were called "Bravado" and "Manifesto." The MC tried to keep spirits up, leading a rousing chant of "Don't tax the Jacks!"

Bernie Gunning from Lusk, who was dressed as a shower, was getting a lot of attention for her outfit. She had a curtain rail around her neck with shower head spewing silvery tinsel rising above it. The curtain draped around her said: "Time to turn the tap off and shut this shower down."

This was Bernie's first protest. "I have two teenage children, my husband isn't working at the moment, I'm in a low paid job and I'm paying out enough as it is. I want my free water. I'm not paying for it to come through my tap and I shouldn't have to."

She has no time for the Government. "Get them out!" And who would she put in? "God only knows," says Bernie.

Apart from the strong Sinn Féin presence, the New Land League people were selling T-shirts and badges with the logo "Stop the sale of Ireland – water, oil and gas." Members of another group, The Hub Ireland, were wearing T-shirts with "No way we already pay" on the front and images of the men who died in the Easter Rising on the back above the message, "1916

– We died for your right to water."

The scenes in O'Connell Street were very different to what took place there last month, when tens of thousands of people took to the capital's main street to protest against the water charges. But the Government would be unwise to conclude that one small, overly political demonstration means that opposition to the changes and/or the way Irish Water has gone about introducing them is on the wane.

Because on a wet day, all over the country, people still got out and marched in protest.

And they are still angry.

NOVEMBER 6TH 2014

Dancing in the strasse before the Wall came tumbling down in '89

Denis Staunton

In August 1986, 25 years after the Berlin Wall was built and just three years before it came down, the West Berlin radio station I was working for sent me onto the Kurfürstendamm to do a vox pop. How many West Berliners thought the Wall would still be standing in another 25 years? After a couple of hours stopping passers-by, I couldn't find one who believed the Wall would be gone in their lifetime. I got the feeling that most of them wanted life inside their walled enclave to stay just the way it was, and I didn't blame them.

I had arrived in the city the previous year aged 24, with no money and few apparent prospects after an abandoned Classics degree and a short, forgettable career as a professional actor. I did have an introduction to a man called Peter Leonhardt Braun, the head of documentaries at Sender Freies Berlin, the city's public service broadcaster. He decided that the brief history of disappointment and underachievement that was my life thus far was so gripping a story that

Health minister Leo Varadkar at the Fighting Blindness' Retina Conference in Croke Park, Dublin.
Photograph: Conor McCabe.

it must be shared with the broader public. He would arrange for me to be interviewed on the radio and listeners would be so impressed that they would call up to offer me work and a place to live and I would be on my way. In fact, there was an English language station across the street, so why didn't I go over and see if they too would like to interview me about my extraordinary life?

I had my doubts, but as I made my way across the street they were pushed out of the way by the force of flattery and my growing sense that Herr Braun was probably right and I really did have an amazing story to tell. The English radio station manager listened quietly as I spun it out, enjoying the sound of my own voice all the more as it went on until I realised I was losing his attention and I finally stopped.

"Well we don't want to interview you, obviously," he said. "But I think we can offer you a job".

I enjoyed the serious-sounding title of Senior Reporter but my main function was to interview visiting celebrities (an elastic category, then as now) and to report on entertainment and nightlife, including a review of bars and nightclubs broadcast live from the location during the daily breakfast show. This meant that most of my life was lived at night within a West Berlin subculture that stayed out all night, every night.

After the Wall went up in 1961, most of West Berlin's big business and heavy industry, patriotic and civic-spirited as ever, fled to West Germany and many workers followed suit. To prevent further population decline, the government in Bonn poured massive subsidies into West Berlin, much of it into construction – and into the hands of corrupt public officials and developers. An enclave of western democracy and the free market system surrounded by communist East Germany, West Berlin was also a showcase for the western system.

Travel between West Germany and West Berlin was cumbersome, with just four transit roads through East Germany, which started and ended with intimidating border checks, limited air connections and rail

23

journeys interrupted by inspections by armed border police. Two measures in particular helped to make the city attractive to a certain kind of young German – the abolition of the Polizeistunde, or statutory closing time, for bars and clubs soon after the Wall went up and the exemption from military service for young Germans living in West Berlin.

Low rents, especially in the districts closest to the Wall, and the easy availability of part-time work meant that if you worked two or three nights a week in a bar, you earned enough to live modestly but comfortably. Even part-time staff in the more fashionable places could become celebrities and if they had an interesting look, minor cult figures. Bar staff not only drank free themselves but could offer their friends (and staff from other bars) free drinks all night so it sometimes seemed that nobody was paying for anything at all.

The lack of economic pressure and the sense of being cut off from the surrounding world encouraged creative experimentation, free from any ambition to be professional or successful. Groups like Die Tödliche Doris produced music, art and performances without any consideration for the financial value of the final product or critical approval. Art and nightlife in West Berlin were entangled, with many of the most interesting artists working in bars and clubs. Some opened their own places, such as Kumpelnest 3000, where the wonderful, deaf waiter Gunter Trube held sway – and chose the music. Exil, a Viennese restaurant in Kreuzberg, was run by the Austrian writer and critical theorist Oswald Wiener. And Anderes Ufer, the first openly gay venue in Germany to leave its door open and allow the guests inside to be seen through a window from the street, transformed its interior décor completely for a new exhibition every month.

Despite the perfect conditions for creativity, most of the idlers I knew in West Berlin were not producing any art, or even pretending to be. Most just focused on living, enjoying the freedom the city offered to make up life as you went along. This was especially true for

Rob Kearney of Ireland evades Jannie du Plessis of South Africa during his team's 29-15 win against the visitors at the Avia Stadium on November 8th 2014. Photograph: Cathal Noonan/Inpho

those of us who were gay, for many of whom West Berlin provided the first experience of living openly and happily as ourselves. Most Germans live in small towns of fewer than 100,000 people and West Berlin was full of young gay men from such places, which were still deeply conservative in the 1980's. Unlike its Anglo-Saxon equivalent, German gay culture remains rooted in its century-long history and each generation absorbs some of the cultural memories of its predecessors. So in the 1980s, when only a very special kind of young gay American still thrilled to the sound of Judy Garland or the Broadway musical theatre, every gay German in his 20s knew all the songs of Marlene Dietrich and Zarah Leander, to say nothing of the squealing 1970s Schlager of Marianne Rosenberg. You could spend all your time just being gay in West Berlin and many did, working in gay places, hanging out with gay friends and meeting an awful lot of gay strangers.

Germans living in West Berlin seldom visited East Berlin. You crossed on foot through Checkpoint Charlie or by the S Bahn railway through Friedrichstrasse Station, past grim, unsmiling border guards. The excitement was greater if you were carrying contraband, as I often was, usually in the form of books or music for people I knew in the East. The music of The Smiths was a particular favourite and I usually had a couple of cassettes of their mournful hits hidden somewhere on my way over.

Levi jeans and Dr Marten boots were also highly prized so one often crossed into the East wearing layers of clothes, to return later wearing some frayed replacements you had picked up over there. You had to be back in the West by midnight but there was usually time for a raucous session in one of the bars in Prenzlauer Berg, often ending in a deep, pointless conversation about politics. We usually agreed that both capitalism and state socialism had their pros and cons but we all knew without saying anything on which side of the Wall we'd prefer to be living.

I left West Berlin for London in 1988 and when I moved back two years later, it was gone, and so was my idle youth. The centre of Berlin shifted eastwards, Prenzlauer Berg and Mitte became the favoured districts for young Germans from the west and the old club scene of West Berlin was overtaken by vast new temples of Techno in the East.

The more dynamic of my West Berlin friends moved eastwards too and, a little older now, were happy to embrace the new opportunities to get rich and make a name for themselves. During the next 10 years that I lived in Berlin, always in the west of the city, I'd sometimes look around and ask myself where everyone had gone. Many of the expatriates left Berlin altogether, to return to New York or California or to find a new adventure somewhere else. But it took me a while to realise that many of the old faces from West Berlin's nightlife had vanished because they were dead.

Many parents learned that their sons, some still in their 20s, were gay the same day they heard they were dying. Many of those who stayed in Berlin to die are buried in a small cemetery in Schoeneberg, which I occasionally visit when I go back there. When I do, I think about the short, insubstantial, unremembered lives of so many who shone so brightly at night all those years ago and how, like West Berlin itself, it's now as if they'd never been there at all.

NOVEMBER 7TH 2014

Letters between Brian Lenihan and Trichet pivotal in Irish history

Arthur Beesley

The exchange of letters between the then president of the European Central Bank Jean-Claude Trichet and the late Brian Lenihan reveals the then finance minister came under extraordinary pressure to submit to the will of the European Central Bank (ECB) in the run-up to Ireland's bailout in the final weeks of 2010.

This was the culmination of a toxic confluence of events which led inexorably to a crippling loss of investor confidence in Ireland's ever-growing debt and, ultimately, to a humiliating international rescue by Europe and the IMF.

With that came the surrender of Irish economic sovereignty and the collapse of the Fianna Fáil-Green Party government.

By any standard, these were historic events.

So what exactly happened? And what do the letters tell us?

Two years previously, in the aftermath of the Lehman Brothers bankruptcy, the government administration had guaranteed the liabilities of the Irish banks. That fateful undertaking left the State in a perilous position as recession deepened, magnifying banking losses and driving the public finances further and further into disarray.

The banks became ever more reliant on emergency ECB support, intensifying concern in Europe and beyond that Ireland would not be able to survive the storm without external aid.

This is the essential backdrop to the exchange of correspondence between Lenihan and Trichet, the assertive Frenchman who had led the ECB since 2003.

Europe had spent the first half of 2010 in a funk over the collapse of the public finances in Greece, whose EU/IMF bailout followed months of discord and controversy. As summer turned to autumn, Ireland came to feel the heat of contagion in a big way.

Faced with ever-increasing pressure in September 2010, the government had already withdrawn from private debt markets. The objective was to cultivate investor confidence in time for a return to the markets in early 2011.

However, it did not work out that way. As the rescue bill for Anglo Irish Bank and other Irish lenders expanded beyond all expectation, investors took fright. The ECB started buying up Irish sovereign bonds in September, support which could be withdrawn at any

time because it called into question the ban on the central bank printing money for member states.

By the first week of October, the interest rate on Irish 10-year debt was already 6.5 per cent, a level that would be impossible to sustain.

Irreversible pressure was building, greatly increasing the strain on taoiseach Brian Cowen and all who served in his administration.

In the days before the first Trichet letter, on October 15th, Lenihan had a meeting with IMF officials at the fund's headquarters in Washington. Moreover, European Commission officials were also in Merrion Street examining plans for a four-year fiscal retrenchment, which would see the introduction of €6 billion in cuts and tax increases in the 2011 budget. In this letter, Trichet addressed Lenihan both as "Minister for Finance" and "Tánaiste", the latter in error as the post was then held by Mary Coughlan. With emergency ECB bank funding for Ireland rising rapidly, the two men had already spoken by phone. Trichet welcomed Dublin's moves to develop a stringent financial plan to fix the public finances over the course of the following four years.

Yet he was also highly concerned about the "extraordinarily" large provision of ECB funding for Ireland's banks in previous weeks. This brought the bank close to infringing its own rules against the printing of money for member states, a practice known as "monetary financing" in the parlance of economics.

Hence a warning from Trichet that such support could not be relied on in perpetuity and his demand that a four-year fiscal plan should be based on "cautious" growth forecasts and a strong programme of fiscal reforms.

"I would like to re-emphasise that the current large provision of liquidity by the Eurosystem and the Central Bank of Ireland to entities such as Anglo Irish Bank should not be taken for granted as a long-term solution ... The Governing Council cannot commit to maintaining the size of its funding to these institutions on a permanent basis," wrote Trichet.

"Future decisions by the Governing Council of the

Curtis, aged 7, from Crumlin in Dublin, at the unveiling by An Post of a new Christmas stamp in which she features dressed as an angel.   Photograph: Dara Mac Donaill

ECB regarding the terms of the liquidity provision to Irish banks will thus need to take into account appropriate progress in the area of fiscal consolidation, structural reforms and financial sector restructuring." This was a crucial point. The bailout may still have been weeks away, but Trichet was already laying down the principle that further aid would have to be matched by significant, ongoing efforts in Dublin to repair the public finances and put the banks on a sounder footing.

By the time Lenihan responded, on November 4th, the situation had worsened considerably. The immediate catalyst was a declaration on the structure of any future bailouts which was issued in Deauville, France, by German chancellor Angela Merkel and then French president Nicolas Sarkozy.

Unhappy that European taxpayers were on the hook for the Greek bailout, the "Merkozy" duo resolved that private creditors would have to make contributions to any further rescue of any other euro zone country.

The Deauville declaration spooked markets. Ireland was, by then, first in line in the danger zone.

Irish debt took an immediate hit, with the interest rate on 10-year bonds approaching 7 per cent. There was despair in Irish government circles, for the development meant it would be even more difficult for Dublin to succeed in its plan to make a smooth return to private debt markets at the start of 2011.

All of this weighed on Lenihan as he submitted his response to Trichet, with enclosures containing global and Irish media reports about the turmoil sparked by Deauville.

"You will no doubt have noted the very adverse developments in the markets in recent days in relation to the widening spread of Irish Government bonds against the German bund," the minister wrote. "This issue gives rise to very serious concerns for the Irish Government particularly in relation to the potential impact on the credibility of the very significant budgetary adjustments which we have developed working closely with the European authorities. I know that this concern is one that is strongly shared by you."

Citing the disruption on markets after Deauville,

Lenihan said already difficult market conditions were being worsened.

"I am sure that you will agree that it [is] imperative that comments particularly from senior political figures within the euro zone are consistent in their content and do not, as an unintended consequence, undermine the efforts of member states such as Ireland to address the serious difficulties that they are continuing to confront."

Lenihan had unveiled the €6 billion adjustment target for the 2011 budget on the day this letter was sent. That same day, Trichet publicly welcomed moves to frontload retrenchment in the four-year plan and said the overall endeavour was "not insufficient".

But the markets were unimpressed. The situation seemed to grow more uncertain by the day.

The public illustration of distress was the spike in bond yields. In private, Ireland's banks were drawing down more and more emergency ECB funds. In January, the ECB's exposure to domestic banks stood at €90 billion. By November, it stood at €140 billion. The ECB was increasingly anxious that this represented one quarter of its total lending, which it saw as an "unprecedented level of exposure" for a country such as Ireland.

After all, the State's share capital in the central bank was less than 1 per cent.

Hope seemed to be evaporating.

Within the ECB and the European Commission, officials privately concluded that Ireland would not be able to avoid a bailout. In Dublin Lenihan authorised tentative contact with the IMF. As the situation worsened, however, the finance minister wondered whether a specific rescue package for the banks might be possible.

Cowen wanted the ECB to buy up more Irish bonds, which it refused to do. For all the promises from Dublin to do the right thing in the four-year plan, the argument was advanced in the ECB's headquarters in Frankfurt that Ireland was not facing up to its problems.

Three points are relevant.

First, the European and global authorities were worried that a repeat of delays over the Greek rescue would result in contagion from Ireland to other weakened countries if a bailout was not quickly arranged.

Second, concern about the turmoil prompted by the Deauville declaration led to an intervention at a Group of 20 meeting in Seoul, South Korea, to dilute the commitment made by Merkel and Sarkozy.

Third, Anglo Irish Bank was now so enfeebled that there was even concern in the Obama administration that it might renege on financial obligations, triggering a new wave of instability in global markets. By mid-November, informal contacts were under way between Brussels, Berlin and other capitals about preparations for an Irish rescue. All of this was denied by the government, although steps were by then in train for that inevitability.

A delegation of top Irish officials travelled on Sunday, November 14th for secret talks in Brussels, an engagement which continued the following day. Increasingly, implausible denials from Cowen and other government figures merely heightened the sense of chaos in Dublin. The government believed it could maximise its hand in the negotiation by delaying the formal application for aid.

This did not go down well in the outside world.

Even after euro zone finance ministers gave a discreet mandate for "short and focused" preparations for a rescue plan, Irish banks suffered their biggest one-day loss of retail deposits on Wednesday, November 17th. The response was swift. Central Bank governor Patrick Honohan went on RTÉ radio early the next day to declare a rescue plan involving "tens of billions of euro" was in the works. As if to emphasise that the game was up, IMF mission chief to Ireland Ajai Chopra arrived in Dublin that very morning. A bailout could hardly be avoided at this point, yet still there was no formal application from the government. Trichet's second letter to Lenihan came the next day, Friday, November 19th.

Again addressing him as "Tánaiste", Trichet issued the now infamous threat that emergency ECB support for Ireland's banks was on the line. Not only that, but he made it clear that this was the position of the entire ECB governing council.

"It is only if we receive in writing a commitment from the Irish Government vis-à-vis the Eurosystem on the four following points that we can authorise further provisions of [emergency liquidity assistance] to Irish financial institutions," wrote the ECB chief.

The first, rather salient condition was the required formal request from Dublin for financial support. The other conditions centred on a continuation of the effort to repair the public finances and a reinforcement of the banks. The ECB chief also sought a guarantee from the State on the repayment to the central bank of emergency funds given to the Irish banks.

The threat to ECB support for the Irish banks greatly aggrieved Lenihan, Cowen and the rest of the government. While only two days passed before Lenihan confirmed the application would be made in a return letter to Trichet, the minister made no mention of his sense of betrayal by the ECB chief. The rescue programme under discussion would be both workable and effective, he said.

"I hope that this will provide some reassurance to the Governing Council and that you will be able to reiterate in a public way the continuing practical support of the ECB for the liquidity position of the Irish banks, to help reassure the market on this crucial point," Lenihan wrote.

"You know that we here will not be lacking in the will to do all that is necessary on our part to protect our economy and people and to play our role in the Eurosystem."

The point of no return had already been reached by the time Trichet issued his threat, but his intervention illustrates just how weakened the government was as it entered the formal negotiation.

Another week passed before the deal was ultimately done, but not before the ECB refused permission for the government to impose losses on senior bank bondholders.

The antagonism between Dublin and Frankfurt was all too clear.

NOVEMBER 17TH 2014

A day in the life at the State's immigration offices

Carl O'Brien

It begins shortly after 4am. Dressed in winter hats and wrapped in blankets, the first applicants arrive at the front door of the Irish Naturalisation and Immigration Service office on Dublin's Burgh Quay. Within an hour there are women with buggies and small children, men in suits, students with backpacks, all queuing silently for re-entry visas or identification cards.

The line snakes from the front door of the building, down Corn Exchange Place, along Poolbeg Street and back on to Hawkins Street, almost wrapping around the entire block. Many have snatched a few hours of sleep. Others, based outside Dublin, say they have slept on friends' sofas or waited overnight in McDonald's.

Lucas is one of them. He wraps his jacket around him to keep out the cold. It is dark and chilly – but at least it's not raining. He has been here for half an hour now and the queue keeps growing behind him. "I came here at 6am the last time and didn't get seen," Lucas says. "I was number 280 in the queue. I won't make that mistake again."

The system works like this: once you get inside, a case worker gives you a numbered ticket. There are only a limited number of these tickets each day. Lucas does a quick tot in his head: he reckons he's number 61 in the queue. He's hopeful that he'll get a ticket before they are all issued.

The queue starts to shuffle forwards at about 7.30am. Inside. there aren't enough seats to cater for the volume of people. A mother and her children are sitting on the floor in the corner of the room. Not far away, there's a couple trying to get some sleep, pressed

People queuing during the night on Dublin's Poolbeg Street waiting to enter the Garda National Immigration Bureau. Photograph: Cyril Byrne.

up against a window which faces out to the street. Privacy and dignity are in short supply here.

Some people who can't get out of work ask friends to queue for them for a ticket. Outside, an entrepreneurial woman walks among those still queuing, offering her ticket quietly for €50.

"It's soul-destroying," says Jonathan, the partner of a Brazilian who has been queueing. "You end up wasting countless hours during this pointless waiting game." Lucas, who has taken a day off his work at a local restaurant, tries to see the lighter side of it. "I know all about queues at home in Venezuela. We're experts at it – but this is bad, even by our standards."

A student at the Royal College of Surgeons says she can't get her head around why everyone has to show up in person. "Why do we have to renew our papers every year?" she asks. "Why not get a visa for the duration of my five-year course? Or get it stamped in a Garda stations. That's what happens in other countries."

Denise Charlton, chief executive of the Immigrant Council, says the queues are symptoms of an immigration system which is failing. New legislation has been promised repeatedly, but there is still

no sign of it. "Our system is very bureaucratic and discretionary. It's all over the place. If there was clear legislation and a proper framework, it would help."

A Department of Justice spokesman says immigrants are required to present in person, in common with many other jurisdictions. "This is necessary and unavoidable for establishment of identity and as an anti-fraud measure and is the practice of immigration services worldwide."

This is one of the busiest offices in the State, with some of the longest opening hours of any public service. "About 130,000 persons attend the Burgh Quay office each year, which presents ongoing logistical challenges," he says. While there have been "no unmanageable issues" with queues, the department spokesman adds that officials are anxious that queuing be reduced to an absolute minimum.

A spokesman for the Garda National Immigration Bureau says that due to large numbers of foreign nationals presenting at the office in recent weeks, it has recently opened the office on Saturdays.

In the meantime, Lucas has finally got his papers. It is early afternoon and about eight hours since he joined the queue. By now, his good humour had drained away. "It does make me angry. I'm a taxpayer, I work hard, but this isn't a fair way to be treated. I don't think Irish citizens would stand for it," he says.

Jonathan, one of the few Irish people standing in this queue, feels embarrassed by the treatment of visitors and residents. "Céad míle fáilte? Yeah, right," he says.

NOVEMBER 17TH 2014

Murphy's 'peaceful protest' damages water charge campaign

Carl O'Brien

The tens of thousands of people who turned out in peaceful protests across the State over recent weeks have much to be proud of. They appear to have forced the Government to backtrack on excessive water charges and drop invasive plans to use PPS numbers. They have exposed plans that could lead to the privatisation of water.

However, some of the protesters who assembled at Jobstown, Tallaght on Saturday have managed the impossible.

They have won public sympathy for Tánaiste Joan Burton at a time when the Government is floundering in a sea of ineptitude and controversy.

That's what happens when a mob calls the deputy leader of the State a "c**t", spits at her entourage, flings a range of missiles – including a brick – and attempts to overturn her car, all the while chanting "peaceful protest".

The setting was a graduation ceremony at An Cosán, a local community group that has provided second-chance education to thousands of people in the local areas for the past 25 years or more.

Graduates and their families had gathered to celebrate a considerable achievement. It should have been the proudest of days. But an air of menace, intimidation and mob rule overshadowed the event.

As graduates filed out of the building as part of their academic procession, the scene turned ugly as protesters swarmed around the Tánaiste and hemmed

An anti-water charges protester makes an obscene gesture at Tanaiste Joan Burton who was trapped in her car in Jobstown, Tallaght, by protesters who refused to allow her leave. Photograph: Crispin Rodwell

her and some of the graduates against a metal fence. Video footage shows Burton surrounded later by dozens of chanting protesters, who used placards to bang on the vehicle, and being struck in the face by an unidentified object.

Paul Murphy, the newly elected Socialist TD, can be seen in the crowd with a loudhailer leading the chanting.

His insistence yesterday on calling the event a "peaceful protest" – even in the face of extensive video footage which shows otherwise from some of the others present – has the Orwellian chill of doublespeak about it.

Murphy denies that protesters tried to overturn the ministerial car and said that a small number of young men, who were initially not involved in the anti-water charge protest, were responsible for eggs being thrown.

"All protesters behaved in a peaceful manner," he said. What he fails to recognise is the consequences if a mob descends into a frenzy.

In essence, Saturday's protest wasn't even about water charges. It was about which political grouping gets to take ownership of the opposition to the tax.

Murphy's election owes much to outflanking Sinn Féin on the water charges issue and highlights the fact that some of the party's TDs were going to pay the charges.

Sinn Féin responded by reversing its position and, last week, staging a sit-in protest in the Dáil.

The weekend's protest seemed to have upped the ante even further.

Murphy and his supporters should recognise that genuinely peaceful protest works. And that the vast majority of Irish people have no time for violence and intimidation.

Murphy's description of the protest as peaceful crossed a line at the weekend.

He damaged the very campaign that he is seeking to progress.

The fact that he can't even see that is even more disturbing.

NOVEMBER 22ND 2014

Coalition must stand its ground or face freefall

Stephen Collins

The priority for the Government parties, now that they have finally produced their solution to the water controversy, is to stop retreating in the face of protest and stand their ground against political opponents inside and outside the Dáil.

Since the beginning of the year the Coalition has been unnerved by one controversy after another. The scent of blood has encouraged an assault from all quarters that threatened to push it into the kind of freefall that overwhelmed the Fianna Fáil-Green Party coalition. While some basic mistakes were made in handling the water issue, the reason the Government lost control so completely was it conveyed an impression of weakness at every stage in the controversy. This was in stark contrast to the impression of competence allied to toughness it displayed during its first three years in office.

One Fine Gael TD remarked during the week that he got far more grief during the protests over the household charge in 2012 than he got over water, but people ultimately accepted the property tax because the Government never gave any sign of backing down. "What backbenchers can't live with is being told to go out and defend a policy only to see Ministers backing down when the protests get too hot. We have had to endure this on a few issues over the past year but we won't tolerate it again," he added.

The irony is that the wobbles began to develop just as the economic turnaround began to take hold and the tough decisions taken during the first three years of the Coalition's term began to bear fruit.

Fine Gael and Labour should have been able to capitalise on the economic recovery to provide a smooth run-in to the general election in around 12 months' time but, at this stage, the best they can hope

Newly appointed Garda Commissioner Nóirín O'Sullivan giving her first press conference at Garda Headquarters in the Phoenix Park. Photograph: Alan Betson

for is to minimise the damage the errors of the past year have done to their electoral prospects.

Alan Kelly, the new Minister for the Environment, has done a good job in bringing certainty to the water charges issue and other Ministers will need to do the same in their areas of responsibility. Mind you it is not only the Government parties that have suffered water damage. The Opposition parties and Independents have also discovered the pitfalls of a complex issue whose contours keep changing. Sinn Féin did a spectacular U-turn, with party leader Gerry Adams and most of his TDs initially saying they would pay the charges and then changing their minds when they calculated that the popular mood was running the other way.

It is common enough for Governments to do U-turns in the face of protest, but for an Opposition party to change its mind in such a short time is something quite unusual.

The Sinn Féin turnaround was prompted by the spectacle of the hard left appearing to outflank it, with TDs such as Paul Murphy, Ruth Coppinger and Richard Boyd Barrett saying they would not pay under any circumstances.

Emboldened by their success, the Trotskyites went too far last weekend with the disgraceful assault on Tánaiste Joan Burton in Jobstown and the encouragement of mob rule, which left her trapped in her car for more than two hours.

It was all orchestrated by newly elected TD Paul Murphy, who maintained afterwards that what had happened was a peaceful protest, despite the evidence of video footage which clearly showed Burton being struck in the face with an object before being trapped in her car and subjected to deeply unpleasant abuse.

Burton sought to play down the incident at the time, but its threatening quality was obvious for all to see on the television screens. Traumatic and all as the incident must have been for her, it was the first break the Coalition got since the beginning of the controversy.

Apart from its sheer nastiness, the incident at Jobstown focused attention on the lack of any coherent alternative policies being offered by those involved in encouraging protest.

When Wicklow Independent Stephen Donnelly intervened in the Dáil on Thursday in support of Paul Murphy, the Tánaiste could not resist remarking:

"This is the alliance of the Tea Party and Trotskyist. This is a new political party in Ireland."

So much of what passes for Opposition in the Dáil simply amounts to rejection of necessary taxation measures coupled with demands for unlimited extra spending on socially desirable objectives. It is also no accident that the variety of parties and individuals from far left to far right who, at the height of the crisis, advocated policies such as defaulting on debt and allowing banks collapse are to the forefront in opposing everything designed to get the economy back on an even keel.

The people who would have suffered most if there had been a financial collapse are those who depend on the State for welfare payments, pensions or salaries, but that is not something that bothered those who are now doing everything they can to make Ireland ungovernable.

There is clearly a constituency for crude anti-establishment politics in Ireland, just as there is across Europe where parties such as Ukip and the National Front in France are thriving. Over the next 12 months the Coalition parties will need to be far more assertive and coherent in explaining their policies to the electorate if they want voters to turn away from the temptations being offered by the peddlers of protest.

NOVEMBER 28TH 2014

Booze cruise: Conor Pope's winter wine shopping spree

Conor Pope

Going on a leisurely cruise to France in search of amazing wine that's being sold for a song seemed like a brilliant idea last summer, when the plan was hatched. But it's November now, and with the enormous raindrops hurling themselves against our windscreen, and the man from Met Éireann promising gales and tormented seas for the ferry crossing from Rosslare to Cherbourg, it doesn't seem quite so brilliant.

We pull into a windswept Rosslare Harbour and join a small queue of cars crammed with furniture and miserable-looking people waiting for the Stena Line ship to depart.

Ferry crossings at the height of summer are said to be jolly affairs, with face painters and parties for children. Our winter crossing is less jolly. There are no face painters, no happy children or parents with smiling eyes. Just morose truckers drinking cider with whiskey chasers and feeding money into poker machines. Bryan O'Brien and I spend 90 seconds taking in the ferry's other delights. Then we join the truckers.

Our mission is to beat the taxman. The Republic has the highest duty on wine in the EU, at €3.48 a bottle. Duty on wine has jumped by 62 per cent in two years, and now more than half of the cost of a €9 bottle of wine in Ireland is tax.

More than 80 per cent of all the wine in the Republic costs between €8 and €12 a bottle. When all taxes are added, they make up €4.28 of the price of the cheapest bottle; another €3.20 goes on distribution and packaging, leaving just 52c for the wine. A €12 bottle of wine attracts €5.02 in tax and €4.80 in other costs, meaning the wine costs just €2.18.

If we travel to France and buy wine for personal use we'll be relieved of the need to pay duty and much of the distribution cost. The cost of the trip, over and back, will be €500, and we plan to spend €1,000 on wine. Then we'll be quids in.

We have booked a cabin, but it's not yet 10pm, so we play cards and watch Friends on a small television in the bar. We wander out on deck, but the rain, wind and swell drive us back indoors. When we eventually reach our cabin the rough seas rock us to an uneasy sleep.

Dawn breaks. We've had dinner, been to the bar, played cards, slept and had breakfast, and there's still six hours before we dock in Cherbourg.

Conor Pope does his Christmas drinks shopping. Photographs: Bryan O'Brien

Some of our fellow travellers have brought their own food. A man beside me in the bar forks a breakfast of tuna from a tin into his mouth, accompanied by unbuttered white bread. He looks so sad that I want to give him a hug.

The wine had better be amazing.

When we dock the cameraman makes a song and dance about setting up the satnav. "We don't want to get lost. The turnaround is very tight," he says. He's right. We have to get off the boat, find the wine shops, buy the wine, load it into the boot and get back on the boat in less than four hours.

An alternative would be to stay overnight in Cherbourg, but that would add hotel accommodation and the cost of feeding and entertaining ourselves for 48 hours into the equation, and the purpose of our trip is to save money.

Eventually he gets the satnav working. "Drive 500 metres," it says in a Derry accent. We do. "You have reached your destination," it says unexpectedly.

Our destination is a giant Carrefour supermarket. I knew it was close but didn't expect it to be this close. And I didn't expect it to be in a straight line from the port. I feel a pang of guilt for making the cameraman buy the satnav. Still, it should come in handy when we're looking for the other wine shops.

The Carrefour is vast, and two wide aisles are given over to booze. There are hundreds of wines, ranging in price from less than €2 to well over €500. There's no tasting on offer, and no one to ask about what we should buy, so we try our luck elsewhere.

Everyone says Normandie Wines is the place to go. I give the cameraman the address. He keys it into the satnav. We start driving. "You have reached your destination," the Derry woman tells us almost immediately. The shop is across the road from the supermarket. The satnav is looking like a bad investment.

Normandie Wines is unpromising from the outside. It's small, and the windows are heavily barred. It's a different story inside.

Wines from more than 40 regions are stacked high along four narrow aisles. There are, perhaps, 100 varieties of red, maybe 80 whites and one small aisle devoted to bubbles. The wines range in price from about €2 to more than €50.

"Most people buy the wines for between €3 and €5," says Denis Moulin, its manager. "That is how you make the biggest savings. It is because of the taxes, you see. They are very high in Ireland, no? We get a lot of Irish coming in looking for wine for a big party or a wedding or just for themselves. We have a lot of people who come back again and again."

You might think it impossible to produce a good wine that sells at €4, but it isn't in France. The wines in the range are perfectly acceptable – and would easily set you back €12 at home. Wines that sell here for €9.50 cost more than €25 at home.

Moulin tells me that people from Ireland tend to spend "anywhere between €500 and €1,000. If you have come such a long way you might as well stock up, no?"

A couple of other Irish people are in the shop. They're delighted to talk but reluctant to be identified. "We're planning to buy 700 bottles," one man from Dublin says. "They should last us a couple of years. And coming up to Christmas we'll go through a fair bit, with presents and the like for neighbours and family."

A trucker from Co Meath interrupts us. Unlike us, he hasn't come over just to stock up; he's just passing through. "I didn't come up in the truck, because I didn't want this guy to get too excited," he says, pointing at Moulin. "I buy a lot of wine. Most of it is for my daughters. They're terrible for the drink; they take after their mother that way."

We have time to kill, so we stop off at Cave Mancel. It's posher than Normandie Wines. "We used to get a lot of Irish people in past years, but with the economic crisis the numbers have fallen, and now we get very few," Sophie Mancel, its owner, says. "I think the boat is expensive, and that is putting many people off. We don't sell cheap wines. Our focus is on quality wines."

We buy some and return to the boat. All told we've spent about €1,200 on wine. It would set us back €3,200 at home.

Getting into the car is a chore, but the ferry back is a breeze, because the weather is better and we are better at managing our time.

It has taken less than 48 hours to save €2,000. Is it worth it? Absolutely. The only downside is that we have to drink all the wine now.

Conor Pope on video: http://bcove.me/zv08f6pp

DECEMBER 3RD 2014

Left, right – what do labels matter when a homeless man dies on a freezing night?

Kathy Sheridan

The urge to attach labels to people is human. It makes life simpler. But labels stick if left unchallenged, so when a member of Aosdána tweeted that last week's column was an example of "the class war credentials – pro-establishment – of the Irish media", I reread it to see how I had offended and perhaps to atone.

To recap: I wrote that in my experience the people whom Paul Murphy TD describes as "ordinary" and "afraid of the government" can be startlingly outspoken when senior politicians come to canvass. If the gentleman tweeter disputes this, he has never been on a canvass.

The column also described politicians' routine self-abasement before a demanding electorate in the perpetual mission to mind the seat, while suggesting that the same electorate should examine the mote in its own eye, given its abrupt U-turn towards Fianna Fáil in 2007.

Would an alternative government have acted differently from the incorporeal FF/Green cabinet on the night of the bank guarantee in 2008? Who knows. We do know that the electorate voted for the party it believed would keep the property ball rolling, choosing in the process to overlook Bertie Ahern's tribunal adventures. Who disputes any of this now?

The column was a call to remember past pitfalls, to inform ourselves about the bigger picture outside our own sectoral interests and to be alert to siren voices of all political hues. Basic common sense.

In any event, the old-fashioned language of class war

Candles light the doorway on Dublin's Molesworth Street where homeless man John Corrie was found dead.
Photograph: Aidan Crawley

seems profoundly inadequate to the current ferment. This paper for example has relentlessly pursued the issues around homelessness. The measured voice of Br Kevin Crowley describing unanswered phones as he sought shelter for a mother and children on Monday demands something more than name-calling or brazen politicking over where precisely a 43-year-old man died outdoors on a freezing night. Where are the solutions? In the name of decency, if an entrepreneur like Niall Mellon can organise a building blitz in South Africa to provide hundreds of homes in a week, why can it not be done in this country?

Tonight, among even those with roofs over their heads, there will be people of every class – whatever that means – too fearful to turn on the heating. Who are the "ordinary" people now? They are the scandalously low-paid and the unemployed. They are the manufacturer nearly crazed with stress; the suicidal retailer in a dying town; the prudent couple who lost their hard-won pension in the crash.

At a time in history when virtually everyone, including the governor of the Bank of England and the head of the International Monetary Fund, is questioning the wisdom of an economic system that leaves humanity dangling at the mercy of amoral financiers and their market bagmen, it seems self-defeating to reduce any individual to the strait jacket of a label. As a strategy, it's hardly designed to win converts to a cause.

History is littered with individuals who defied pigeon-holing. Otto von Bismarck was an arch-conservative who also happened to introduce the world's first welfare state policies (public industrial accident insurance in 1871 and public health insurance in 1883). Thomas Jefferson was "right-wing" in his support for free trade (including in slaves) but "left-wing" in his hostility to banking and belief in great devolution of power. It was the aristocratic Benjamin Disraeli – the British Conservative who served twice as prime minister – not William Gladstone, who was concerned with the "two nations" that the industrial revolution was creating.

The above examples come from Ha-Joon Chang – economist and author of 23 Things They Don't Tell You about Capitalism – who holds there is no single way to define right and left, either in parties or individuals: "There are many different dimensions along which we divide them and these criteria differ according to the time and the place."

This is why the language of the Taoiseach with his talk of "the divide in Irish society", in which the "choice will be a Fine Gael-led government or a group possibly led by Sinn Féin", is so dispiriting. For more than six miserable, frightening years, the citizenry has been asked to unite in sacrifice – and overlook blindingly obvious unfairness. Now we have a leadership entrenching national division. Michael Noonan's description of an emerging "clear left/right choice", must have Labour stalwarts scratching their heads. Where do they fit into these strait-jacket labels a year from an election?

This is the problem with phoney wars. Labels polarise. They entrench people in their foxholes. Instead of promoting critical thinking, they reduce debate to poster slogans and facile one-liners.

Above all, they are a poisonous distraction from the important questions.

The words of Ireland rugby captain Ciaran Fitzgerald still resonate since 1985 – and a decade when 200,000 people emigrated, unemployment reached nearly 18 per cent and the national debt was more than 140 per cent of gross national product: "Where's your f--king pride?"

DECEMBER 4TH 2014

Mary Lou detonates alleged Ansbacher list

Miriam Lord

Another no-warning blast from Mary Lou. You'd think Sinn Féin could find somebody to telephone the poor Ceann Comhairle and give him the heads up.

Seán Barrett seemed to be caught on the hop, although we're not quite sure whether this was by accident or design.

The Ceann Comhairle was slow to act when Mary Lou proceeded to detonate a list of alleged offshore account holders in the middle of a packed Dáil chamber yesterday morning.

Actually, when we say packed, we really mean sparsely populated. Even the Taoiseach had to sit on his own for most of Leaders' Questions.

Had he known Mary Lou was going to stage another spectacular , he would have taken in a few ministers for protection.

But then, how was Enda to know she would switch her weekly stunt from Thursday to Wednesday?

It's normally Joan Burton who absorbs the onslaught from across the floor.

She doesn't seem to mind it at all. In fact, the Tánaiste returns fire with alarming relish.

It's hell for backbenchers cowering in the trenches when Joan and Mary Lou have to be dug out of each other.

Furthermore, Enda would have been feeling very chilled out yesterday morning, having spent an agreeable evening at a Christmas shindig in Dublin's Pantibar with Cork TD Jerry Buttimer and other members of Fine Gael's LGBT group.

(We have it on disreputable authority that when the Taoiseach was given the name of the venue he thought he was off to a lingerie party and had hoped to pick up a stocking filler for the missus. But he got over his disappointment and enjoyed the festive drinks with his colleagues.)

The Taoiseach turning up at one of Dublin's most popular gay bars caused quite a stir on social media, where some people said, rather unkindly, that Enda's appearance was a stunt.

But if it was, nobody was talking about it in Leinster House, where Mary Lou McDonald once more demonstrated her superiority in the age old art of political distraction.

Give her a mirror and she'd probably try to upstage herself.

The session began with a return to the issue of

homelessness. Fianna Fáil's Micheál McGrath, standing in for his party leader, said that if the death this week of homeless man Jonathan Corrie "is to mean anything, it has to be a catalyst for change".

The Taoiseach didn't disagree with him.

There wouldn't have been much surprise had Mary Lou (Gerry Adams is on a trip to the Middle East) kept up the pressure on the Government's response to the growing homelessness crisis, which is affecting individuals and families in the private rental sector.

Perhaps she would address the state of our ambulance service. Or maybe she might have raised the case of the women who suffered the appalling procedure of symphysiotomy and are now very unhappy with the redress package which was put in place for them.

Maureen O'Sullivan of the Technical Group later raised this subject, pointing out that the Government has ignored recommendations from the United Nations Human Rights Committee on the implementation of the scheme.

She quoted the chairman of that committee who said: "I simply don't understand how the State can look the other way at what seems to have been systematic assault on people who weren't in a position to resist or even give consent in many cases. We called for prosecutions explicitly and I would hope, I have to hope, that the recommendation won't be ignored." He shouldn't hope. Because the Taoiseach gave him no cause for it yesterday.

Nor did he have an answer for O'Sullivan when she asked why there has been no focus on the "perpetrators" who inflicted such harm and pain on these blameless women.

But back to Mary Lou McDonald, with a nice list of options to choose from if she wanted to get tough on the Taoiseach. Why should Joan have all the fun? Whereupon she brought up the dreaded Ansbacher accounts, which some of us first heard about nearly 20 years ago at the McCracken tribunal.

There have been many investigations into them since then.

However, Mary Lou was most anxious to tell the

Caption: Siobhan and Aisling Devine from Coolock in Dublin enjoying themselves at the Geansai Nollaig (Christmas Sweater) world record attempt on O'Connell St. Photograph: Dara Mac Donaill

Dáil about allegations made by a whistleblower about named senior politicians whom he alleges held offshore Ansbacher accounts.

A curious subject to bring up, given that the Public Accounts Committee is still actively considering what to do about the dossier in light of recent legal advice.

McDonald is a member of the PAC and her solo-run yesterday annoyed quite a few of her colleagues on this independent Dáil Committee.

In the middle of her contribution on this file of allegations – which has been investigated on a number of occasions down through the years, she named the people mentioned in it in a very deliberate fashion.

This took the rest of the chamber by surprise.

However, she was at pains to point out "it's not a case of me making allegations against anyone . . . but they come from a very credible source."

In naming politicians, some of whom saw their heyday in the 1970s and most of whom are long retired from active politics, Mary Lou stressed she was just "echoing the serious allegations that have been brought forward by the whistleblower that are quite serious."

Among those names was an "S Barrett. Mary Lou said it slowly and clearly, so we could get the full import.

The Ceann Comhairle intervened. "Sorry, are you making these allegations in the chamber?"

One wondered if Seán Barrett had been holding back, reluctant to take on the Sinn Féin deputy leader, who has been doing her best to drive him to distraction with distractions.

And he snapped, rather sourly: " I wish to state quite categorically, in case anybody is under any doubts when you say 'S Barrett', it doesn't apply to me".

No. That concerns wholly unsubstantiated allegations against one Sylvester Barrett, a Fianna Fáil minister back in old God's time.

You have to hand it to Sinn Féin, the party which likes to remind people that their colourful legacy is not up for inspection.

This leaves members free to focus on dark periods they might see in other party's political pasts, while roundly condemning anyone who tries to shine a similar light on the murkier aspects of Sinn Féin's past.

Whistleblowers who do not criticise the party or the republican movement are embraced.

Those who dissent are not so royally entertained, as Maíria Cahill discovered.

Just because they have no legacy to stand on, doesn't mean you can't step on their toes.

Another tour de force from Mary Lou.

DECEMBER 5TH 2014

Yeats in love
Irishman's Diary

Frank McNally

We'll hear a lot in this decade of centenaries about patriots who died for Ireland. But spare a thought for poor Maud Gonne who, despite living to old age, made a different, and near-ultimate, sacrifice.

In refusing all the advances of WB Yeats, including four marriage proposals, she knowingly allowed him to place her on a pedestal, where she would be gawked at by future generations. And she must have guessed that images of her beauty, as preserved for posterity by mere photographs, would never stand comparison with the love-lorn exaggerations of one of the world's greatest poets.

Whereas even a short-lived affair might have shut him up. It would doubtless have ended badly. Then Yeats's early love poems would have been counterbalanced by the literary equivalent of the divorce album, and the pressure would have been off Maud in every way thereafter.

Instead, knowing well that it would only encourage further effusions about her perfection, she turned him

Russian president Vladimir Putin at a concert honouring the Kremlin's security staff.
Photograph: Alexei Druzhinin/Reuters

down repeatedly, over decades, in the interests of the greater good. Here she is in 1914 – almost a quarter century into the siege — explaining yet again why she won't marry him, while insisting he's happier single:
"Oh yes you are, because you make beautiful poetry out of what you call your unhappiness and you are happy in that. Marriage would be such a dull affair. Poets should never marry. The world should thank me for not marrying you."
And with that, Yeats is off again to build her a new, even higher pedestal in verse. Nor was it just in poetry – a medium where the usual rules of sanity are suspended – that he eulogised her.
Here he is [from 1913] recalling their first meeting, in apparently sober prose:
"I had never thought to see in a living woman [such] great beauty. It belonged to famous pictures, to poetry, to some legendary past. A complexion like the blossom of apples, and yet the face and body had the beauty of lineaments, which Blake calls the highest beauty because it changes least from youth to age, and a stature so great that she seemed of divine race."

It can't just be me, vulgarian that I am, who reads such descriptions of Gonne and then looks at her photographs before concluding, mystified, that you had to be there. She certainly had striking features. But even allowing a 20 per cent discount on the apple blossoms, which black and white photographs could hardly capture, the best I can allow is that she was handsome.
One might be tempted to attribute some of Yeats's ardour to the fact that, great poet aside, he was also a world-class eccentric. And yet he wasn't unusual in worshipping Gonne. A sister of the poet, Lolly Yeats, wrote of an early visit to their house and the already-famous beauty "who is marching on to glory over the hearts of the Dublin youths".
With the clinical eye of a fellow female, she described Maud as "tall and very stylish and well dressed in a careless way". But another contemporary, Mary Colum, sounded almost as smitten as the male Yeats. Gonne's beauty was "startling in its greatness, its dignity, its strangeness," she wrote, and "people's hearts stopped beating" when they saw her.

41

That and all the other quotations above are taken from a charming new book on the subject, which attempts to explain Gonne's fatal attraction, albeit more with comic intent than as an exercise in literary analysis.

Yeats in Love is by the Sligo artist and illustrator Annie West and it traces the whole tortured affair through a series of climactic events, including the various proposals, from the 1880s to the poet's old age.

Its opulent, full-colour drawings don't attempt to capture Maud's apple-blossoms, never mind her Blakean lineaments. But the wit of the pictures is accompanied by well-chosen words, including some of the poems to which Yeats was driven on his regular rebounds. And West's gentle style sits well with the subject: she treads softly, treading on dreams.

Mind you, in a preface for the book, Theo Dorgan advances the possibility that the poet, at least in later years, was not as far gone about Maud as it suited him to pretend, even to himself. Dorgan's suspicion is that there was mutual role-playing and that "the old boy was putting it on a bit". I suspect he's right. If so, even the poet might have enjoyed West's affectionate joke, which is at least as handsome as Maud was, and is available (at €34.99) from good bookshops and anniewest.com.

DECEMBER 6TH 2014

Pigs and Nazis mark curious times in American politics

Simon Carswell

Amid the recent uproar over white cops escaping criminal charges for killing black men on the job, you may have missed two of the stranger political stories in the United States:

about pigs and Nazis.

New Jersey governor Chris Christie has angered animal rights activists by vetoing for a second time a Bill that would have outlawed pig gestation crates in the Garden State. The crates are small, metal cages that house pregnant sows. They are so small that it is impossible for the hogs to turn around.

The crates are already banned in nine states, including California and Colorado, and are being phased out in Australia and New Zealand.

A majority of New Jersey people support the ban and Democrats and Republicans overwhelmingly supported the Bill blocking their use, but not Christie, a Republican in his second term. He's in the minority on this issue in New Jersey. The move is all the more bizarre when you consider that the state is not really a pig producer: New Jersey has about 300 pig farmers and fewer than 10,000 hogs. In fact, the state's only notable porcine connection may be the fictional Satriale's pork store from the HBO mafia drama The Sopranos.

Christie labelled the ban a "solution in search of a problem" and a "political movement masquerading as substantive policy".

Three facts might better explain the ambitious New Jersey governor's position on the crates: Iowa is the country's largest pork producer with 6,300 pig farmers and 20.5 million hogs; Iowa is the first state in the country to pick nominees in presidential elections; and Christie is mulling a run for the White House in 2016.

From a political perspective, Iowa is important for the New Jersey governor. The state's hog industry is worth $6.5 billion (€5.2 billion), so it is politically expedient for him to keep Iowans happy. Christie has visited Iowa four times in the past year, a sign of his future intentions.

Terry Brandstad, the governor of Iowa, admitted on Monday that he had lobbied Christie to veto the crate-ban Bill again. He heaped praise on Christie for his veto so the New Jersey governor has won over at least one key political ally in an electorally influential state by continuing to make life difficult for pregnant

42

New Jersey pigs.

The move has of course irked many, notably Hollywood singer-actor Cher, who said that it would damage Christie's presidential hopes. "Iowa pig farmers, why must you torture preg pigs?" she wrote on Twitter. "U put them in crates & lock em down so they can't move. C. Christie, UR despicable bully 4get POTUS."

Asked about Cher's condemnation, Brandstad told the local Iowa newspaper, the Des Moines Register: "Yeah, I saw that. They know a lot about pig production in Hollywood."

Meanwhile, in Washington on Thursday, the Senate passed the curiously named Bill No Social Security for Nazis Act, HR 5739 by unanimous consent. The Bill passed the House of Representatives in a 420 to 0 vote the previous day.

This Congress, split by the Democrat-led Senate and Republican-led House, is on track to set a new record – at least in modern times – for the fewest number of Bills ever passed, so when Capitol Hill politicians can agree on something, it is a moment worth noting and indeed cherishing. (Not that any politician would jeopardise their careers by coming out in support of social welfare for retired Nazis.)

"Thank you, Nazis," said political satirist Stephen Colbert on the Colbert Report in a note of gratitude to the fascist movement for being able to bring together Democrats and Republicans for a brief moment.

The Bill arose following an Associated Press investigation last month which said that dozens of suspected Nazi war criminals forced to leave the US were collecting millions of dollars in social welfare payments from the American government due to a loophole in the law.

AP reported that at least four former German soldiers still living were in receipt of US social security cheques. They include Martin Hartmann, a former SS guard at the Sachsenhausen death camp in Germany, and Jakob Denzinger, who patrolled the grounds at Auschwitz in Poland. Hartmann moved from Arizona to Berlin in 2007 before being stripped of his US citizenship. Denzinger left Ohio for Germany in 1989 and now lives in Croatia.

"While the number of Nazis receiving social security is few, allowing payments to continue is an insult to those who suffered at the hands of the Nazis," said Congressman Sam Johnson, a Republican from Texas and a US Air Force veteran who sponsored the legislation that now awaits Barack Obama's signature. So, a good week for Congress and a bad week for Nazis and New Jersey pigs.

DECEMBER 12TH 2014

Mosab Hassan Yousef: son of Hamas founder to Israeli agent

Tara Brady

I'm almost surprised to find Mosab Hassan Yousef sitting casually in a Mayfair bar. Yes, I knew he was coming. And yes, this is precisely where we were supposed to meet. But having spent a decade working as an informant for Israel's internal security service Shin Bet, Yousef should, one thinks, have arrived in heavy disguise with a squadron of bodyguards. Or at least sit far away from the windows.

Instead, he shrugs and orders some food: "I live my life normally," says the 36-year-old, who relocated to San Diego six years ago. "I try to look forward."

Between 1997 and 2007, Yousef, as recorded by the new documentary The Green Prince, was one of Shin Bet's most valuable operatives.

It's not just that he was operating at the highest levels of Hamas. Yousef is the oldest son of Hassan Yousef, one of the founding leaders of that organisation. For years, he was his father's closest confidant

Mosab Hassan Yousef, as portrayed in the documentary on his life as an Israeli agent, The Green Prince.

and aide. And for many of those years, he was supplying information to the Israelis that allowed them to prevent dozens of suicide attacks and political assassinations, including a 2001 plot to kill Shimon Peres.

So how did a youngster who was first arrested, aged 10, for throwing rocks at Israeli settlers end up working for the other side?

"The analogy that I like a lot is Plato's cave," he says. "I went through different political systems and governments and terrorist groups and war zones. I have lived under Islam and in the free world. And you come to realise that many people are looking at the wall watching a bunch of shadows. Their perception of truth is completely distorted."

Yousef first began to question his Islamic faith when, in 1996, the Israelis jailed him in a Hamas-controlled prison wing, where he saw Hamas operatives, including his uncle, torture and kill prisoners they suspected of cooperating with the Israelis.

"Everybody was afraid in prison, including my uncle," he recalls. "Everybody was afraid to oppose torture and killing. I was afraid. In that society, we didn't have rights."

His abhorrence for Hamas activities within the prison – and what he saw as the Shin Bet's relatively humane interrogation methods – prompted him to become an informant.

But Yousef's situation was further complicated by his friendship with Gonen ben Yitzhak, his former Shin Bet handler. That relationship forms the spine of the fascinating new film.

"At the beginning it was very hard to see him as a person," says Yousef. "I already had certain perceptions of what an Israeli secret-services agent was like. But in time my perception became more accurate. I came to see humanity in him and in other agents that I worked with.

"They had families. They had children. They had good qualities. They had bad qualities. They were human beings. That brought me to question the nature of my father and Hamas. Hamas wanted to destroy everything that was Israeli or Jewish or American."

How does he feel listening to western Europeans who are sympathetic towards the Palestinian cause? "That's just stupidity," he says. Does he mean ignorance?

"No. No. No. I mean stupidity. When we criticise Israel, we are criticising ourselves. Israelis are no different from people who live in western Europe. Israel is basically an extension of western civilisation and its values.

"Jews and Christians have liberty. They can choose to believe what they believe. They can choose to worship however they want to worship.

"When we use that liberty and choose to identify ourselves with radical movements, with people who live in the darkness, people who don't believe in the western model, who don't believe in democracy: then we are mistaken."

He scarcely pauses for breath. "And how would people here in London or in Ireland or in Germany act if a terrorist group or neighbouring country started launching missiles? You need to understand that war is ugly."

In 1999, Yousef met a British missionary who introduced him to Christianity. He was baptised in 2005, but is not affiliated with any particular denomination.

"I don't read the Bible or go to church," he tells me. "I believe that religion is a necessary evil. Just like the government, I did not leave Islam to become a Christian. But Christianity really helped me to escape from the Islamic mindset. I still follow the idea of loving our enemies and of unconditional forgiveness."

His conversion came as a shock to his family, although they remained in contact with Yousef until 2010 when his autobiography, Son of Hamas: A Gripping Account of Terror, Betrayal, Political Intrigue, and Unthinkable Choices, was published.

"I had given them an idea what was coming," he says. "But from that moment I've had no contact."

His family has faced persecution since his confessional emerged. But Yousef stands firmly over his decision and believes that his actions have saved lives.

"If we blame Hamas, we need also to blame the ideology that inspires them. If we fight Hamas or any radicals or fundamentalist groups, we need to understand that we are fighting their ideology. Islam is their foundation. If we're not aware of this, we increase the chance that terror will win over peace.

"Islamic ideology is an aggressive and dangerous ideology, inspired by Muhammad, the founder of Islam. It's very clear from Islamic texts and from the Qur'an that it is a violent ideology. People who say that it is peaceful, they have no clue. It's a sick religion, born in a sick man's mind."

But surely Islam isn't simply a monolith? What about the newer, feminist voices within the faith? What

Mosab Hassan Yousef, as himself.

about Taqwacore punk music and other Islamic subcultures?

"Attempts to reform are great. But there can be no reform while there is no separation of mosque and state. In Islamic countries, non-Muslims have to pay a tax to live there. Christianity has evolved. Judaism has evolved. Islam is still in the seventh century.

"Muslims have to realise this is a bunch of crap. For as long as they believe that this is the word of God, that it is good for every time, that it is good for every civilization, they will never be compatible with life nowadays."

Really? But Yousef has previously described his father as a good man.

"That is how the confusion happens. There are good Muslims, just doing their thing, raising their family. They take care of their wife and members of their society.

45

"They're productive. They're well educated. But my father's project is an Islamic project. He had people killed. Just as Muhammad carried a sword and invaded other civilisations and took women and took property. These are the facts. But for me there is nothing darker than hating a human being. I want to choose a different way."

DECEMBER 18TH 2014

Ghosts of Christmas past: deep roots of Irish winter traditions

Dick Ahlstrom

People look to the skies at Christmas, some watching for a Yuletide star pointing the way and others for flying reindeer and a jolly character dressed in a red suit.

More seasonal symbolism is offered by the passage graves of Newgrange, Dowth and Knowth along the River Boyne. Renewal and rebirth at the rising of the sun is the shared theme expressed by the builders of these 5,000-year-old monuments and by the Christian churches.

It is no accident that the winter solstice and Christmas fall so close together on the calendar, as older festivals have given way to modern versions. The names change but the themes remain closely linked. Only the hardy will brave the dawn cold on December 21st to see the sunrise at Newgrange, and the lucky few assembled in the far recesses of that large grave will hope to see the magic once again as the sun begins its journey towards spring.

The astronomical alignments achieved during the monument's construction attest to the importance of astronomy to the ancient people who built it. And astronomy was there again in the Christmas story

as the Wise Men from the east delivered their gifts, guided by the light of a star that pointed the way.

Today it is much easier to peruse the stars, since you can take the car rather than having to ride a camel for weeks.

The Kerry International Dark-Sky Reserve is an ideal place for viewing the night sky, and it is one of only three Gold Tier reserves on the planet, as determined by the International Dark Sky Association. From there you can watch for a star or for that character riding the reindeer-pulled sleigh; it's entirely up to you.

"What you will see is the Milky Way; you have to have a black sky to see [its] band," says the Kerry Reserve's manager, Julie Ormonde. "You can see the Andromeda galaxy with the naked eye. You are seeing things 2½ million light years away."

Our fascination with the night sky is not the only common point linking present to past. Many of the social traditions we enjoy today date back hundreds of years, and in some cases even earlier.

"Christmas was the major festival of the year for Christian Ireland and there is a whole nexus of traditions surrounding it," says Críostóir Mac Cárthaigh, an archivist at the National Folklore Collection at University College Dublin.

Many seasonal traditions that are very familiar to us date from a distant past. Holly and ivy were used to decorate the house because of their wintertime colour, and, in the case of holly, the bright red berries. Mistletoe was also there as an evergreen, but the notion of using it to capture a kiss was an American practice.

"There was also a big emphasis on the perambulatory traditions: going house visiting and presenting folk dramas," says Mac Cárthaigh. The December 26th visitation of the wren boys is an example.

"The wren tradition appears to be very old, likely back to prehistory," he says. "The wren boys seem to be part of a wider western European tradition, but it survives to the present in Ireland. A French scholar has studied this, and she argues that the sacrifice of the wren at this time of year is paying the debt of

Julia Ormonde of the Kerry International Dark-Sky Reserve from where stars two and a half million light years away may be observed. Photograph: Michael Sheehan.

nature: spilling blood as an offering and fertilising the ground."

There was also a powerful community aspect to this. "There is a very strong social dimension to the folk dramas. They were inclusive: the more houses involved, the better," he says. "If somebody was shunned and got no visit from the boys, or if you were a difficult neighbour or wouldn't accept social norms, this was important."

While the wren boys were native Irish and Norman, the mummers were found in the Pale. "The mummers replaced an older wren tradition across most of Ulster and a good swathe of the east coast: areas of plantation," he says. "They put on complex dramas revolving around death and then resuscitation."

These performances were followed by drinking and feasting, all of which would look familiar to us today. Research, whether related to astronomy or to social conduct from 400 years ago, allows us to better understand where we came from and where we are headed as 2015 beckons.

DECEMBER 20 2014

The magic of the winter solstice

Michael Viney

Solstice is a fine soft word to slip off the tongue. It comes, the web tells me, via Old French from the Latin solstitium – sol for the sun and sistere, to stand still, which was one way of understanding Earth's significant tilt tomorrow and the consequent shortest day of the year.

Mistle thrushes at mistletoe by Michael Viney.

The wilder corners of west Connacht abound in big rocks – standing, carved or aligned – with a role in Stone Age calendars and magic. The east coast's great megalithic monuments, Knowth and Dowth, open their stony hearts to the rise of the sun at dawns around the winter solstice. The west has simple rows of rocks, lining up with the sun as it sets into some chosen mountain notch in Connemara or Mayo.

Around the corner of my coast, Croagh Patrick's pyramidal sanctity has warranted several such marvels. They include a row of boulders on a mound in a saltmarsh (at Killadangan, five kilometres west of Westport) where, at 1.45pm tomorrow, they should align spot on with the sun as it dips into a niche in the shoulder of the Reek.

More spectacular is the happening on a clear evening on August 24th, when, from a carved rock at Boheh, on a hillside east of the Reek, the setting sun appears to roll down the edge of the mountain's seaward scarp like a flaming Catherine wheel.

It will, however, be quite dark tomorrow by the time I join friends at their annual winter-solstice party, complete with bonfire to celebrate the true turning of the year. While its ruddy light may not quite reach Croagh Patrick, across the bay, the mountain's looming presence and the roar of surf on the shore always give the evening a proper druidic spice.

Little is known about the druids of Ireland, considering their role as professional power brokers in dealings with Iron Age nature. What I find intriguing about them is how – or whether – they managed their magic without mistletoe.

Notable now as a predator's wand at Christmas office parties, it was then the indispensable "golden bough" of druids throughout the Celtic continent.

This was the title of the monumental study of magic and religion by the Scottish anthropologist Sir James George Frazer, first published in 1922. The Roman Pliny, in his natural history, was first to link druid rituals with the parasitic plant, but it was Frazer who traced its role in so much European myth and magic (none of which seems to have involved uninvited osculation).

In Pliny's version white-garbed druids invariably climbed "hard timbered" oaks (Quercus robur) to cut clumps of mistletoe with a golden sickle, then sacrificed two white bulls before a ceremonial feast. The white mistletoe berries, with juice as sticky as semen, was a cure for barrenness in livestock and a panacea for poison and illness.

"All-heal," reported Frazer, was "said to be still the name of the mistletoe in the modern Celtic speech of Brittany, Wales, Ireland and Scotland". Variations of "uile-íoc" do, indeed, appear among the many Irish names for mistletoe collected by the botanist Peter Wyse Jackson in Ireland's Generous Nature, his recent encyclopedia on the uses of wild plants. Relieving epilepsy and hysteria seems to have been among the virtues of Viscum album (although itself somewhat toxic).

On this island it is nowhere widespread in the wild, as Dr Wyse Jackson says, and rates no mention in the widely definitive Webb's Irish Flora. Indeed, it has been generally accepted as an alien plant, spread by berry-eating mistle thrushes from cultivated introductions, such as that in the National Botanic Gardens, at Glasnevin, in the 1800s. This now has Ireland's biggest colony of mistletoe growths, on several kinds of tree, and has been known to offer kissworthy sprigs to visitors to Santa's grotto.

The late decades of the last century brought such an apparent expansion in Irish locations for mistletoe that Dr Charles Nelson (once of Glasnevin, now in Cambridgeshire) invited records from the public. This brought 75 individual reports from 15 counties, north and south.

None of the plants was growing on oaks; instead they were on apple, hawthorn, poplar, willow, sycamore and lime. Their density around Dublin, Nelson suggests, might point to a warming of climate that is allowing mistletoe, flowering from February to April, to be pollinated by the wind and spread by seed, as a naturalised Irish plant.

There is no fossil pollen of Viscus album from Ireland's postglacial deposits or the centuries of the druids. So, unlike the wizards of Britain, they must have made their magic without the "golden bough".

Today, in a commercial pre-Christmas ritual, white vans from Ireland gather at Tenbury Wells, in northwest Worcestershire, where a procession of modern druids launch the auctions of the town's mistletoe festival. The boughs are gathered abundantly from weathered cider-apple trees perhaps half a century old.

There's nothing like keeping up tradition – Happy Christmas!

DECEMBER 23RD 2014

When I close my eyes and think of Christmas . . .'

Fintan O'Toole

When I close my eyes and think of Christmas, I see a fat man in a top hat with a whip. I see lurid stripes of red and yellow. This is not delirium tremens. It is the only Christmas present I can remember from childhood. It is what floats back into memory from the year my mother knitted us a circus.

I know there were other Christmases and other presents. There was a tricycle once but the only thing I remember about it is getting in trouble later when I swapped it for a water pistol. It's the brutal thing about children. They say they want things and you slave and save and you buy them. In return, you get the hysteria and the running around and the novelty wearing off around noon and the kids going back to what they were playing with the day before. And they forget the whole thing.

But I don't forget the knitted circus. There was the fat ringmaster in his scarlet coat. His flesh seemed pudgy and pale. His black top hat with yellow ribbon perfectly matched his black boots with yellow tops and the yellow bib that set off his black beard.

A seasonal face in the crowd at the lighting of the Christmas tree in Dublin's O'Connell Street. Photograph: Dara Mac Donaill.

There was a lion whose ears stuck up between the strands of deep brown wool that made his shaggy mane, above big eyes of dark felt and a snubby black nose. There was a giraffe, his neck as long as his legs, his jagged, irregular spots embroidered in black outlines. There was a brown elephant with yellow and red backcloth and head piece, buttons for eyes and white felt tusks.

A seal with fluffy whiskers balanced a red-and-white ball on his nose. The clown had a conical hat, red ruffs at the end of his sleeves and round his neck and a shock of golden hair. A lady usher wore a blue bellboy-type outfit with a gold stripe down her trousers and a gold band around her pillbox hat.

There were two little white dogs with black patches on one ear and one eye. And there was a big yellow circus ring with red tent poles and a high box for the lion to sit on.

The circus was for five of us – four really because the new baby was too little to care very much.

The only thing that seemed at all odd to us was that Santa hadn't put it in a box. It was just wrapped up in paper. But we didn't mind. It never dawned on us that

the circus was home-made, and I don't think we even registered that it was made of wool.

It simply could not have been produced by the same hands, and with the same material, that created itchy jumpers and shameful scarves. It was entirely lovely and, to us, entirely exclusive. Other kids on the street and in school had boring answers to the question: "What did you get for Christmas?" A doll. A ball. Football boots. Roller skates. We got a whole circus.

It was not until many years later that I realised that the circus was actually made of despair. It had been a hard year, with a new baby coming not long after his predecessor had died in infancy. Then there had been a very long strike – 10 or 12 weeks, I think – that kept my father out of work and devoured all the savings that my mother had for Christmas.

She realised in the dark of November that there would be no money for presents. Even then, when Ireland had not yet been drenched by the full tide of consumerism, this was shameful.

It evoked that dread that parents hate to name – the terror of appearing a failure in the eyes of your kids. It was rock bottom.

And then she saw a book of knitting patterns for a stuffed woollen circus. She remembered later that she had her own evening pattern. She would get us up to bed. My grandfather would go off to the pub. My father would still be at work, doing overtime to recoup his lost earnings.

She would wash out our socks and underwear for the next day and hang them in front of the fire. And then she would sit down and knit a giraffe's tail or a red-and-white ball for a seal's nose. I like to think that the anxiety in her fingers unwound itself little by little as the needles clicked and the yarn looped round itself and these daft creatures began to take their jolly shapes.

Still, when it came to it, when she wrapped the circus and put it under the tree, she was afraid. Afraid that we would see through the cheapness of it all, the remnants of wool, the scraps of felt, the absence of anything that reeked of shops and money.

She need not have been – it reeked instead of sawdust and animal sweat, of colour and fantasy. And somehow, though we knew nothing of where it came from, what lodged it unforgettably in our memories was not just the thrill of the circus but the movement of the hands that made it.

DECEMBER 24TH 2014

Scale of distress is almost too much to process

Ruadhán Mac Cormaic

Her father looks out into the court and inclines his head towards the microphone. "My daughter's dead," he says softly. "I just want her to have dignity, to be put to rest."

To his right, three judges, headed by Mr Justice Nicholas Kearns, their expressions serious and solemn.

To his left, 17 lawyers, squeezed into three rows of seats, and a public gallery filled with more barristers, some doctors and a smattering of onlookers.

Not for the first time, the room falls silent.

The scale of the tragedy, the depth of the distress, seem almost too big to process. Scarcely can a court hearing have felt more pared back, more intense. The atmosphere is grave and purposeful, and it seems heightened by the unfamiliar surroundings.

This is an out-of-term sitting; absent are the gowns and wigs and the trappings of ceremony. Absent too the showmanship, the theatrics: the noise, in other words. Nobody reacts much other than to shake a head, shed a tear or stare off into the distance.

The judges handle proceedings with delicacy and tact, and the evidence proceeds swiftly. We hear from the woman's father, who describes seeing his daughter on life support and feeling she didn't look like herself. Her children know she is sick; they've been told the nurses are "looking after Mummy until the angels come".

We hear from her partner, who tells the court she was happy to be pregnant and that they were planning to move in together. They had talked about names for their baby.

We hear from seven consultants specialising in neurology, obstetrics and intensive care. None argues against switching the machine off. "I don't believe this unborn can survive," says one intensive care specialist. "I would be firmly of the view that the appropriate thing to do is not to continue support," says an obstetrician. "If it were to be continued, we would be going from the extraordinary to the grotesque."

Looming over their contributions is article 40.3.3 of the Constitution – the Eighth Amendment – which sets out the equal right to life of the mother and the unborn and stipulates that the State will vindicate those rights as far as is practicable.

That was uppermost in the minds of the woman's doctors. At one point, a treating neurologist recounts,

51

he and a colleague sat down together and tried to "figure out" the Eighth Amendment.

"We were very uncertain about the legal standing. We didn't know."

He describes having to approach the woman's distraught family and tell them that he couldn't fulfil their request to switch off life support for legal reasons.

In the public gallery, family members hold their hands over their mouths.

Legal submissions will be made by lawyers for each of the parties on Christmas Eve. Lawyers for the woman's father will argue that the Eighth Amendment is not applicable or engaged in this case. They will say that the purpose of the amendment, inserted by referendum in 1983, was to protect the unborn from abortion, not to retain a brain dead woman on life support when medical evidence suggests that there is no real likelihood of a foetus reaching viability.

For its part, the HSE's stance is that the medical evidence indicates there is no reasonable prospect of the foetus being born alive from continued life support, and that therefore it is not practicable to keep the machine on.

The court will also hear from lawyers representing the interests of the unborn and the mother.

In a hospital's intensive care unit, meanwhile, nurses are watching over the body of a woman who was declared brain dead at 5.20pm on December 3rd. At that moment, in the words of one medic, she became a corpse.

Her picture stands by her beside, but she bears "not a whole lot of resemblance" to it, according to Dr Frances Colreavy, an intensive care specialist who visited her. Make-up has been applied to her face because her children came to see her, but the swelling of her eyes is so bad that they do not close. The children found it distressing.

She is connected to a life-support machine and six syringe pumps. She is being fed via a tube through the nose.

Her condition is deteriorating rapidly. She has ongoing infection, presumed to be pneumonia, and her temperature is a high 38 degrees. She appears puffy, her blood pressure is fluctuating and her abdomen shows signs of inflammation and discolouration. She has an open head wound and the brain appears to the naked eye to be rotting. Blood flow to the brain has stopped. Asked whether it was realistic to continue life support, Dr Colreavy replied: "I don't think that is possible or to be recommended." Already, she said, they were in the realm of experimental treatment.

The court rose just before 4.30pm. Lawyers chatted quietly among themselves. Reporters tap-tapped on their laptops. Doctors shook hands with the family and wished them well. Quietly, the room emptied and the crowd fanned out into the darkness.

On December 26th, the court ruled the life support could be switched off and the woman died subsequently

DECEMBER 31ST 2014

Why we need party politics

Colm Keena

During a lecture in Dublin a few years ago the US economist Joseph Stiglitz set out in plain terms an aspect of the modern world that is of particular importance when considering the strain which so many western societies, including Ireland, are now experiencing.

The economist was addressing how the West can best deal with the effects of globalisation, and, if memory serves, then his prescription included classic European policies such as state support for those who lose their jobs, including retraining, and a focus on high quality education. But it was his simple description of the basic facts concerning globalisation that made the most impact on this reporter, and

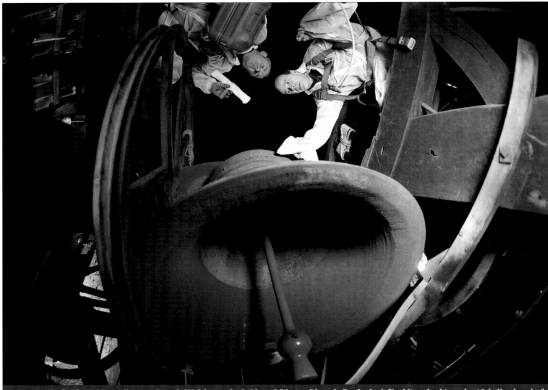

Daire Daly (left) and his colleague Joseph Walshe in the belfry of Christ Church Cathedral, Dublin, checking the 19 bells ahead of their Christmas season's ringing. The oldest bell dates from 1738. Photograph: Julien Behal/Maxwells

watching the increasing amount of rancour that entered Irish public life this year, it is easy to see how the evident frustration that is abroad fits in with the picture painted by Stiglitz.

Globalisation means that labour in poorer countries is competing with labour in the richer, more developed world, and because of this working- and middle-class incomes in the West are no longer growing the way they once did. In some western countries they are stagnating or have even gone into reverse.

Hundreds of millions of people are being lifted out of abject poverty because of this tectonic shift in the distribution of income from labour. By way of an example, Indonesia, with a population of 240 million, expects that its "middle class", which numbered single digit millions at the outset of this century, will top 130 million by 2030. (A middle-class income in Indonesia has been defined as one that exceeds

$3,500 net, in 2005 purchasing power terms.)

Meanwhile, the owners of capital are not just profiting from the fall in labour costs, they also have a global market into which to sell their goods and services. So while for major corporations and the super-rich, the conditions for making ever greater profits have never been better, for the bulk of the population of the developed world, the future is a country filled with challenge.

All of the this feeds into the crisis being faced by party politics in Ireland and the drift seen this year towards nationalism (Sinn Féin), flat-earth socialism (Clare Daly, Paul Murphy), anti-party independents (Ming Flanagan), and other manifestations of people's frustration. This temptation to abandon traditional and centrist political parties is now common in the Western democracies and it would be extraordinary, given the nature of globalisation, if it weren't so.

The question is, what to do? It is a question that policymakers and political parties here and elsewhere have been struggling with for years. This must be part of the reason, I suspect, why Irish "establishment" politicians are so annoyed with the antics of the politicians leading the anti-water protests, who are encouraging the public to believe there is some magical way out of the conundrum the West faces (a united Ireland, a socialist, State-controlled economy, giving a bloody nose to party politics). Of course, the fear that they may lose their seats to these forces is a part of their reaction, but that is not relevant to the debate as to what should be done.

If Ireland, along with other countries in the developed world, is to best manage the challenges being thrown up by globalisation, then what is needed above all is a well-functioning political, economic and social system, be it centre-left or centre-right or dead centre. This is best achieved by having political parties that promote reasonable and serious political programmes, which they can then seek to implement if they get sufficient backing at the polls.

Party politics may be out of favour but people who don't like party politics might find it educational to pay a visit to countries where they run other types of political systems. Frustration, and even rage, is understandable, but people should think carefully before putting anger or fantasy before policy. One of the key drivers of Ireland's recent and spectacular economic crash was the support the electorate gave to unwise and opportunistic politics. It would be nice to think we've learned from our mistake.

There is another reason for turning your back on those who would promote rancour in political debate. During the year a consumer sentiment index run by KBC registered a sudden dip in people's optimism during May. The reason, it was decided, was the local and European elections. The relentless complaining and accusation that people were being exposed to as candidates fought for support, drove the national mood into a slump. We talked ourselves into grumpiness, whereas up to that we had been experiencing increasing hope. The index showed another dip in October, which the bank put down to the water charges row.

Relentlessly negative, rancorous politics is, as well as being worse than useless, bad for your mental health. Ireland is one of the most pleasant places in the world in which to live, stuffed as it is with the nicest, kindest, most well-mannered people on the planet. That's worth remembering.

Happy new year.

JANUARY 6TH 2015

Forty-four lessons for life

Paul Howard (44 years old today)

1 Life is like a toilet roll. The closer you get to the end, the faster it seems to disappear.

2 "I don't know" is the most underrated sentence in the English language.

3 If you can't dance by the age of 18, you're probably never going to be able to dance.

4 You can't make people be who you want them to be. If you don't like the way they are, then you're probably with the wrong people.

5 In January 1962, Decca Records turned down the Beatles in favour of Brian Poole and the Tremeloes. That is all anyone needs to know about rejection.

6 The social contract between humans and dogs might be the best bit of business we have ever done.

7 Securitisation means the exact opposite of how it sounds.

8 Most of us find the middle of the road in the end. Mike Tyson is a vegan. Mick Jagger is doing pilates.

What makes you think you're going to be different?

9 A wise man once told me that whenever he falls out with someone, he asks himself would he go to their funeral if they died tomorrow. If the answer is yes, he thinks: what is so wrong that he can deal with them in death and not in life?

10 Not everyone suits a hat.

11 The North Wind and the Sun, Aesop's fable about the power of gentleness in 112 words: "The North Wind and the Sun had an argument over which of them was the strongest. A traveller came along, wrapped in a warm cloak. They agreed that the one who succeeded in making the traveller remove his cloak should be considered the strongest. The North Wind blew a violent gust in the traveller's face, but the more he blew, the more tightly the traveller pulled the cloak around himself. Eventually, the North Wind gave up. Then it was the Sun's turn. He shone down warmly on the traveller, who immediately removed his cloak. And so the North Wind was obliged to confess that the Sun was the stronger of the two."

12 No one has ever sung a song better than Roy Orbison sang Crawling Back.

13 The person in the world I would most like to meet is whoever came up with the idea of putting yellow boxes on roundabouts. I feel I would have a lot to say to that person.

14 I've discovered that my mother's advice to me

Forty four year old Paul Howard (right), altar ego of Ross O'Carroll-Kelly, at home in his garden in Avoca, Co Wicklow. Photograph: Eric Luke

about DIY – "Do it once and do it right" – can be applied to hundreds of situations, including marriage.

15 About once a week, I find it helps to remember the words of Subh Milis by Séamus Ó Néill. "Bhí subh milis, Ar bhaschrann an dorais, Ach mhúch mé an corraí, Ionam d'éirigh, Mar smaoinigh mé ar an lá, A bheas an baschrann glan, Agus an láimh bheag, Ar iarraidh." ("There was jam on the door handle, But I suppressed the anger that rose up in me, Because I thought of the day that the door handle would be clean, And the little hand would be gone.")

16 Brown to live, blue to neutral . . . Actually, let me check that and come back to you.

17 There comes a point, when you're staring down the barrel of middle age, when you realise that almost all of the stuff you've spent your life amassing is going into a skip when you die. That realisation is very liberating.

18 Never smoking in the first place will save you years of trying to quit.

19 Returning from abroad to discover that someone has put milk and bread in your fridge is to remember how much you missed home while you were away.

20 If everyone stopped to smell the roses, we'd still be waiting for the industrial revolution.

21 To win in love, stop keeping score.

22 Some advice that my grandfather gave to my father, which has served me well in life: "Find out which way the crowd is moving, son, then run like hell in the other direction."

23 I am forever shocked by how petty I can be in the battle for the elbow rest on an airplane.

24 In arguments, forget who's right and remember what's right.

25 "Let it breathe" is good advice when it comes to wine, cheese and a great many situations.

26 A cup of tea tastes 40 per cent better if someone else makes it.

27 Sometimes good things come to an end so better things can come to a beginning.

28 A shut mouth gathers no foot.

29 To try to make someone laugh is a very noble ambition.

30 People fought for my right to vote. But they also fought for my right not to vote. When you've lived long enough to see politicians come to believe the opposite of the things they once believe in, you realise there is no shame in abstaining.

31 Perfection is something we seek in everyone except ourselves.

32 Money is as relevant to happiness as the stock market news is to a chimpanzee.

33 A doctor told me recently that once you reach the age of 40, you've got to start thinking of your body as a vintage car that's never going to be in factory condition again. All you can do is keep it going as best you can by doing running repairs. Every year I find out how right he was.

34 Arguing with strangers on the internet is like wrestling with a pig on a barnyard floor. No one learns anything and all anyone gets is dirty.

35 This old Irish proverb: "If you lose an hour in the morning, you'll end up chasing it all day."

36 Few things give a man as much of a sense of power as catching a fish or poking a fire with a big stick.

37 Nothing bad will ever happen in this country that isn't terrific news for certain middle-class professionals.

38 A day without music is a day without joy.

39 If PG Wodehouse and Damon Runyon were the only authors I ever read, I would consider myself well-read.

40 It is hard to get down off a high horse gracefully. I know this better than most.

41 No man over the age of 30 should wear combat trousers.

42 There's no harm in being embarrassed by the things you did when you were younger. It will save you the trouble of having a midlife crisis later on.

43 It is a healthy thing to take some time out once in a while to laugh at yourself. There's a good chance you're more ridiculous than you realise.

44 Yes, it's brown to live and blue to neutral.

JANUARY 7TH 2015

David Drumm 'not remotely credible', says US judge

Simon Carswell in Washington

Former Anglo Irish Bank chief executive David Drumm has been denied a write-off of more than €10 million in debts after a US judge found him "not remotely credible" and his conduct "both knowing and fraudulent" in statements he made to an American bankruptcy court.

In a damning judgment of the former banker that strips him of a chance for a clean financial start, US Bankruptcy Judge Frank Bailey found that statements made by Mr Drumm (48) were "replete with knowingly false statements, failures to disclose, efforts to misdirect, and outright lies."

"Such conduct disqualifies a debtor from the privilege of a discharge in our system of bankruptcy," said the judge in a ruling issued in Boston.

Judge Bailey issued his 122-page judgment seven months after the end of a six-day trial of a legal action taken by Mr Drumm's former bank, now known as Irish Bank Resolution Corporation.

Mr Drumm moved to the Boston area in June 2009, six months after his resignation from Anglo, and filed for bankruptcy in October 2010 after failing to reach a settlement with the bank over outstanding debts.

The nationalised bank, which is owed €9 million by Mr Drumm arising mostly from loans to buy shares in the now defunct lender, sought to prevent Mr Drumm from writing off his debts through US bankruptcy.

IBRC alleged that Mr Drumm under oath knowingly and fraudulently failed to disclose and otherwise concealed cash and property transfers totalling more than €1 million, which amounted to most assets he owned solely or jointly with his wife Lorraine, to his wife's sole ownership.

The bulk of the cash transfers took place in the final four months of 2008 at a time when he was chief executive of Anglo and the bank's share price was

"Not remotely credible" – former Anglo banker David Drumm. Photograph: Josh Reynolds

Stephanie Roche, Irish footballer and Puskas Award nominee for the Goal of the Year, turns a few heads at the FIFA Ballon d'Or ceremony in Switzerland. Photograph: Alexander Hassenstein/Getty Images

plummeting and the financial institution was facing collapse.

In a major win for the bank, the judge ruled that IBRC and the other plaintiff in the case, the court official overseeing Mr Drumm's bankruptcy, had "established cause to deny him a discharge many times over."

In all, the judge ruled that there were 30 counts out of 52 objections on which the bank and trustee had established cause to deny him a discharge.

The ruling exposes Mr Drumm to further legal actions by the bank, which can pursue him for any past income he has earned or future income.

Mr Drumm's "so stupid" defence in the case - that he mistakenly failed to disclose transfers to his wife in financial statements to the court when he filed for bankruptcy in October 2010 - was rubbished by the judge.

The judge said Mr Drumm's co-operation with his trustee, disclosing information about his finances in a piecemeal fashion from October 2010 to May 2011, was "limited, delayed and shaped to his purposes".

Analysing Mr Drumm's character, the judge described him as "a quick thinker, adept in testimony intended to deflect, misdirect, avoid, fabricate."

"His accounting and knowledge of financial affairs is detailed, precise, almost obsessive. He is confident in his strategising, and by the time he filed his bankruptcy petition, he had been planning and strategising for this eventuality for over two years," said the judge.

Mr Drumm was "no bumbler," he said in the opinion,

"and clearly a controlling type, he knew what he was doing."

Judge Bailey rejected Lorraine Drumm's testimony that she would "like a million euro" of her own in the autumn of 2008 because she feared the worsening banking crisis might spell the end of her marriage or the death of her husband from a stress-induced heart attack.

"Each of them was motivated first and foremost by desire to shelter their assets from seizure by Drumm's creditors, especially [Anglo Irish Bank]," said the judge.

"Their salutary concern to protect Mrs Drumm and their children gave rise to action because creditors would soon be seizing family assets."

The judge said that Mr Drumm was "highly motivated" to protect a home in Wellesley near Boston that the couple bought in 2009 for $2 million, accusing him of withholding information about the property and controlling its release "for some perceived strategic advantage."

The former banker elected not to disclose certain information to the court showing that his withholding of information was "not accidental."

"He doled out the truth only when he sensed he could gain an advantage in doing so," said the judge.

Mr Drumm's release of information about a €250,000 mortgage drawn on a house he owned in Skerries, Co Dublin was intended to hinder and delay his trustee and "even more, IBRC and the interested public."

The judge found it "difficult to believe" that Mr Drumm had failed to disclose to the court and "forgotten" about the sale of two cars, a Range Rover and a BMW, and the transfer of a total of €56,000 in proceeds from the sale of the vehicles to a bank account held solely by his wife.

"Drumm had no trouble remembering many other transfers he had effected even further back in time, yet he omitted virtually every direct transfer to Mrs Drumm and several that were liquidations whose proceeds he transferred to Mrs Drumm," said Judge Bailey.

JANUARY 8TH 2015

'I heard screams. People were running. There were no sirens yet'

Lara Marlowe in Paris

The killers arrived between 11.00am and 11.30am local time yesterday, when the satirical weekly Charlie Hebdo, known for its provocative cartoons mocking Islam, held its weekly editorial meeting.

Two black-clad men, wearing balaclavas and toting assault rifles, entered the lobby of number 10, rue Nicolas Appert and ordered the receptionist to take them to the editor, Stéphane Charbonnier, known as "Charb".

They burst into the conference room and shot 10 people dead, one by one, including Charbonnier and the well-known cartoonists Cabu, Tignous and Wolinski.

The economist Bernard Maris, who was the biographer of John Maynard Keynes and a frequent radio commentator, was a guest at the editorial meeting. He too was shot dead. The attack claimed the lives of 12 French people, including two policemen. Some of the magazine's staff fled to the roof for safety.

"It's a horrible, unbelievable scene," said police officer Emmanuel Quemener of the Alliance police union, briefing journalists at the police line outside. "These are acts of war. Opening fire at close range with a Kalashnikov . . . It was extremely violent. The police know there are these kinds of weapons in the Paris region but I've never seen anyone killed with them at close range."

The getaway car, a small, black Citroen, parked some 50m away with its doors open, waited for the killers

The murders in Paris sparked pan-European demonstrations of support for free speech, crystallised by the slogan Je suis Charlie (I am Charlie), displayed at solidarity gatherings, including this one outside the French embassy in Rome. Photograph: Allesandro Bianchi

in the Allé Verte, perpendicular to the rue Nicolas Appert.

The magazine's previous headquarters, near the Porte de Bagnolet, was fire-bombed in November 2011, when it published a special issue titled "Sharia Hebdo" to mark the election of an Islamist government in Tunisia. Staff joked that it was edited by the Prophet Muhammad.

Twenty-four-seven French police protection, and Charbonnier's permanent police bodyguard, proved totally inadequate. The bodyguard was one of the two police fatalities. An amateur video shot from a window shows the death of the second policeman, from the local 11th district commissariat, in the street outside. He lies wounded on the pavement, face down, tries to push himself up and looks over his shoulder at the approaching gunman, raising both hands in a pleading gesture. The gunman shoots him dead and the murderers proceed, with no great urgency, to their car.

A journalist working at a press agency near Charlie Hebdo said the assailants cried "Allahu Akbar", then "We have killed Charlie Hebdo", and "We have avenged the prophet." Another witness told me he heard them speaking Arabic.

One witness spoke of three killers, but the gunmen got in the front seat of the Citroen and it's not certain there was a third man in the back. At a press conference, Paris prosecutor François Molins said they exchanged fire with police patrols three times as they fled.

The killers collided with another car at the Place du Colonel Fabien, injuring its driver. They then abandoned the Citroen in the rue de Meaux, in northeast Paris, where they also dropped a Kalashnikov charger. They stole a Renault Clio at gunpoint and the police lost track of them.

The police's failure to apprehend the perpetrators of

the most lethal terrorist attack on French territory in decades seems inexplicable. French authorities blocked all the exits from Paris and launched a city-wide manhunt. Members of the public with information were asked to call a freephone number.

Men and women who live and work in this normally quiet neighbourhood between the Bastille and the Place de la République said they were in shock, and worried about the future. "This sort of thing happens to people around the world every day, but we're not used to it," said Gérard (63), a photo engraver. "I heard shooting. I looked out the window and saw a black car with two guys in it, from behind. A police car came towards it from the other direction but it reversed under a rain of bullets."

Police said the gunmen carried out the operation with military precision. A group of Jewish students from the nearby École Progress private lycée came to stare at the scene of the crime from behind the police line. All were aged between 17 and 19.

"France is at war with itself," said one young man. "This is a war against radical Islam."

"Leave France. Go to Israel. That's what I intend to do," said a young woman. "We're not safe here. Even if there's war in Israel we'll be safer there than here."

An older man, who appeared to be a North African Arab, stood nearby, listening and scowling.

Around the corner in the rue Saint-Sabin, Myriam Bensadoun (59), an employee at the local creche, told me: "This is a war of religion, between Catholics and Muslims. For sure."

She listened to shooting for at least 10 minutes. "Then I heard screams. People were running in every direction. There were no sirens yet. There was an eerie kind of silence. The sirens came 15 or 20 minutes later."

"There are good Muslims and bad Muslims," said Sofiane (28), who works in a homeless shelter. "I'm a Muslim – it shows, doesn't it? My wife is French. My children are French. I came here from Morocco when I was 14. For years, everyone has been trying to sully the image of Islam. True Islam is about peace and helping people . . . We're targeted . . . Islam is the most targeted religion in the world."

Several French leaders alluded to war in reacting to the massacre. "It is in these days of war that a people show their determination to save what is most precious to them," said the French centrist politician François Bayrou. Jean-Christophe Lagarde, the president of the centrist UDI, said the slain policemen must be considered "martyrs of the republic".

The killings at Charlie Hebdo underline the chasm between legitimist and extremist Islam. In Cairo, Al Azhar, the leading authority of Sunni Islam, "strongly" condemned "this terrorist attack". Dalil Boubakeur, the rector of the Grand Mosque in Paris and the president of Council of French Muslims, called it "a deafening declaration of war".

JANUARY 10TH 2015

It was over in less than a minute: For France a dark, disorienting week reached a brutal end

Ruadhán Mac Cormaic and Lara Marlowe in Paris

Dusk was settling over Porte de Vincennes. Flashing blue lights illuminated the darkening thoroughfare, where hundreds of armed police had taken up position, their guns trained at the supermarket door. Teams of paramedics looked on from a hastily assembled field hospital. Neighbours crouched to watch from their apartment windows. An uneasy calm hung in the air. Suddenly, four loud explosions boomed in quick succession. Then a brief pause followed by a round of intense, rapid gunfire, making a sound so deep and insistent it was as if the ground beneath us was being thumped by some great force. As the gunfire echoed around the streets, the supermarket door opened and

A gunman shoots dead a wounded French policeman, Ahmed Merabet, who is shown lying on the ground, his arms raised, as the attacker and his accomplice flee the offices of the French satirical paper Charlie Hebdo where they murdered 11 people. Photograph: Reuters (still from amateur camera phone video).

more than half a dozen people, dazed and screaming, ran out towards the police. Among them was a man clutching an infant to his chest.

A police commando, hit by a bullet from the shop, fell to the ground. Two colleagues grabbed him by the uniform and hauled him along the ground to safety before joining the stream of black suits pouring into the shop. More shots. A fleet of ambulances moved in.

It was chaotic and bloody, and it was all over in less than a minute. For France, a dark, disorienting week had reached its violent conclusion. Three men suspected of two terror attacks in as many days were killed in separate shoot-outs after taking hostages in the city and its eastern outskirts.

The raid on the kosher supermarket at Porte de Vincennes, where four hostages were also killed, came within minutes of police storming a printworks in Dammartin-en-Goële, close to Charles de Gaulle airport, where the two brothers suspected of killing 12 journalists and policemen in an attack on Charlie

Hebdo magazine on Wednesday were shot dead by police. The atrocity at the offices of the satirical title was the worst terrorist attack in France in more than half a century.

The Charlie Hebdo killings prompted a global outpouring of outrage and revulsion, with tens of thousands of people turning out at rallies and vigils in support of press freedom under the slogan "Je Suis Charlie".

In a national television address, French president François Hollande concluded an extraordinary day by solemnly appealing for national unity after what he called "a tragedy for the nation".

He will join other national and foreign leaders at a "silent rally" in Paris tomorrow. German chancellor Angela Merkel, British prime minister David Cameron, Spain's Mariano Rajoy and Matteo Renzi of Italy have said they will also attend.

The decision to launch simultaneous raids was taken by Mr Hollande at a meeting with his prime minister and ministers for the interior and justice.

Above: Some of the Charlie Hebdo shooting victims (clockwise from top left) : Charlie Hebdo publishing director Stephane Charbonnier; economist and journalist Bernard Maris; cartoonists Georges Wolinski (left) and Jean Cabut (known as Cabu); cartoonist Bernard Verlhac (aka Tignous).

Right: The two terrorists, believed linked to al-Qaeda, brothers Said Kouachi (left) and Cherif Kouachi who were later shot dead by police.

Brothers Chérif (32) and Said Kouachi (34) had holed themselves up in the printworks on Friday morning as police closed in on them after a huge two-day manhunt across northern France. Officials said the pair were acquaintances of Amedi Coulibaly, who is suspected of killing a policewoman in Montrouge in southern Paris on Thursday before taking hostages at the supermarket. Gael Fabiano, of the UNSA police union, told The Irish Times Coulibaly walked into the shop firing a Kalashnikov. It was, Mr Hollande said, "an appalling anti-Semitic act".

The hostage taken by the Kouachi brothers at the printworks survived uninjured. A second employee managed to hide from the two gunmen under a sink, escaping unharmed after being able to speak to police on the phone and describe the building's layout.

When the raid began, the brothers ran from the building, shooting 50 rounds of ammunition. A local politician had earlier said they had told negotiators they wanted "to die as martyrs".

BFM TV revealed that it had been in telephone contact with Coulibaly and Chérif Kouachi during the sieges. In a calm voice, Kouachi told the television channel he was financed by Anwar al-Awlaki, the

People in Paris show their solidarity for the victims of the Charlie Hebdo terrorist attack.
Photograph: Thubault Camus/Associated Press.

US-born leader of al-Qaeda in the Arabian Peninsula, and that he and Said worked for al-Qaeda in Yemen. Earlier this week, police found an Islamic State flag in the boot of the brothers' abandoned Citroen.

In a second recorded conversation, Coulibaly told BFM they had synchronised the Charlie Hebdo and Montrouge attacks. He said he had targeted the Paris shop "because it was Jewish", that he was holding 16 hostages, and that four people had died when he entered the supermarket. He said he had been mandated by Islamic State.

Citing reliable police and judicial sources, French media reported that police timed their raid on the supermarket as Coulilaby was at prayer: he reportedly used the shop's phone and failed to hang up properly.

The sieges put an already tense city on edge. Dammartin-en-Goële was sealed off, its residents ordered to stay at home, its children under lockdown in their schools while helicopters circled overhead. At Porte de Vincennes, a busy transport hub and a gateway to the city from the east, traffic was stopped and Metro stations closed. The nearby Paris ring-road lay eerily quiet and deserted.

"I'm in shock," said Jean-Marc Sellam, watching events from the police cordon. "But I've been in shock for 48 hours." His friend's niece, in her early 20s, was among the hostages. Around him, hundreds of police, including dozens of plain-clothes officers with handguns, streamed towards the scene.

French Jewish leaders called for vigilance. With the city on high alert, synagogues shut their doors and the mayor's office ordered the closure of shops on rue des Rosiers, a street known for its Jewish-run shops and bakeries.

The violence has raised questions about the surveillance of radical Islamists, religion and censorship in a country where Islam and immigration are already fraught political themes.

Chérif Kouachi, one of the Charlie Hebdo attackers, was known to police and intelligence services after being convicted of terrorism charges in 2008 for ties to a network sending jihadis to fight US forces in Iraq.

Prime minister Manuel Valls greeted the surviving Charlie Hebdo journalists as they arrived for work at the headquarters of Libération, which has provided them with office-space and computers. They plan to bring out the paper as planned next Wednesday, and to print a million copies.

JANUARY 13TH 2015

My Health Experience: 'I can still move my arms enough to put them round my wife'

Peter Carvosso

I wish I had been a little less cynical about the ice bucket campaign last summer, joking with my wife that the sooner they introduced the water tax the better.

Well, that came back to haunt Mr Smart-Ass Carvosso.

Just a few weeks later, a doctor who looked disconcertingly like Jim Carrey, the comic actor with the impossibly wide smile, gave me some news that wasn't funny at all. In this role he was Scary Carrey as he told me I had the illness all those celebrities got a soaking for.

The doctor, Peter Widdess-Walsh, is a very warm man, and this shines through his professional presentation. I almost felt sorry for him as he struggled to come out with the words: motor neurone disease.

It's the one that became well known in Ireland after RTÉ's Colm Murray revealed in 2012 he was suffering from it. I was editor of the Irish Independent Weekend Review at the time, and we ran a front cover with a picture of him, lauding his courage as he faced up to this terrifying illness that shuts down your body but not your mind.

Peter Carvosso.

I'm sure he was braver than I am. I haven't even had the courage to Google it yet. I've been too scared to ask the doctors any hard questions.

I suspect that my wonderful wife knows more about my prospects than I do, but I'm frightened to ask her. I joke with them all that I'm in Cairo's river: de Nile.

It all started, although I had no idea at the time, just a few months ago. I had a pain in the top of my left shoulder when I lifted my arm. It didn't bother me: I just put it down to wear and tear.

I love fly-fishing for trout and would spend hours on my favourite rivers – the Liffey, the Nore and the Anner – wading upstream looking for the tell-tale rings that show where a fish is sipping in an olive or perhaps a sedge. This summer I found myself getting tired quickly and said to my wife that age was beginning to creep up on me. The weariness vanished on those rare days when the trout went mad for the fly, a syndrome every angler will recognise.

It was difficult getting in and out of the river, and one day I had a real scare when I got stuck in a boggy bit of bankside.

I must have known something was seriously wrong, because I started taking pictures of the loveliest pools as memories for when I couldn't fish again.

I caught my last trout, a handsome little half-pounder, on the beautiful Nore at Thomastown, Co Kilkenny. I gave him a special little tickle as I gently put him in the water to swim away.

The final line in my angling diary says: "Last cast?" And I put the fly I used – a black and peacock spider, since you ask – into a box by itself.

So long, Spiderman.

The next clue that something was wrong was when I had to put an extra notch in my belt.

I had needed to lose a bit of belly, the product of my liking a glass of wine and the occasional whiskey. In the spring, as an experiment, I decided to give up the drink for a few months. So, I had a new teetotal tum. That, I thought in my innocence, explained the weight loss.

The next step, or rather non-step, in my decline was a pain in my left calf which left me with a bit of a limp. I put that down to one of our three-hour country hikes.

Over the next few weeks my walking got worse; I could scarcely make half a mile round the block. I felt that my arms were getting weaker, too.

Another symptom was a slight difficulty swallowing, which meant I wasn't eating as much as I should.

And to cap it all I was sleeping badly, waking up every couple of hours and fretting.

Then I weighed myself and was shocked to find that I'd lost about two stone.

A typical man, it was only then that I thought I'd better get checked out by my GP. I told her what had happened and said I thought it must be cancer. Then, to my amazement, I burst into tears and blubbed for the next 10 minutes as she dabbed my eyes with tissues.

She got the ball rolling with blood tests, X-rays and a trip to a psychiatrist to see if anxiety was causing my weight loss, or vice versa.

The tests all came back okay, which just made me think they were looking in the wrong place.

Next I rehearsed that old chestnut – anyone who sees a psychiatrist needs their head examined – as I sat down with Dr Ian Schneider in St John of God Hospital.

He went into action immediately. He admitted me for a short time while the hospital monitored me, boosted my food intake with special protein supplements, arranged a rake of tests at the Blackrock Clinic and tried to allay my very real worries.

I suppose anyone would feel fearful about a psychiatric hospital, but I felt safe and cared for. Almost embarrassingly so. The doctors, nurses, physio, occupational therapy people and social workers were extraordinary. I felt like saying, that's enough about me; how are you? Just good manners, really.

My response to everything was that my head would be grand as soon as I put on weight and could walk properly again.

At the Blackrock Clinic, they stuck cameras down me, up me, scanned me from head to toe and did even more exotic blood tests. Every day the nurses gave me more good news: no cancer, good heart, lungs and liver. They told me I didn't have diseases I'd never even heard of.

I was a very healthy 60-something, apart from shuffling around like a drunk penguin and gulping for air as if I'd just finished a 10-second 100m race.

Poolbeg Lighthouse in Dublin, sitting among waves and white horses as storm winds whip the sea.
Photograph: Eric Luke/Irish Times

Emily Duiffy from Desmond College in Limerick with her novel portable bubble wrap cover for the homeless at the BT Young Scientist Competition. Photograph: Alan Betson

The next step was a visit to a neurologist in Blackrock. There were more tests, including an MRI brain scan, which freaked me out completely until I remembered I was a stiff-upper-lip Englishman and started to behave myself.

Everyone was seriously concerned about my breathing, which I had put down to panicking about my other ailments.

After dinner they put me on a breathing mask, and at 10pm Dr Widdess-Walsh came in to deliver the grim news. That was a few weeks ago and I'm still in the clinic.

My next instalment will be about how you cope when you hear your life will be much shorter than you'd expected. All with the help of the fantastic staff here and my family.

The problem is that I can type with only one finger. But I'm hoping to be able to raise the finger to MND for a while longer.

For the moment I'm happy that I can still move my arms enough to put them around my wife, squeeze her and pretend for a few moments that nothing is wrong.

Peter Carvosso hoped to write further about his diagnosis and living with MND but died on January 19th.

JANUARY 16TH 2015

How I learned to start worrying and love the angst

Hilary Fannin

I suppose it's a seasonal thing: this need for reappraisal, this new-broom feeling that pops up with the lost turkey thermometer (a bit late now, mate) when you open the kitchen drawer to shove the electricity bill out of sight.

My resolutions this year are exactly the same as my resolutions last year: work more, drink less and don't forget to worm the cat.

Snow in Omagh makes driving difficult. Photograph: Niall Carson/Press Association.

I feel like a goldfish with a three-second memory function; a fiftysomething, wrinkled goldfish, that is, with a persistent spare tyre and a mouthful of overpriced root-canal work, but a goldfish nonetheless.

There's something decidedly goldfishy about facing four-square into another year, resolving to pull up your baggy socks and rein in billowing distractions, and then, in the time it takes to circuit your bowl, failing and forgetting, only to remember and resolve, again and again. Reigniting oneself each new year with the same spent match.

Mind you, the myth that goldfish have a three-second memory has been blown clean out of the scientific water, apparently. According to some rabidly dull article I found in the dentist's waiting room, goldfish can – wait for it – outshine trout in cognitive functioning.

Trout? You must be codding me. Those perspicacious freshwater fellows?

You could have knocked me down with a sterilised toothpick.

Apparently goldfish can actually remember things for about five months. That Christmas compromise gift (no, you cannot have a puppy) swimming around in its tiny glass dome on top of the children's bedside locker and slowly turning an alarming shade of mud green is not actually thrown into a lather of wonder every time it swims past that ornamental aquarium castle you bought it on Ebay. Its little guppy mouth is not opening for another sprinkling of shrimp pellets. It's trying to tell you that it's bored out of its underestimated brain and is having an aqua-stential crisis that's going to last until May, when its five months are up and it can forget again.

Anyway, where was I? Oh yep, failed and failing resolutions. Aside from "work more, drink less" (which is probably a slight improvement on "work less, drink more", which I had been contemplating), I have had one original impulse this January, one notion I might manage to remain faithful to. I thought, in 2015, that I might try to embrace anxiety.

Don't ask me for the statistics (look, I have significant problems counting beyond 10) but they say – whoever they are – that about one in six of us is prone to anxiety.

Personally I think you'd want to be truly off your rocker not to be feeling anxious in this shaky age of global warming, feral social media, unflattering leisurewear and decorative contact lenses.

So it's consoling to predict that anxiety will be the new cool.

There is a current television advertising campaign for a very expensive perfume, a brand synonymous with opulence and luxury, which makes neurosis and mild depression look aspirational, a wannabe lifestyle choice.

You know the one I mean: the ad artily slows down You're the One That I Want, from Grease and features an awfully worried-looking, albeit beautiful, woman wading out of a frothy ocean in bone-dry surfing gear, her golden locks barely dampened, in search of her lover, only to find a handwritten note from him, saying "To my heart I must be true".

The lover, an anxious chap, with his knitted brow and five o'clock shadow, is so busy negotiating his existential despair, his fancy car and his Malibu-style beach house that he can't manage to do up his dicky bow properly.

The fretful pair eventually reunite in a gothic concert-hall box, but only after a lot of foreboding looks and troubled perfume-spraying.

I like the ad (as in "Oh God, look at this awful ad"). It's a festival of mild depression and good tailoring, which seems to imply that it's no longer enough to be rich and thin, we now also need to be steeped in an alluring personal crisis.

So that's it: rather than trying to banish negatives and stamp out the pins and needles of paranoia by running around the park, eating a balanced diet and avoiding caffeine, bank managers, parent-teacher meetings, gin, deadlines and effortlessly elegant people, I'm simply going to embrace my angst.

Ask any alarmingly intelligent goldfish: anxiety is a cultural condition, a function of the times we live in. Learn to love it.

JANUARY 17TH 2015

Planning tribunal which garnered huge interest comes to naught

Paul Cullen

The planning tribunal, in its heyday, was box office. For years, nightly news led with the latest from Dublin Castle, where the public gallery was regularly packed to capacity. Evidence was re-enacted on the radio and as cabaret theatre.

In 2002, ordinary citizens queued around the block when the chairman, Mr Justice Feargus Flood, published his damning report on the payments made to former Fianna Fáil minister Ray Burke.

Flood retired and the tribunal moved on to other things – mostly involving Frank Dunlop or Bertie Ahern. Burke and the businessmen who bribed him were told to pay their own legal costs, although the criminal proceedings expected by some never materialised. The tribunal, now chaired by Mr Justice Alan Mahon, completed its hearings and published a final report in 2012.

End of story, or so it seemed, with only the substantial legal costs of hundreds of witnesses remaining to be paid. Yet, this turned out to be far from the end of the tale for a tribunal that always had the whiff of controversy about it.

Years after the hearings into Burke and former planning official George Redmond, a succession of legal challenges has unpicked its work to such an extent that those early years now seem largely to have been a waste of time.

All of those who appeared before the tribunal in this era, even those found to have been corrupt, are getting their legal costs; in Burke's case, these may run to €5 million. Findings that they hindered and obstructed the inquiry have been withdrawn. The corruption findings against Redmond have been withdrawn and it is expected corruption findings against others will also be retracted.

So how did it come to this? How did a tribunal with a massive budget, widespread public support and copious material to investigate end up falling flat on its face? Whose fault is it and who should foot the bill?

While this unravelling of the tribunal stems from legal actions taken by witnesses, the judiciary has long had its doubts about the tribunal process, and the planning tribunal in particular.

As far back as 1999, a High Court judge was describing the tribunal's powers to make orders as "draconian". A former taxing master in the court called tribunals "the Frankenstein of modern Irish society".

Mr Justice Adrian Hardiman of the Supreme Court, one of the tribunal's chief critics over many years, complained about the "grotesque" cost of tribunals and their duration, which he characterised as "nothing less than appalling".

For many years, the tribunal enjoyed the protection conferred by widespread public and political support, but, as the years passed and the bills mounted, disillusionment set in and the courts began to look critically at its workings.

The start of the unravelling can be traced back to a seemingly innocuous ruling made by Mr Justice Flood in January 1999. In it, he ruled that he would only circulate documents to other parties when he found them to be relevant to an issue. Fast forward to 2005, when property developer Owen O'Callaghan won a legal battle against the tribunal for access to the unedited versions of documents held by the inquiry.

As far as O'Callaghan was concerned, the missing bits were very relevant; his lawyers claimed the tribunal concealed parts of the documents containing "wild" allegations against him by whistleblower Tom Gilmartin.

This ruling opened the door for other parties – if they could afford the litigation – to seek the unredacted versions of documents supplied to them by the tribunal. One such witness was Joseph Murphy jnr,

Taoiseach Enda Kenny and Tanaiste Joan Burton testing virtual reality goggles at the Plan for Jobs 2015 event in Dublin... and Martyn Turner's take, a day later.

Photograph: CyrilByrne/Irish Times

a wealthy businessman found by the tribunal to have made a corrupt payment to Burke.

In Murphy's case, the whistleblower on which the tribunal based this finding was James Gogarty, the original "star witness" in Dublin Castle. The octogenarian former boss of Murphy's company, best known for his, "Will we get a receipt? Will we fuck" line, died in 2005.

In 2010, the Supreme Court ruled in favour of Murphy and a colleague, Frank Reynolds. The court said it was a "cause of concern" that Mr Justice Flood had edited Gogarty's interviews and statements in a manner which cut out serious allegations against at least four prominent people.

Mr Justice Hardiman, now in the Supreme Court, linked the concealment of this potentially "explosive" material to the credibility of Gogarty. Effectively, he was asking whether Gogarty was to be believed on his main allegations if he was making these other, seemingly implausible, allegations.

Murphy's litigation was aimed only at securing his legal costs, which were duly awarded. The court also quashed the finding of hindering and obstructing on the basis that this was a criminal offence which only the courts could decide. The Murphy ruling blew a hole in the tribunal's defence of its procedures and others were happy to march through that hole.

Redmond, whose own action had stalled for want of resources and confidence about winning, revived his case. The tribunal threw in the towel and Redmond, once an avid tennis player, won game, set and match when his case was settled just before Christmas.

Now the tribunal, having studied the Murphy judgment, not only withdrew the hindering and obstruction findings against Redmond and awarded him his costs, but it also undertook to withdraw all findings of corruption.

Redmond was in the clear, and it followed that the findings against others mentioned in the tribunal report on him – Murphy, Reynolds and builder Michael Bailey – would also have to be dropped.

What though about the tribunal's second interim report, the one that became a bestseller? In the Murphy decision, Mr Justice Nial Fennelly stated "it would be wrong, unjust and anomalous if the court were to be permitted to reach a conclusion that the findings in the third interim report [on Redmond] were invalid but allow the second [on Burke] to stand".

On the basis of this comment, the tribunal has no choice but to redact the second interim report by removing the hindering and obstruction findings against Burke and the businessmen who made payments to him. It may well go further and remove all corruption findings contained in the report.

It doesn't stop there. O'Callaghan is pursuing a legal action aimed at overturning the findings of the tribunal in relation to him. The success of publican Charlie Chawke – one of Bertie Ahern's "dig-out" friends – in overturning a finding of non-co-operation by the tribunal and winning his costs may

encourage others to challenge some of the findings of the final report of the tribunal.

Mr Justice Mahon says the final cost of the tribunal will be less than €159 million, considerably less than previous estimates. It is also true that the matters uncovered by the inquiry led to Revenue investigations that netted the Exchequer large sums of money in tax settlements.

Yet, the failure of the inquiry to make its findings watertight and the lack of any substantial follow-up to its reports, are causes for concern. Set up to allay public cynicism about corruption in the planning process, the tribunal has added to that disillusionment. Just as it was said about the beef tribunal that the only person threatened with jail was the journalist who revealed the scandal, one of the few parties at the planning tribunal left to pay its own legal bills is this newspaper, which published the revelations about Ahern's finances that led to him being investigated publicly by the tribunal.

JANUARY 19TH 2015

Brave Leo Varadkar gives it to us straight

Miriam Lord

Leo Varadkar was a teenager when he came out as openly Fine Gael.

The early signs were there. His mother now understands why, at the tender age of seven, young Leo confided that he wanted to be the Minister for Health.

At the time "she was mortified".

Minister for Health Varadkar is still saying things that stop people in their tracks.

Some see it as his biggest failing – he's too straight sometimes for our nod and wink political culture.

Yesterday morning, he shocked the political establishment by telling RTÉ's Miriam O'Callaghan that "a politician should trust people with the truth". Then he shocked the nation by revealing that he is still only 36 years old.

It was his birthday.

Doing anything on the big day?

"Not doing anything special."

Nothing?

Nothing, apart from becoming the first Irish Cabinet Minister to publicly come out as gay.

It came as news to a lot of people, including some from his own parliamentary party.

But to others it came as a relief. For months, Varadkar had been biding his time, building up to an announcement he really shouldn't have had to make.

It should be nobody's business but his own, except that isn't how things work at the sharp end of his trade.

With a referendum on marriage equality drawing near and issues such as surrogacy legislation and the ban on gay men giving blood on his immediate agenda, he knew he had to go public about his sexuality.

"I don't want anyone to think I've a hidden agenda or that I'm not being fully honest with them," he said. And Leo also knew he just couldn't talk in "a detached" manner about subjects he feels passionate about.

"I want to be an equal citizen in my own country." That is a astonishing declaration for a Cabinet Minister and PFT (potential future Taoiseach) to make.

Leo's brave declaration will also put a stop to the gallop of the gossipmongers.

It is true that certain media organisations have been itching to "out" him. Queries were regularly submitted to his department seeking information about his personal life. Certain photographers were

Health Minister and Fine Gael TD Leo Varadakar talking to Miriam O'Callaghan during his RTE radio interview in which he spoke about being gay. Photograph: Aidan Crawley

keeping an eye on his movements.

He had to time his announcement between health controversies. He had a small window of opportunity yesterday.

For those aware of where his interview was heading, it made for difficult listening. Everyone else must have wondered why Miriam was taking the scenic route through Leo's childhood and assorted nuggets of family trivia.

He sounded nervous as he tip-toed with Miriam towards the main reason for their chat.

She finally, excruciatingly, broached it.

"You are, by all accounts, very eligible. But you haven't settled down yet, have you?"

The words haltingly spoken, but laden with meaning. Leo wound up for his big admission, swallowing hard as he talked about how he values his privacy and the privacy of his family and friends.

Miriam let him go round the houses until he finally got to the point . . . "so, but em, but em, I am, I am a gay man. It's not a secret, but not something that everybody would necessarily know. But it isn't something I've spoken publicly about before."

And that was it. Done.

He said it wasn't a big deal for him anymore.

But for once, straight-talking Leo was being a little sparing with the truth. It is a big deal, and he knows it.

It shouldn't be, but it is.

There was something very touching about the interview. Cabinet Minister Leo talking about telling his big sister and friends and how he told his parents. How his mother was worried at first that he might get beaten up in the street or have his sexuality used against him in his political career.

"The only thing she wanted for me was to be happy."

Then, of course, he had to tell the Boss. Enda immediately drew on his extensive knowledge of The Gays.

"Have you ever been to the Pantibar?" he asked his Minister for Health. Leo said he was never in the place.

"There you are, Varadkar, I'm ahead of you already!" chortled the Taoiseach.

Who'd have thought it? On a Sunday morning, after Mass, roast in the oven, lovely Miriam on the radio and a Government Minister telling the whole country that he's gay and happy and still the same fella he was before they heard his news.

And the sky didn't cave in and Sunday morning went on as normal.

Afterwards, Leo, with a big weight lifted off his shoulders, went out for a run to clear his head.

FEBRUARY 4TH 2015

Emotional inflation in the internet age

Frank McNally

Has anyone else noticed a big upsurge of late in the number of people claiming to be "incredibly excited"? The latest example I've seen was the singer Hozier, who declared himself "incredibly excited" about performing at this week's Grammy Awards. And all right, that's a reasonable excuse for excitement. But it's also an exception.

Certain classes of people – PR consultants are a high-risk group – are now wont to get "incredibly excited" at the launch of a new brand of odour-eating shoe inserts. Or if not excited, they're "incredibly proud", as Aer Lingus declared itself in a statement the other day after winning an award.

Note the implication in these statements that the level of emotion is very unusual for the person or persons in question. If somebody tells you he's "incredibly proud" about something, he's also hinting that humility is his normal state. If "incredibly excited", he's asking you to believe he's not usually given to such giddy sentiment. And yet for those of us who are naturally humble, and grounded, the apparent ubiquity these days of extreme pride and excitement can be a challenge. After all, if so many other people can work themselves into a fervour, the rest of us must be emotionally stunted.

The ability to find things "stunning" is another example of the phenomenon. You see the word a lot now, especially on social media, and most often applied to pictures of sunsets, or a harvest moon, or mountain scenery. And sometimes the views in question are indeed spectacular.

But if you believe Twitter, the incidence of people being stunned by pictures is now so high that the company should introduce concussion protocols. Henceforth if a user is stunned twice in the same week, there should be mandatory medical assessment. ("How many fingers am I holding up? Twelve? Sorry pal –no more Twitter pictures for you until after the next full moon.")

Again though, the natural human tendency is that, underwhelmed by things other people find "stunning", you fear it must be you, and wonder if you should ask the doctor about putting you on emotional Viagra, so that you can get your responses up to standard.

You need to remind yourselves at these times, as I do, that the people claiming to be stunned or incredibly excited may just be working in parts of the economy where verbal hyperinflation of sentiment has become the norm.

Witness, for example, what happened to the word "passionate" over the last decade. It used to be hard currency, reserved for the feelings of poets and lovers. Then it was co-opted into company boardrooms as the entry-level adjective for describing how enthusiastic you were about your job. Now it's printed by the wheelbarrow load, like the interwar German mark, with similar value.

But there seems to be a particular urge for people to exaggerate when on social media. No doubt a lot of it this is about the need to grab attention, which you won't do by flagging, say, "almost interesting pictures of tonight's full moon". Better risk disappointing the viewer (especially given the chance that he'll think it's him) than be invisible.

And then too, of course, with so many human interactions now taking place remotely, people are more free to exaggerate. Even on an old-fashioned person-to-person phone call, for example, you would

John Gibson of Massey Bros, funeral directors, walks in front of his company's latest way of saying farewell to lately departed motorbikers – a Harley-Davidson Electra Glide hearse.   Photograph: Brenda Fitzsimons

have had to support a claim to be "incredibly excited" with suitable sound effects: a vocal tremor, heavy breathing, etc. If you weren't really feeling it, this would be hard work.

It's the same with the concept, so popular in the internet age, of things being "laugh out loud" funny. Yes, we've all seen solitary people laugh out loud while reading on a bus or train, or in a cafe.

But it's a fairly unusual event. So much so that the person who does it will be embarrassed and try to suppress the laughter. Or if he doesn't, and laughs freely, others will quickly feel the urge to move away from him, in case he's an axe murderer.

Whereas when communicating by email, or text, removed from the risk of visual inspection, you can quite brazenly claim that something has made you LOL, or even ROFLMAO, while in reality sitting glum-faced on the No 13 bus.

Never mind that there isn't room to roll on the floor, or that if it were physically possible to laugh your ass off, there'd be a lot of gyms out of business. You can even accompany your exaggeration with one of those little smiley faces. There's one for every sentiment, and they don't call them "emoti-cons" for nothing.

FEBRUARY 4TH 2015

Why catwalk snapper Anna Bauer has packed her paintbrushes for Dublin

Deirdre McQuillan

She has captured every major figure in fashion in her book Backstage, shot campaign imagery for Céline, Victoria Beckham, Zara and others, has photographed leading culinary and sports stars as well as travel stories from all over the world. Now,

in a surprise move, the German photographer Anna Bauer, who had been based in New York, has put a very successful career on hold to study for an MFA in painting in NCAD in Dublin and has settled down to a new life in Stoneybatter.

In a recent issue of the Gentlewoman magazine, the camera was turned on her for a change, as she modelled gowns from Lanvin, Marc Jacobs and others, her fitness from body rolling and boxing very much in evidence.

"It was fun to dress up," says Bauer, who is togged out in wet- weather cycling gear when we meet in a Dublin cafe. She is bright and articulate with a wide, disarming smile. She chose Ireland to study because she needed a break from New York after 12 years.

"I enjoy painting so much. It is so different to photography and Dublin takes me out of everything and I can really concentrate." Her parents have a house in Tipperary, close to Dromineer, where her brothers race a Shannon One sailing boat. The mother of one of their friends, who had studied at NCAD, triggered Bauer's interest in studying there. She moved to Dublin in September, and within a few days she had joined the Newmarket Food Co-op and Arbour Hill boxing club. "I like communities," she says.

Bauer is from Marburg in Germany, home of the brothers Grimm. She grew up on a big farm, and after school she interned with a commercial photographer in Hamburg. That was followed by a period as a carpenter, "as I wanted something more grounded", but she ended up moving to New York in 2002 to study for a BFA at the School of Visual Arts. "It takes a certain determination to be a photographer, but after assisting others, I slowly got my own jobs."

Her first was photographing musicians for Fader magazine. At the time the magazine's creative director was Phil Bicker, who had been one of the first to shoot Kate Moss for the Face years earlier in London. Later Bauer travelled the world for Gourmet magazine for two years, photographing chefs and locations until the magazine folded. In 2006 her pictures ended up in the National Portrait Gallery competition in London; one of the judges, Jenny Dyson, founder of a

Artist Anna Baurer in her studio on Dublin's Thomas Street. Photograph: Cyril Byrne

London Fashion Week freesheet, commissioned her to take photos backstage in 2007.

With the encouragement of Sean Cunningham, a well-known runway photographer, Bauer moved on to Paris on the last leg of the season. There her backstage work caught the attention of Fabien Baron, editor-in-chief of Interview magazine. He published eight pages of her portraits of musicians, artists and fashion insiders for a 40th-anniversary special edition.

This ultimately resulted in the publication of Backstage. Using a heavy, large- format camera, she captured major industry figures such as Anna Wintour, Karl Lagerfeld, Kate Moss, Cate Blanchett and Kanye West, along with backstage models, hairdressers and make-up artists. The directness, honesty and unity of these black-and-white portraits capture the transience of the industry.

Bauer's big break came when Céline hired her to shoot backstage at its show, which was then followed by Victoria Beckham. "Then I started making money and ended up shooting more fashion. It's a hard world to break into – it's a hardworking world – and people are very dedicated, especially those doing hair and make-up. It is amazing the amount of skill and

talent during fashion weeks. I have a big respect for the runway photographers; the last picture in my book is an homage to them because they don't get a lot of credit."

Her camera, like a modern version of the old Gandolfi, demands a different interaction from the subjects than digital snaps.

"People have to concentrate for two minutes and it does something to them. Mario Testino [a celebrated Peruvian photographer] took a long time, but did it in the end. He likes to control images himself. Karl Lagerfeld was so nice and has an appreciation of photography, though my flash wouldn't go off and I was so nervous."

Keeping fit is important to her. In New York she started boxing with legendary Panamanian trainer Hector Roca in Gleason's, an old boxing gym in Brooklyn. Last summer she did a shoot with him and soccer player Franck Ribéry for Audi magazine.

"When they spar with you in New York, they tone down, but here sparring is rougher, and they start boxing at seven and eight and everybody wants to be Katie Taylor," she says.

Painting and boxing relate to each other in a bizarre

way, she says. "In each case you don't know what is going to happen. In boxing you do know that someone wants to punch you, but you are really on your own in the ring. Both share an unknown outcome. I have not yet figured out why I like boxing, but I do think the world would be a better place if people started to do more martial arts."

A love of colour drew her to painting. "I started with acrylics in New York, and with oil-painting classes, and I really like it, though it is very difficult." In NCAD she has her own studio and is tutored by painter Robert Armstrong, working on colour and shape, and course director Declan Long. The painter Vicky Uslé, daughter of the Spanish painter Juan Uslé is a friend and "my other teacher".

In June and July she plans to return to New York to shoot, make money and then come back. "Photography, when it works, is a great way to earn an income. I have no idea what painting will do and whether or not it will be lucrative, but I really enjoy doing things, and painting is very physical, though it will remain separate to photography. It's a different mindset."

FEBRUARY 7TH 2015

Robbie Henshaw is focused on winning above all else

Gerry Thornley

The first thing that strikes you about Robbie Henshaw is how grounded and level-headed he is. Aside from a striking physicality which is unusual for an Irish midfielder, that maturity and sensibility ought to be a help. After all, it can't be easy being the anointed one.

With Gavin Duffy injured at the start of the season before last, no sooner was Henshaw pitched into the team and Eric Elwood declaring him a definite international of the future, since when Brian O'Driscoll has publicly declared his faith in Henshaw's ability to have a long international career in the Ireland midfield.

Recalling Elwood's declaration that he was destined to play for Ireland even though was barely out of school and still only 19, Henshaw admits with a smile: "I was totally shell-shocked. 'What's he on about here?' And then obviously Brian saying that has given me the confidence to kick on and just not look back and keep moving forward.

"I suppose it does put a bit of pressure on me," he concedes, though you'd never think it in his demeanour or his performances, "but I just try and stay positive all the time and keep putting out consistent performances and that's how I keep my confidence up."

It says everything about the 21-year-old's rapid progress that he looked the one nailed-on certainty to play in the Ireland midfield against Italy, be it at '12' or '13', and accordingly he is, along with the celebrated pair of Paul O'Connell and Johnny Sexton, one of the three players to feature in Three's striking series of TV commercials called "All It Takes is Everything".

"I've seen some of it, yeah," says Henshaw of the ads, in which Sexton turns into a butterfly whereas the young centre turns into a ball of fire. "It looks good. I'd take the fire ahead of the butterflies any day."

That he has been identified as one of the three poster boys, as it were, for the series, is quite something considering this will be his Six Nations debut. "Yeah, I know. It's all part of the game I suppose these days."

Last season he was 24th man in four of Ireland's Six Nations matches, including their coronation as champions in Paris in O'Driscoll's last game, which gave him a taste of things to come and how Joe Schmidt's meticulous attention to detail also incorporated planning for the future.

"I think that has prepared me, definitely for this year. I know what matchday is like. I know what the build up is like, the hotel. Even though you know you're not

Robbie Henshaw by Morgan Treacy/Inpho.

going to be playing but there is the slightest chance that you will be playing, so you have to be prepared. It was, very memorable when their number eight was held up in the end and we got that turnover. It was a great feeling to get the win, even sitting in the stands, but it's a new challenge this year."

"I do want it more this year. I know I was there or thereabouts last year but I was on the outskirts of it, but definitely I want it this year and I want to try and compete for it."

O'Driscoll's generosity of spirit, and being acutely conscious that even he must pass on the jersey (and assuredly took it on to new levels) has helped Henshaw no end. Following on from chats at pitch-side, or over coffee or over a computer last season, Henshaw says they have remained "close" and receives texts before and after games.

"He'd give me the good and the bad of a game, how I did and what I could improve on. It's great that he actually came on board and helped me last year in camp. He didn't have to at all. He just went out of his way and that shows his character as well.

"He was a genius at most things in the game, and he went through lines of attack, lines in defence, when to come up hard off the line and when to hold back and just not bite in. Things like that and just a bit of passing skills. We used to do one-on-one passing and stuff like that after training. All parts of the game he would help me with."

As events transpired, last autumn he was given the relatively unfamiliar number '12' jersey inside Jared Payne, but with a little help from the equally generous Gordon D'Arcy, wasn't fazed by it, and was quick to see positives from the switch. "Darce said: 'if you can play '13' you can play '12'. It's just one slot in, just do the same things and stay connected with your 10 and your 13. There's a good side to it. I can run physical hard lines and I can try and put in some big hits whereas there's more traffic coming down the way . . . I think that's a positive that I will be taking out of it, that I can possibly gear up for putting in some massive tackles."

The nephew of the former Connacht prop David, Henshaw is built for the modern game. His career has already been celebrated on YouTube with his penchant for big hits, and he admits the collisions are

80

one of his favourite aspects of the game.

He describes his uncle as "quite short and light, but for the size of him he was really strong. He has massive arms on him like and was short and stocky but really well built." He also recalls his uncle being on an All-Ireland League winning team alongside Keith Wood in the frontrow.

Henshaw's dad, Tony, also played prop for Buccaneers and occasionally for Connacht, and having introduced his son to the game at about six in the club's mini-rugby section, coached him all the way through to their under-19s; remaining a key confidant. He thus attributes his speed and athleticism to his mother's side of the family, and specifically Audrey's father Joe Craven, "a really good Gaelic footballer" with Athlone GAA club and Westmeath.

"I wasn't sure if I was always going to play rugby. I always drifted between Gaelic and soccer as well." He and the Connacht outhalf Jack Carty were the central defensive pairing for Marist in Athlone, where they won an All-Ireland under-13 schools title. "I was the hammer head. I just headed the ball. He stopped everything coming through on the floor."

Henshaw gave up on the soccer before the Gaelic football, which he admits was a significant complement both in the seasons, and as a skillset, to his rugby. He grew up outside of Athlone, near the Shannon, in Coosan, five minutes from his school. His Dad was an engineer in the cable business, and his mum is a counsellor. "We had a boat and we used to go up and down the river every summer for our holidays and stuff like that."

His first Connacht game as a fan was the Challenge Cup semi-final against Toulon. Being from Athlone, back then it was quite a trek to Galway. "Sonny Bill Williams was playing in the Sportsground, yeah I was amazed by it all."

Tana Umaga was a big hero growing up and Henshaw has a picture of himself and the former All Blacks centre after approaching him in Lansdowne Road not far from his seat at the 2007 November test. Henshaw's star grew as he also won an All-Ireland under-19 title with Buccs, with Carty again a team-mate. Rugby began to dominate his sporting week as he combined Buccs with Marist, who he captained to their first Connacht Schools Senior Cup for 35 years in 2012.

"If I could go back there and relive it I would, it would be one of the things on top of the list. It was just a great feeling going and winning the cup after losing two finals in a row. We beat Sligo Grammar then in the final in the Sportsground. It was a good memorable day. The weather was nice. It was nice and sunny and it wasn't too windy. It was beautiful. I just remember the celebrations and the fans coming running in. And there was a really nice civic reception for us back in Athlone as well."

Cue to his time with the Connacht Academy and under-age set-up, and Nigel Carolan.

"I really like his work and I like his method of coaching as well. He has an eyes-up approach to rugby and letting the players decide as to not going through a system where you have to do certain things; play what you see in front of you and it really is good for young players to try and play what they see and try and create some opportunities and hit holes and make good opportunities."

Aside from his infectious passion, Elwood took a particular interest in Henshaw. "All along the way he just helped me and kept in my ear. His main quote to me was 'if you're good enough you're old enough. Don't worry about your age. Just do what you normally do and do what you have been doing and you'll be able to succeed at this standard'. I've a lot of respect for Eric, for firstly having the balls to pick me and bring me in after schools, a massive call and I'm really grateful for what he has done for me."

Henshaw wouldn't have five caps under his belt if he hadn't played so much rugby with Connacht, and two seasons ago this led to a Wolfhounds debut and then the under-20s in his home ground of Dubarry Park, when Ireland beat their English counterparts 16-15.

"That was right up there apart from a little hiccup; I got sinbinned," he recalls with a smile of the only yellow card of his career to date. "I went up in the air and caught their fullback. I misjudged it. But we came back to win in the end. I loved that, especially as there is a good picture of myself and my Dad and my granddad after the game." It was the first time his grandfather saw him play live. "My Dad says that what is keeping both my grandparents alive at the moment is the rugby. They are so obsessed and fascinated with it, and they're well into their 80s now." His grandfather introduced him to traditional music, and Henshaw can play the accordion, the fiddle and the piano with a fairly unique method.

"He whistled into my ear and I'd play back what I could hear. It was quite incredible, this listening technique. It would have been an old style of a learning tradition."

It comes as less of a surprise that he is also studying Arts with Economics and Geography, in NUI Galway, which he has somehow managed to dovetail with his meteoric rise in rugby. You sense his parents at work there.

They were also there when he made his debut away to the USA two summers ago, and for his second cap against Canada a week later. His third cap, initially as a blood replacement for O'Driscoll, and then late on for Rob Kearney in the defeat to Australia in November 2013, is not such a fond memory.

"It wasn't enjoyable, I didn't enjoy it at all. I felt like I could have given more. The step up to the Australia game was 10 times bigger and it was faster, and I missed a tackle on Michael Hooper in the corner, in the far corner and I felt I could have got him," he admits candidly, looking on the empty Aviva pitch from a quiet function room in the stands.

"Ever since that day I prepared myself to be the best I could for the November that just went and just tried to relive that and say, 'what would you do different and how would you prepare yourself?' And I just kind of left nothing behind and just made sure everything was ticked off."

He looks out on the pitch with a sense of wonder in his eyes, for what stands out is the noise. "You couldn't hear a call from Johnny, you couldn't hear yourself on the pitch. When Tommy [Bowe] got an intercept against Australia I was down on the floor

getting my nose checked, but the sheer and utter buzz and excitement of the crowd amazed me. Lining up and singing the national anthem and then getting the ball in your hands, running and doing your best and enjoying it."

Just for a moment, he does come across as a 21-year-old.

However, reliving his five caps and these fledgling steps in what has all the potential for a significant career, it's clear that while it's all very well playing in the green jersey at the Aviva, as Paris last year reinforced for him, it's all about being part of a winning Ireland team, not just being part of an Ireland team.

"It's about being part of a winning team. It's what makes the feeling so special, to have something good to talk about and brag about, to get out there and put out some really good performances and create some history."

FEBRUARY 18TH 2015

'Never write a story ending with snow'

Arminta Wallace

So whereabouts in New York do you live, I ask the writer Andrew Fox. "Second Avenue," comes the reply. He pronounces "avenue" like a New Yorker born and bred: "avenoo". But when he continues the sentence, I detect the accent of the post-downturn Irish emigrant; cautious, wary of bragging, wanting to keep the Big Apple low-key. "It's a neighbourhood that's between neighbourhoods," he tells me. "Which is kind of what attracted us to it."

A similarly double-edged, insider- outsider energy animates the stories in Fox's debut short-story collection, Over Our Heads. In Stag, two young Irishmen bump into each other in Manhattan, old animosities from across the Atlantic fizzing between them.

In The Navigator, a New York-based Irish father

brings his teenage daughter on her first trip to Ireland, shattering the rose-tinted glasses of distance in the process.

How to Go Home offers a tongue-in-cheek "instruction manual", rendered in brittle staccato: "Open your eyes. Unclench your teeth. Relax your grip on the armrest. Take your iPod and your bad novel from the seat pocket in front of you . . ."

What there isn't, in Over Our Heads, is a story called "Over Our Heads". Is there a deep and meaningful reason for that? "Not really," says Fox. "The process of actually getting a title together took quite a while. The titles of the individual stories are mostly one word. Which is maybe a function of my minimalistic sensibility – but also, just me not being very good at titles."

Now that the book has been christened, he's happy with the way it worked out. " 'Over our heads' is a colloquial expression, so it's close to the way that people generally speak, which was important to me in writing a lot of the stories. Many of them are in the first person and the idea of getting voices for the characters was important. But also there's the sense of being overwhelmed by something."

Fox, a native of Skerries in north Co Dublin, did his primary degree at University College Dublin, followed by an MPhil at Trinity College Dublin. Having studied in Boston, he is currently completing a PhD in New York.

"I started writing stories when I got to Trinity in about 2007," he says. Does he have a typical starting point for a story? Does it begin with an image, a character? Or is it different every time?

"It's probably a situation. Something about a situation will interest me, so I'll begin to figure out a way to write about that. And then in the writing, something will suggest an ending. So the process is to write towards that."

Take Two Fires, of example. What's the story behind that one? "I remember that I wrote it on the grass outside my university in Massachusetts, after a class." The setting for the piece is Chicago's O'Hare Airport, where Fox had found himself laid over for a few hours en route to the the annual conference of the

Writer Andrew Fox by Eric Luke

Association of Writers and Writing Programmes. "I was as sick as a dog. I missed the whole conference. I was in bed the whole time," he recalls.

"I like the idea of starting a story with a fire. So, reading it, you're waiting for the second fire." The story features two colleagues on a cross-country work trip. "I quite like how it turned out," says Fox. "It's an odd one.

"There's a short story in the Denis Johnson collection Jesus' Son called The Two Men. And Johnson tells this story, and it's about one man. And then three or four stories later in the book, there's a story called The Other Man, which begins: 'Oh, but I never told you about the other guy …' I thought there was something a bit fun about that."

The short story is a wonderful form for readers – and for writers. But it's a difficult form to talk about. Or would Fox agree?

"It is, because so much of what you're trying for is openness. Some sort of formal conclusion on the one hand, but also something that doesn't completely close off whatever resonance it has for the reader or in the world around it. To talk about the stories, you have to start saying definitive things – 'this is a story about this' – after spending so much time trying to make them about other things as well.

"I think, though, that the thing I like about writing in the form is precisely that they are hard to describe. And other people's stories that I like the most are the ones that achieve that weird, right thing between a formal conclusiveness and an emotional or thematic ambiguity."

Irish short-story writers are caught in another layer of double-bind. The fact that we've had so many masterclasses here in the craft in the past means that stories are recognised as a serious art form, and given the respect they deserve. For a young writer, on the other hand – Fox is 30 – the very quality of that tradition can be a bit of an albatross around the neck. "You can think of it as an oppressive thing, a weight," he says. "But it's an interesting thing to have behind you when you're learning, because there's such a wealth of stuff that you can read – and steal from –

when you're starting out.

"There are certain things that are off-limits, though. I mean, you never write a story ending with snow."

He stops. He has actually written a story that ended with snow, he confesses. But it's not included in Over Our Heads. "A lot of the work in this book is setting challenges for me as a writer," he says. "Try and do a short story well in the second person. After however long of writing 3,000-word short stories that you can send to magazines, try and write an 8,000-word short story."

The latter is Are You Still There?, the final story in the book. Its sad, wise narrator has clearly travelled a million miles from the raw boys of the opening stories, Pennies and Manhood. It will be fascinating to see where Andrew Fox's literary journey takes him next.

FEBRUARY 20TH 2015

Bill Nighy on success, ambition and the box-office the appeal of older actors

Donald Clarke

It's mid-afternoon in the Soho Hotel, but, for reasons that I never fully establish, the curtains have been drawn against the daylight. Bill Nighy, eternally crisp in a well-fitted suit, opens the door and extends fingers that – thanks to a troublesome condition called Dupuytren's contracture – can never be entirely straightened.

"Yes, hello. Erm, over here I think."

If one didn't already have a handle on Nighy, the experience could be a little unsettling. He could be the butler in a period horror film. Happily, the suave Nighy we know from dozens of British films, soon asserts … No, "asserts" is wrong. He smooths his way

Actor Bill Nighy being interviewed outside a film festival. Photograph: Jemal Countess/Getty Images

into the conversation. He sinks nonchalantly into the chat as one might ease oneself into a vintage Jaguar.

He is fiddling with a handheld device that is currently emitting Van Morrison. "Yes. Hmm? I'm not very good with concerts, but I've seen Van many times," he says. "Last time I saw him I just felt glad to be alive in these times."

Now 65, Nighy has just reunited with the cast of the "grey pound" hit The Best Exotic Marigold Hotel for, yes, The Second Best Exotic Marigold Hotel. Judi Dench, Penelope Wilton, Maggie Smith and Celia Imrie have all travelled to India for further golden-years misunderstandings.

"Old friends? I have been married to Penelope Wilton at least twice before. I have had letter sex with her on the radio. I've been Judi's love interest four or five times. So, yes."

It is fiercely patronising to use the words "grey pound", but it looks as if the industry has finally come to recognise the appeal of older actors. A few mainstream films are now aimed at people who can remember decimalisation.

"The reason I went for the first one was not just because it was in India," he says (more defensively than is strictly necessary). "It was a good script. But you get these marketing ideas. They deal in subsets. Everything must be aimed at audiences between 17 and 34. But they seem to be realising that older people can get out of their armchairs and make it into the cinema."

Nighy is in an interesting place to consider the older performer's place in the entertainment machine. Raised by working-class parents in Surrey, he has been a full-time actor for four decades, but it wasn't until middle-age that he became properly familiar. Following study at the Guilford School of Acting, he worked at the National Theatre and the Everyman in Liverpool. He did the odd bit of telly. His role in the TV series The Men's Room, in 1991, drew some attention. Nighy would argue it took another decade – until Love, Actually – before anybody much recognised him outside the UK.

"Well, I had been only vaguely well-known until then. If you saw me in the street, you might think I was your dentist," he says. "When Love Actually came out I did push it to another level. Look, there are no downsides to this. When it first started it just meant more money and that was welcome for someone who hadn't had enough money for long periods."

He smiles and relaxes into a happy memory. "I'll tell you. The first time I went through a hotel door in LA and the doorman said, 'Hey, Mr Ni-jee. I love your work,' I immediately phoned my agent: that's a couple of extra bucks. There is no downside. It means I can choose my work."

Since then he's popped up in the Pirates of the Caribbean series, the movie Underworld and (inevitably) a Harry Potter film. Good at posh patrician confusion – although his dad managed a garage – Nighy has mapped out a little corner of Hollywood for himself. His pleasure at securing a modicum of comfort can be excused.

How hard was it in the early years? Were there Withnail & I moments?

"There was some of that," he says. "Let me put it this way: I was untaxable for about the first 10 years of my career. I didn't make £500 a year and couldn't be taxed. When you get a family it's different. It's fine being skint when you're on your own. If you have trouble with the rent, you move. That's what everybody else was doing."

He mentions family. Nighy was in an 18-year relationship with the actress Diana Quick – best known as Julia Flyte in Brideshead Revisited – and the couple had a daughter in 1984. Quick and Nighy never made it to the altar. No woman has got him to sign the register since. Is it worth asking why?

"No, I've never been married," he says with a drawl. "There was nowhere for me to go. Marriage is sort of back in now, isn't it? There wasn't a lot if it about back then. Where are you going to go? I have no God. A registry office didn't sound like much. I don't think the tax situation was very beneficial. I don't think anybody would have married me anyway. But it just wasn't a thing you did."

It's funny. Is it not? Had anyone told us, 30 years ago, that gay people might be free to marry in 2015 we would have been delighted, but we might also have wondered whether anyone would still bother with the institution.

"Yeah. It's back with a vengeance."

He has a nice way with a neat phrase. It comes as no enormous surprise to learn Nighy wanted to be a writer when he was a young man. Still hip after all these years, he has the swagger of the beatniks and lost-generation exiles that he sought to emulate while growing up in sleepy Caterham.

What strange tangles life has for us. Before acting caught up with him, Nighy made an attempt to launch himself as the next William S Burroughs. What pulled him away from writing?

"Like everybody else: not doing any writing," he says. "That was my literary career. I really did sit in a room in Paris with a blank piece of paper and a pen. The doorbell went and that was the end of my career. I didn't have the courage of my heroes."

Nighy's dad seems to have had a fair grasp of the direction his son needed to take. Forty years later, lurking in the sepulchral Soho Hotel, Nighy remembers talking to David Frost on that late broadcaster's Al Jazeera show. When things had been looking bleak in the early part of his career, Nighy was tempted to get a VW bus and, as was then the way, make for the oblivion of the open road.

Frost knew the story: "He asked what my dad's name was and turned to the camera and said, 'Alfred Nighy, thank you.' I phoned my sister and my brother said: 'You won't believe this. David Frost just said dad's name.'"

The cool hasn't quite broken down. But he seems quaintly excited. I like your work, Mr Ni-jee.

FEBRUARY 23RD 2015

'I want to tell girls it's not how you look that's important'

Kate Holmquist

"She's amazing, basically. She doesn't get enough publicity compared to the men. I love her. I love boxing: you can take out your anger and any emotions." That's 14-year-old Shannon MacAnaspie talking, having just met her heroine, Katie Taylor, when the boxer was on a visit to Shannon's secondary school, New Cross College, Cappagh, Finglas. "She's an inspiration and a role model. She shows that girls can do whatever they want."

Rebecca O'Grady (15), whom Taylor has her eye on as an upcoming talent, has been kickboxing for four years in Blanchardstown. "You can get your emotions out and control them at the same time," says Rebecca. "Katie Taylor was the only one I watched in the Olympics," says cheerleader Lauryn Groome, adding that you don't have to be a boxer to gain confidence. Why does she love cheerleading? "I love how you have to be really sassy, and put on a smile and personality, and don't hold back. I used to be shy, and now I've got confident. The coaches are inspirational, and my teammates are my best friends."

All three young women have experienced Ireland's Sky Sports Living for Sport programme, of which Taylor is an ambassador. After being piloted at New Cross College, which is in a designated deprived area, the programme has been rolled out to more than 100 schools around Ireland, to thousands of children.

Katie Taylor is involved in it, she says, because "there's not a lot of positive role models of women in newspapers and magazines. I think it puts pressure on girls. They think that the image put out, it's the way you have to look. I want to tell girls, it's not about make-up and how you look that's important; you are so much more than how you look."

Boxer Katie Taylor (second left) with, from left, Rebecca O'Grady, Shannon McAnaspie and Lauryn Groome at New Cross College in Finglas, Dublin. Photograph: Eric Luke.

For girls, participating in physical challenges can be transforming. Research by Chrysalis last year found that 91 per cent of participants improved in self-confidence and self-esteem. Nearly 90 per cent improved their attitudes towards other students, staff, health and the future.

Team sports can be daunting for young people – boys and girls – who are picked last or have no interest in competition. When young people engage in physical activity that they are actually interested in, their optimism and ability to engage with others improves. The Chrysalis research found that 88 per cent of participants engaged more in school life after taking part in the Living for Sport programme, while 84 per cent engaged more in learning and 81 per cent found their behaviour in school improved. Meanwhile, 92 per cent of teachers felt that the programme had a strong positive impact on the development of teamwork skills. Social skills and communication skills were also found to have improved, by 90 per cent.

Unfortunately, many girls will do whatever they can to skip PE. Girls tend to spend many hours in front of the mirror, trying to match up to a skinny, fake-tanned, toned stereotype, rather than exercising.

Katie Taylor is one of the few Irish female sporting role models for girls. "We don't see enough about her in the media," says Shannon MacAnaspie.

Taylor is a bit of an enigma, appearing shy on camera and always on-message to a frighteningly professional degree, with her father and coach, Peter, hovering nearby. Yet, after sparring with students in the gym at New Cross College, she appears energised, warm and authentic, and she takes a genuine interest in the young people.

Between interviews with a range of sports journalists (all male and all preoccupied with her wrist injury), she takes kickboxer Rebecca aside and walks down the hall with her. The pair talk about training and competition nerves. It's a moment that Rebecca is unlikely to forget, as Taylor makes the youngster the star.

Taylor says the message she wants to give young people is that "sport is a great way to keep fit. It's a stress reliever. You're clearing your mind during a workout. Boxing is a great sport for girls; it's really safe."

She handles the pressure of competition well. "I have confidence in my own ability, and my father is very supportive," she says.

She thinks she is a "better, stronger" boxer now than in the Olympics, where she won gold. She is in awe of Brian O'Driscoll and Conor McGregor, but while she enjoys watching UFC, she tells me she has no plans to do it herself, despite what has been reported. Many of us watched the Olympics just to see Taylor. In the boxing ring, she appears heroic, aggressive, larger than life. Meeting her, it's a shock to see how small she is, at 5ft 5in and 60kg, and she is still girlish at 28.

She is currently preparing for the European Games in June, with a view also to Olympic qualification. Her absence from the Women's National Senior Elite Championships in early January gave Debbie O'Reilly a chance.

But while Taylor is a lightweight in the ring, she's no lightweight when it comes to being critical of a media obsessed with male sports, rugby and soccer in particular.

She's not surprised to hear of schools where boys' rugby teams have their own locker rooms and gyms, while the girls playing team sports have no such luxuries and are mentioned in the smallest paragraph in the school newsletter.

Taylor also mentions Olympic runner Sonia O'Sullivan as a role model, but the first two heroes she mentions are male. Is that because the female role models are not there? Or because they don't get enough media attention?

Taylor believes that sports media definitely prioritise male sports. "It's harder for women to get recognition than for men in the media, because sport is male-dominated. The only answer is to keeping winning competitions and you have to work harder than the men."

Many other female athletes agree, including two

Ireland football captain Robbie Keane introduces President Michael D Higgins to fellow members of the LA Galaxy team during a visit to Áras an Uachtaráin. Photograph: Colin Keegan/Collins.

other mentors in the Living for Sport programme, basketball champion Aoife McDermott and athlete Jessie Barr, who are visiting New Cross College along with Taylor.

"I'm lucky to be in a mixed sport with men and women," says Barr, whose brother, Thomas Barr, is also an athlete. "Men and women train together, we go to the gym with them and we do it way better, and we meet at the same competitions, so sport builds confidence in girls and builds genuine, close friendships.

"I went from a small primary school to a big secondary, and the way I got to know people was through sport. Girls doing sports together, nobody cares what you look like. PE was a bad word when I was in school, but that's changing. Suddenly it's okay for girls to train."

Aoife McDermott, who is 6ft tall, says: "I had low confidence and self-esteem due to my height. Then I played basketball and gained confidence. Representing my country is a huge honour, but I do notice that women's sports never gets enough coverage.

"Even in basketball, where the Irish women's 3x3 has reached the European finals and Olympics, the women were very much an afterthought to the men. Yet women basketball players are far superior to the men. The National Cup final in 2014 was described as one of the best games ever played, yet the men got more coverage. It's annoying because you would love to get as much recognition."

Another of the mentors, Christy Toye, of the Donegal senior football team, agrees with his female sporting colleagues. "Women don't get enough coverage in the media. The boys in charge have to sort that out," he says.

What's it like to feel physically powerful as a woman? To be able to get into a boxing ring without fear and to punch an opponent into surrender? Taylor shies away from the question slightly. "Everyone has different gifts and talents. I feel privileged to do what I'm doing," she says.

The popularity of boxing is huge among women in gyms in Ireland and the US. Go to almost any gym and you'll see grown women taking our their frustrations on a punching bag.

"So, teach me to box," I ask her.

"Just close your eyes and swing," she says with a grin. It's hard to imagine a better motto for getting on in life, especially for Irish women, who tend not to be assertive enough, and who do better in education but lose out in the postgraduate and jobs markets when it comes to high-status positions. Earlier this month, Louise Glennon, of the National Women's Council of Ireland, said she hoped the Government would reach its target of at least 40 per cent representation of women on State boards while it is in office.

Just as important as the message to engage in physical, confidence-building activity, says Taylor, is to "have a passion and follow your dreams. Nothing is impossible when you believe in yourself".

But how do we get girls and young women to truly believe that? For New Cross PE teacher Eimear Cullen, the Living for Sport programme "is a medium for young people to go on a journey for what they really want in life".

Pat Carolan, principal of New Cross, says that in a designated disadvantaged school, "sport can be used as a means to help these kids aim higher".

Katie Taylor is certainly showing that in the way she lives. No make-up, hair in a rough ponytail, ordinary sports clothes with no fluorescent Lycra, Taylor practises what she preaches.

Year of the Goat sees Hong Kong more divided than ever on China

Clifford Coonan

The Year of the Goat (or Sheep, or Ram, or Ewe) is only a few days old, and people in Hong Kong are speed-walking back to work, while across the border in Shenzhen, people are still on holiday for another few days.

Chinese New Year is a holiday with very different characteristics, depending on which version of China you find yourself in.

The world's biggest annual migration, which takes place in mainland China every year, sees hundreds of millions of Chinese people head back to their family homes for a week of reunions, of tidying their parents' houses, of avoiding questions about why they aren't married.

For many migrant workers, it means a time of wrenching loneliness at the prospect of going back to the city for work for another year, of making decisions about whether to change job and, this year, of worrying about whether slowing economic growth will make for a troubled year ahead.

Copious amounts of baijiu are drunk, people watch the Chinese New Year Gala TV show – although this year, only 690 million people tuned in, an eight-year low. The content was heavily focused on Xi Jinping's crackdown on corruption, and this does not seem to have set many hearts a-flutter.

In Hong Kong, a Special Adminstrative Region of China, but a territory with its own laws and, yes, traditions, Chinese New Year is the same but different. Since Hong Kong was handed back to Chinese rule in 1997, the law of "one country, two systems" also applies to Lunar New Year traditions.

People also visit their families bringing tangerine trees bearing red envelopes of money, "lai see" gifts to spread the fortune at the changing year.

Red flowers abound, the lights in the skyscrapers spell out the Chinese characters for goat.

The whole holiday is a flurry of red envelopes, children gather them up and for them it's like making your Confirmation for Irish Catholics, except it comes around every year. One young friend of ours picked up more than €120 on New Year's Day alone in the little red packets.

Restaurants are full, although the Apple store was closed – it's so strange to see shops shuttered in consumption-frenzied Hong Kong during daylight.

The temples are full in both Hong Kong and the mainland. Day three of Chinese New Year is known as "Tsek Hau", or "red mouth", a day on which you avoid your family because you are very likely to have a huge fight.

In some ways, the current tensions between Hong Kong and China are an extended version of "red mouth day".

Most Hong Kong people come from mainland China originally, either from Shanghai or the east

Models Karen Fitzpatrick (left) in a Zia Ocean Silk Organza full skirt, and Sarah Morrissey in a Harriet Ocean Jersey Evening Gown, at the launch of the Louise Kennedy Spring/Summer collection. Photograph: Dara MacDonaill.

Newly commissioned officers of the Defence Forces celebrate at their passing-out ceremony at the Cadet School of the Military College in The Curragh, Co Kildare. Photograph: Brenda Fitzsimons

coast, or neighbouring Guangdong, many of them after the revolution which brought the Communists to power in 1949.

The Year of the Goat sees a Hong Kong more divided than ever on how to deal with mainland China, especially since the Occupy Central protests last year, which closed off large chunks of the city after Beijing's refusal to grant a fully democratic election for the city's chief executive in 2017.

Many in Hong Kong bitterly resented the way Occupy shut the city down, and said it only fuelled perceptions in China that Hong Kongers were spoiled and ungrateful.

A sizeable number of people, no fans of Beijing's heavy-handed way of dealing with Hong Kong, felt Western media coverage of the Umbrella Movement was too one-sided, and didn't reflect the complexity of the situation. They fear it will just fuel Beijing's mantra that foreign elements are responsible for stirring up unrest.

The musicians John Legend and Common were the subject of wide debate on Twitter after they name-checked the Occupy Central pro-democracy protests in their acceptance speech for best song at the Oscars, but their remarks went unmentioned in TV coverage in the territory.

In the run-up to the New Year, a campus election at the University of Hong Kong turned into an attack on mainland Chinese candidates, which shows just how tens things are here since the Occupy movement. The People's Daily, the official organ of China's ruling Communist Party, says things are getting tougher for the 150,000 Chinese mainland students and young people living in Hong Kong as they were being singled out as "collateral targets".

But some bridges are going to be difficult to span, and this goes beyond the impact of Occupy Central, or Beijing's efforts to muzzle democratic impulses in the former Crown colony.

In a Hong Kong hotel on New Year's Eve, a young mainland girl flounced past in a hotel lobby, moaning to her parents in northern Chinese dialect: "I hate Hong Kong."

And it cuts both ways. When a mainland tourist

muscles his way past us in a queue for a clothes shop changing room to take our booth, the shop assistant rolls his eyes and says: "Mainlanders".

FEBRUARY 27TH 2015

The jailing of water protesters: intimidation at the heart of the matter

Noel Whelan

Anyone listening to some of the media coverage and political rhetoric in the last week would be forgiven for thinking that the courts have been imprisoning people for protesting against water charges and water metering. This is simply not the case.

In fact what happened last week was that a High Court judge imprisoned four people for repeatedly harassing and intimidating workers. The court imprisoned them only after it had given them the option of avoiding time in jail by apologising for breaching a court order and undertaking not to intimidate installers again.

The mass opposition to water charges has been one of the largest and most effective protest movements in the history of the State. Not only did it give rise to massive marches but it also forced a significant shift in policy.

It has been an almost entirely peaceful movement. There has been a small element within the anti-water charge protest movement, however, which has been nasty and intimidating. When suggestions first arose last autumn that some water protesters were intimidating water-meter installers it was dismissed as establishment spin.

However, in October, GMC/Sierra, a company involved in installing meters, sought a court injunction to protect its workers who, it argued, were being harassed by some protesters. After a court hearing which included several days of evidence and submissions from the company and the water protesters, a High Court judge found that harassment had occurred and granted an order prohibiting protesters from being within 20m of meter-installing works. The court did so, not as some randomly chosen exclusion zone, but as the best way of ensuring the workers were not interfered with or intimidated.

In the last few weeks, the same judge has heard extensive evidence alleging seven named persons had, on various occasions last December, deliberately breached the order of November 5th.

In a balanced judgment delivered last week, the judge discounted some of the incidents where he was not satisfied interference was proven. He also found two of the people about whom allegations of breach had been made had not done so and later granted them their costs. He held the other five however had breached the court order.

One of those five, through his solicitor, indicated a willingness to apologise and to make a commitment not to interfere with installing again.

The other four, through their counsel, told the court they were not prepared to enter any bond which might have enabled the court to suspend any sentence nor were they prepared to make an undertaking not to breach the order again. The court correctly concluded these four were therefore effectively inviting the court to imprison them.

Before imposing 28-day sentences on two and 56-day sentences on the other two, the judge emphasised that people have the right to protest peacefully and this right was the bedrock of a democratic society. Establishing and maintaining the rule of law was also a fundamental imperative to a democratic society.

The judge reiterated that sending someone to prison for contempt of court should only be done as a last resort: "with manifest caution and great reluctance".

The basis of the court's decision lay not in any sense of insult to the court but rather the necessity to protect workers. The judge found the incidents observed on video, amounted to "harassment and intimidation of

Martyn Turner's take on the Taoiseach as the film Birdman hits the screens...

workers in their lawful work" and it was "unfair and cowardly" the workers were "subjected to ongoing harassment and intimidation on a daily basis as they simply set about carrying out their lawful duties".

The court found some of the incidents were being carefully orchestrated to generate and provoke civil disobedience, in contrast to the actions of the many people who have carried out peaceful protests against water charges. The court said video evidence showed "distinct small groups of people persistently move in around and encircle the workers who are attempting to install water meters".

Again this week the judge offered those imprisoned the opportunity to be released by purging their contempt.

These four were sent to jail not because they protested against water meters or water charges but because they harassed workers. They remain in jail only because they refuse to give an undertaking not to continue to do so.

One would expect politicians of the left to welcome this court decision as a vindication of the rights of ordinary workers to go about their jobs without undue interference. Such is the convoluted logic of some of those now most prominent on the left wing of our politics, however, that the opposite has been the case.

MARCH 5TH 2015

O'Donnell accused of 'being perched in his tower in the castle'

Kathy Sheridan

Nothing about Brian O'Donnell's confident demeanour suggested he was the common-or-garden subject of a trespass order. He took his seat in the barristers' bench a minute after Mr Justice Brian McGovern had taken his, removed

94

Solicitor Brian O'Donnell returning to Gorse Hill, a house on Killiney Head in Dublin, from which he was refusing to move so it could be sold to help pay some of his €70 million bank debt. The gates was opened by John Martin, a member of the so-called New Land League that was supporting O'Donnell.   Photograph: Alan Betson

his coat and apologised urbanely for his tardiness. Then, within minutes, he was demanding that the judge withdraw from the case. While Blake, his solicitor son seated in the public gallery with his siblings, hurried up and down with scribbled notes for him, the father accused the judge of having a "relationship" of some kind with the plaintiffs.

"My wife never sued Kavanagh Fennell [the receivers involved in this case]," responded the judge. "Well, it was in the newspaper," said O'Donnell (who had apparently stumbled across such a report in The Irish Times, written by Mary Carolan, although he claimed he never reads the press).

Court No 1 was then treated to the spectacle of a judge effectively being cross-examined in his own court, obliged to explain, inter alia, that he and his wife had no outstanding mortgages with Bank of Ireland.

Meanwhile, Blake had settled finally into the solicitors' side of the bench, whispering constantly and passing notes, while his father insisted that he and his wife – currently occupying the mansion known as Gorse Hill – had never before been involved in proceedings against Gorse Hill and so demanded the right to be heard separately.

He had a slew of complaints, mainly on points exceedingly familiar to all who had been involved in the case against his children – but they were "separate people", he said, whose legal team had never invited him to discuss the case.

He wanted more time to consider his case, he said, and he wanted to cross-examine the receiver and a named bank executive, "famously known as The Sniper", upon which Cian Ferriter SC for the bank, leaped up amid titters around the court, to defend the "sniper's" good name.

The Land League defended, 'bog standard' home, Gorse Hill. Photograph: Collins

Meanwhile, Jerry Beades from the New Land League – described by O'Donnell as a "friend" – was in the gallery to hear Ferriter call O'Donnell "in truth, a Walter Mitty". The couple had flown in last weekend from their "permanent home" in England "to take up occupation . . . in a tactical manoeuvre", said Ferriter. And now Brian O'Donnell was "perched up in his tower in the castle behind the walls, sending out his Gallowglass – this so-called, self-styled Land League . . ." to spread the word. He read a line from the league's charter, which refers to "a corrupt judicial and court system".

"These," he said, looking straight at the judge, "are the friends Mr O'Donnell has brought in to assist his cause."

At one point, Mr Justice McGovern made an effort to posit the Gorse Hill case where ordinary homeowners could understand it. "If I own my house and I have a mortgage, I have a right of residence – but if I default, I may have a receiver put in."

"But in this case the company is the person," replied O'Donnell, about a property he had earlier referred to as "in effect, a family home".

That line of argument soon lost its charm for members of the public.

By 4pm, few were there to witness Brian O'Donnell leave the court, reprieved for another day.

"The O'Donnells are very simple people for people that have had such wealth," said Mr Beades outside court. "They weren't a helicopter jet style, they lived a very very simple life, and that's what my comment was in the context of, that it wasn't palatial.

"It's a substantial property in Killiney, and as somebody in the construction sector, when I would speak of a property a lot of these homes nowadays have sophisticated hi-fis and tvs and internet and everything else. It's a very bog standard house, and that's what my comment was last night."

MARCH 7TH 2015

Portadown news

Róisín Ingle

People keep asking me about Queenie. "How is Queenie?" they keep saying as though she is their long lost friend. "Why have you not written about her for so long?" And, the one she's especially delighted about, "I really miss Queenie". The truth is I've not been spending much time up North with my in-laws-in-waiting. I've been very busy you know. Then a call came to say Queenie was in hospital. By the time we made it up there she was out again. We heard all about it though and here follows the news from Portadown.

The first thing to say is that Queenie only felt like she had the flu. Couldn't quite get heat into her bones, even with the radiators on full blast. She always has the heating on full blast. Every time I'm up there, I find myself nearly overcome with the heat and begin to fret that the next interesting biological phase of my life is about to occur, but then I realise it's just Queenie and her desire to simulate Sahara desert conditions in her home at all times.

She felt unwell, weak, shivery, but never thought she'd need to be hospitalised. Christine, her daughter who is a nurse, called around to her house, took one look at her face and bundled her into the car to the hospital. They sat in A&E for hours before she was admitted. Cellulitis, they said it was. "A spreading bacterial infection of the skin and tissues beneath the skin." Her face ached and had swollen up, the swelling

Students in Trinity College, Dublin, during their version of Holi, the Indian festival of colours. Photograph: Cyril Byrne.

making the beautifully symmetrical shape of butterfly wings, one on each cheek.

I'm not saying Queenie is vain, but she spent most of her time in hospital with the sheet pulled up over her head afraid that someone she knows would see her. The doctor came over one day and asked would she mind if a few of his medical students took a look at the swelling. Queenie said she didn't mind at all and took the sheet down from her face. She quite enjoyed being gaped at by these young strangers, the doctor telling his students "you will never see a better example of this again, look closely, see the way the swelling is in the shape of a butterfly".

While she would have died if anyone she knew saw her in this condition, she revelled in her status as a medical rarity. The students asked could they touch her face and she let them. Their timid hands making feathery strokes around the hard, swollen parts of her. When they'd finally gone she pulled the sheet back up over her head. She was sure she'd seen someone from work visiting another patient and she couldn't afford for a picture to get back to the women at the office.

Ever resourceful, she found ways to distract herself in hospital. At one point she became heavily embroiled in remote control wars. If there is one thing Queenie likes it is her daily dose of Deal or No Deal. There was only one remote control though, which meant that whoever in the ward had it could exert a significant amount of control over everyone else. She overheard an orderly telling someone about the time the remote control went missing and that's when she had the idea.

She waited until it was quiet, with patients dozing and not many staff about, then hid the remote down the side of the bed, covered by some magazines. Her fellow patients weren't very happy about it, mounting a search for the bit of black plastic, but if it meant Queenie could watch Noel Edmonds in peace then it was worth it.

When the time came, she tried to subtly retrieve the remote from under the magazines but it was a bit of a struggle and it was only when she finally got the thing out that she realised she was being watched by a doctor. "So that's where it is," he said, his voice thick with bemused disapproval, as Queenie feigned surprise at discovering the remote. She watched Deal or No Deal anyway. Nobody could actually prove anything.

The doctors gave her special cream for her face. Paraffin based. I'm not saying she's vain but she sat up slathering the stuff on her cheeks as the swelling subsided and when people asked her what cream she used she mentioned some fancy, expensive brand instead of admitting it was medical ointment. Now she's back at work, although soon to retire, with her normal face, and there's no photographic evidence of the medically-interesting butterfly. I won't leave it so long to get my next fix of her. When I left Portadown my own face ached. From laughing. "How is Queenie?" The same. She is beautifully, wonderfully the same.

MARCH 7TH 2015

A history of modern Ireland in 60 ironies

Diarmaid Ferriter

The supreme irony of the presence and the declarations of the New Land League ["we help big and small . . . the house is very much a bog standard house"] at the palatial home of solicitor Brian O'Donnell on Vico Road in Killiney this week prompted the following compilation of a history of modern Ireland in 60 ironies.

1 "No man has the right to fix the boundary of the march of a nation." (Charles Stewart Parnell, in 1885, the year before the men of the House of Commons defeated the first Home Rule Bill).

2 "Parnell, by his public misconduct, has utterly disqualified himself." (The Catholic bishops on the

Ian Bailey leaving the High Court after losing his civil action against the State over his arrest as a suspect in the Sophie Toscan du Plantier murder in 1996. Photograph: Cyril Byrne

Parnell divorce scandal, 1891).

3 Fair rent, free sale, fixity of tenure.

4 Ulster will fight and Ulster will be right.

5 "Those of us who thought Home Rule as something utterly inadequate were a very small minority, without influence, impotent." (Desmond FitzGerald on those who planned the 1916 Rising).

6 Our gallant allies in Europe.

7 "Ireland, the last unliberated white community on the face of the globe." (Erskine Childers in 1919).

8 "We declare the right of the people of Ireland to the ownership of Ireland and to the unfettered control of Irish destinies." (Democratic Programme of the First Dáil, 1919).

9 "All right to private property must be subordinated to the public right and welfare." (Democratic Programme).

10 "It shall be the first duty of the government of the Republic to make provision for the physical, mental and spiritual well-being of the children, to secure that no child shall suffer hunger or cold from lack of food, clothing or shelter." (Democratic Programme).

11 "The number of people who live a parasitic existence is increasing." (James Burke, minister for local government, 1924).

12 "The Evil one is ever setting his snares for unwary feet … his traps for the innocent are chiefly the dance hall, the bad book, the motion picture." (Catholic bishops' pastoral, 1927).

13 "Well Done Mayo!" (Front page of the Catholic Bulletin in 1931 after Mayo County Council refused to sanction the appointment of a Protestant librarian).

14 "The government shall be responsible to Dáil Éireann." (article 28 of the Irish Constitution, 1937)

15 "All citizens shall, as human persons, be held equal before the law." (article 40 of the Irish Constitution)

16 "There is no one in this country who is not getting proper food." (taoiseach Éamon de Valera in 1943).

17 "The Ireland which we dreamed of would be the home of a people who valued material wealth only as the basis of right living, of a people who were satisfied with frugal comfort and devoted their leisure to things of the spirit." (Éamon de Valera, 1943).

18 "I cannot conceive any sadism emanating from men who were trained to have devotion to a very high purpose." (minister for education Seán Moylan, speaking in 1954 about the Christian Brothers.)

19 Fine Gael's Just Society.

20 "Class distinction is almost entirely absent in this country." (Judge Barra O'Briain at Limerick Circuit Court, 1963).

21 Fianna Fáil: the Republican Party.

22 "The Seventies will be socialist." (Brendan Corish, 1967).

23 "Charlie always had the uncomplicated belief that the greater good was served by him getting what he wanted." (Terry Keane on Charles Haughey)

24 Practising lapsed Catholics.

25 The Right to Life.

26 "We are tactically, strategically, physically and morally opposed to a hunger strike." (Gerry Adams to Bobby Sands at the end of 1980).

27 "Is it correct to rake up the past now?" (Department of Education file in 1982 on a paedophile teacher who had been abusing boys since 1940).

28 Balanced diet.

29 A few drinks.

30 "Everything in moderation."

31 General election manifestoes.

32 Serving the needs of the community.

33 In the interests of fairness for all.

34 Faith of Our Fathers.

35 Tenant Rights.

36 Pluralist education.

37 Free Education.

38 Protecting Irish Purity.

39 The League of Decency.

40 Never! Never! Never!

41 Never Again.

42 The most oppressed people ever.

43 "It's entirely a matter for my old friend of 30 years." (Charles Haughey speaking about Brian Lenihan's possible resignation before he sacked him in 1990).

44 Openness, transparency and accountability.

45 Legitimate expenses.

46 In the national interest.

47 The Irish economic miracle.

48 Decentralisation.

49 "I'm one of the last socialists left in Irish politics." (Bertie Ahern as taoiseach in 2004.)

50 "We will not get into auction politics" (Bertie Ahern during the general election campaign of 2007).

51 "So far, we've had the cheapest bailout in the world." (minister for finance Brian Lenihan in 2009).

52 "It's Frankfurt's way or Labour's way." (Eamon Gilmore, 2011)

53 A democratic revolution.

54 Rural broadband.

55 Water conservation.

56 As far as is practicable.

57 The fighting Irish.

58 The foreseeable future.

59 "Let me be absolutely clear about this."

60 "Paddy likes to know what the story is." (Enda Kenny after the general election in 2011).

MARCH 12TH 2015

Sinn Féin plays victim as McGahon row rages on

Miriam Lord

Why is Sinn Féin being singled out here? It's most unfair.

You can't expect a political party/republican movement the size of Sinn Féin to know about every senior IRA operative who's been accused of sex abuse. And you certainly can't expect the party leader to know, particularly as he was never in the IRA.

The party's Justice Spokesman, Pádraig Mac Lochlainn endeavoured to explain this on Newstalk yesterday morning. Upwards of 30,000 republicans were involved in the "conflict" in Northern Ireland, any of whom could have been abusers. (Law of averages and all that.)

So many people could have been at it. Impossible to know.

Meanwhile Gerry Adams, for two days running, has been very hurt at the notion that Sinn Féin alone seems to taking the rap for allegedly turning a blind eye over the years to sex abusers operating within the wider republican ranks. Like, wasn't everyone at it? Isn't everyone?

That's why he's very much in favour of a "process". This will be across the board and an all-Ireland body, for everybody. Martin McGuinness came up with the idea. Gerry is very annoyed at Enda because he isn't responding to Martin's suggestion.

Whatever about his party having questions to answer, he said he is sure members of Fianna Fáil and members of Fine Gael have been through the courts

Martyn Turner on Gerry Adams and snakes

Greek prime minister Alexis Tsipras glances at his German counterpart, Angela Merkel, during the playing of their respective national anthems when they met in Berlin for talks on Greece's financial problems.   Photograph: Sean Gallup/Getty

charged with offences.

He didn't make a distinction about the nature of those courts, though. They were not Kangaroo Courts.

And the Sinn Féin leader repeated for the second day that whoever raped teenager Paudie McGahon "did not act in my name, or the name of Sinn Féin" or in the name of those people who "suffered for the republican cause" over the years.

So the abuse was not done in the name of the IRA, but in whose name were the alleged cover-ups committed? And what does it matter?

Gerry Adams, and his party, accept that both Maíria Cahill and Paudie McGahon were raped.Both allege they were assaulted by senior figures in the republican movement.

This is why things get hazy for Gerry Adams, who has been President of Sinn Féin for over 30 years and insists he was never a member of the IRA.

Before he went into the Dáil yesterday afternoon, he did the round of radio stations following Tuesday

night's compelling edition of Spotlight, in which McGahon told of his rape, how he was threatened with murder by the IRA man who carried it out and how that individual later returned from exile to live in his area.

Broadcaster Pat Kenny asked Gerry Adams if he knows the name of the alleged rapist and he said he did.

"A prominent republican activist, is this a fair description of him?"

And Adams replied: "Let me say if he is, he didn't do any of this, if its true, in the name of the republican cause or in my name."

If he is? One would expect a man of Gerry's top-level experience to recognise a senior activist.

Former Louth TD Arthur Morgan pitched up on his local station, LMFM.

Around the same time his former leader was agreeing that he knew the name of the alleged rapist, Morgan said: "I don't know the identity of the man . . . I don't know if I know him or not."

And he was the man supposedly keeping Gerry in the loop.

McGahon said it was Morgan who told him his abuser was back in the area. But the former TD said it happened the other way around.

So Paudie tells Arthur that this senior IRA man who raped him is back in Louth. But, strangely, the victim never said where the man was living.

"I've no idea where the guy is – I'd no idea then, I've still no idea where he was."

But, said the interviewer, you knew a child rapist was living locally? Not at all, said the former TD. "Not locally, not locally . . . it wasn't in our region."

Most confusing.

And back in Leinster House, the Taoiseach insisted that questions remained unanswered.

"I listened this morning to the interview given by the president of Sinn Féin, Deputy Adams and found it quite incredible. If this happened to any other leader of any other party down here . . ."

He paused.

Labour's Robert Dowds filled in the missing words: "He'd would be gone. She'd be gone."

But Gerry Adams insisted there had been no cover-ups.

But he can't say where senior republicans who allegedly abused children, exiled by kangaroo courts to other parts of Ireland, might be living.

As he said earlier on radio, it's not his or his party's job to carry out investigations.

Enda outlined what would normally happen. "If a similar situation were to arise for the leader of Fianna Fáil, for myself or for the leader of the Labour Party, we would be expected not only to ask the relevant questions but to find out who ordered the kangaroo court, who attended it and where they are now. If a member of any branch of Fine Gael around the country was exiled, I would find him or her in 10 minutes."

Which is true.

MARCH 16TH 2015

37 signs that you might be Irish

Jennifer O'Connell

At this time of the year, everyone is claiming to be Irish. And with an estimated 70 million of us out there, sure they might as well.

But how Irish are you, really? Are you as "Irish" as a pint of green beer and a sexy leprechaun costume? Or as Irish as road frontage, Burdock's chips and the Late Late Toy Show? Here are 37 signs that you might be Irish, as opposed to "Irish".

1 The list of things you are least likely to do on St Patrick's Day starts with pouring green food dye in the toilet bowl in order to persuade the young people of the household that a leprechaun visited overnight.

2 Other "traditions" you will not be participating in include making leprechaun traps, eating corned beef, drinking anything green, planting peas, pinching passers-by if they're not wearing green, taking part in a 5k beer run, wishing anyone a happy "St Pat's" or "St Patty's" or even "St Paddy's" day. (If you have done or intend to do any of the above, take your passport out. Does it read "United States of America"?)

3 Students of the English language are taught that there is not one plural form of the word "you". As yizzer know, that's correct. There is not one plural form but many, including youse, ye, yiz, yizzer, yousuns and you goys. There are some super-plural forms (youse-all and youses) possessive plurals (ye'er and yousers) and there's even a reflexive form. Don't be losing the run of yizzerer selves, now.

4 You understand that the phrase "This? Sure that's only Penneys" – is actually a form of humble bragging.

5 When abroad, you're secretly bursting for someone to ask you where you're from.

6 There's nothing that can't be cured by either flat 7Up or Sudocrem.

7 You know that, in property terms, "bog standard" actually means an outdoor swimming pool, tennis courts, stunning sea views and rock stars for neighbours.

8 Conversely, "an exceptional family home" is a bog-standard bungalow, while "palatial" means there's a porch tacked on to the front.

9 You think Light Touch Regulation would be quite a good name for a band, but you're worried it's too soon.

10 You still haven't forgiven Dick Moran for the affair.

11 You never really blamed Miley, though.

12 Grievances are measured in units of 800 years.

13 You've been involved in at least one discussion in your lifetime about Anne Doyle's necklaces.

14 You have a Bono story.

15 You can quote at least one line from The Snapper.

16 You know the Galway Tent is not a no-frills campsite near Ballinasloe, but a dismal episode in Ireland's recent past.

17 You still secretly believe a tan is healthy.

18 When people of other nationalities ask you if you speak "Gaelic", the only phrase that comes to mind is "An bhfuil cead agam dul go dtí an leithreas?"

19 You remember exactly where you were when you heard that Brian Cowen interview on Morning Ireland.

20 Any drive longer than four hours needs to be fuelled by a stop at the petrol station for Club Orange and crisps.

21 But you can't think of anywhere you could drive that takes longer than four hours.

22 The only reason you ever look forward to the weather forecast is to see what Jean Byrne might be wearing.

23 You'd sooner be accused of torturing puppies than of having notions.

24 To paraphrase Yeats, you have enough residual misery in you to sustain you through temporary periods of joy.

25 When somebody asks how you are, there are really only two answers necessary. "Not bad now" can mean you're at death's door while "Not bad at all" might mean you've won the lottery. It's all in the tone.

26 If Tom Cruise walked into the pub, you'd let on you hadn't a notion who he was.

27 You once saluted an actor from Fair City in the street, but only because you mistook him for someone you knew.

28 You appreciate that there's a lot more than just semantics at stake in the differences between the phrases the north, the North, Northern Ireland, the northern part of this island, the north of Ireland, these islands, Britain and Ireland, the British Isles, Ulster and the six counties, but you might be hard-pressed to explain it in a way that a foreigner would understand.

29 You think we missed a trick not sending Rubberbandits to Eurovision.

30 You've never been drunk, but you may have been half-cut, hammered, fluthered, rat-arsed, ruined, blotto, blitzed, banjaxed, buckled, trolleyed, twisted, wasted, locked, legless, langers, lamped, lit, mouldy, manky, spannered, scuttered, sloshed, stocious, steamin', plastered, paralytic, ossified, gargled, gee-eyed, in the horrors, out of your tree, off your face, on the batter, out of your bin, slightly shook or suffering a bit of nasal congestion.

31 Most likely, though, you just had a bad pint.

32 Or else it was the curry chips on the way home.

33 Next time, you'll have a pint of milk to line your stomach.

34 You're always up for a party, but the phrase "We all partied" is likely to make you turn to the drink.

35 You would like to see a special UN resolution

passed against Irish people who emigrate and adopt the accent of their new country.

36 You think there should be something about the immersion in this list.

37 You have an Irish birth cert and/or an Irish passport. That's usually a fairly reliable sign.

MARCH 23RD 2015

Memories are made of this as brilliant Ireland seize the day

Gerry Thornley

The old championship's 121st edition will not go down in history as its best, not when so much of the 'samey' first four weeks was so forgettable. But it sure as hell provided its best ever

climax and, most likely, simply its day of days.

To complete an idyllic weekend, the Irish Women's team regained their Six Nations crown with a 73-3 win over Scotland yesterday, but you couldn't have scripted Saturday's events. With Ireland's 40-10 win over Scotland eclipsing Welsh efforts in Rome and setting England a target of beating France by 26 points or more, "allez les bleus" duly echoed around Murrayfield, and heaven knows how many bars elsewhere, as Irish supporters roared on Philippe Saint-André's side.

An estimated 10,000-plus Irish supporters watched on various screens around Murrayfield as darkness gradually descended – living and dying with every torturous twist and turn from Twickenham as England eventually won 55-35 and fell one converted try short of snatching the trophy.

In those fateful last few minutes, you spared a thought for Ian Madigan, after he uncharacteristically missed a last-minute penalty to compound two previous misses by Johnny Sexton. Joe Schmidt was not alone

Paul O'Connell (front) and Cian Healy of Ireland tackle Stuart Hogg of Scotland during Ireland's final game of the 2015 Six Nations which they won 40–10, securing them the Championship.   Photograph: Dan Sheridan/Inpho

Jamie Heaslip's try-preventing tackle on Scotland's Stuart Hogg. Photograph: Cathal Noonan/Inpho

in presuming that when Nigel Owens awarded France a penalty in overtime, that the game was over – only to discover seconds later, like many thousand shocked and shrieking Irish fans, that France were running the ball.

"I thought the game had finished," said Schmidt, "and then I looked up and thought 'that's not good'."
It was a fittingly madcap end to a madcap game, as Rory Kockott finally kicked the ball dead.

"You forgot that they weren't playing for us, they were looking for a try," said Paul O'Connell with a rueful smile in what he described as "the most strange, bizarre way to win a trophy".

When Ireland were awarded the trophy on the pitch, it was a cue for U2's A Beautiful Day, the Irish Rover and, rather more curiously, Living on a Prayer. In fairness to the Scots, they threw us quite a party.

Reflecting on Twickenham, Schmidt said: "Coming into it, I thought: 'yeah, we've set them a pretty tough target but they're capable'. They go 7-0 up after about four minutes and you go 'aw, that's not what we're looking for'. France bounced back and took the lead and we got excited about that and I don't want to go through it score-by-score – I didn't actually see them all thankfully, it would have been close to the death of me."

"It was emotional," admitted Schmidt, who also managed to put rugby in perspective when he unusually revealed that he would be going abroad with his 11-year-old son Luke to seek more specialist medical attention. Luke had a brain tumour aged four, and now has epilepsy. Schmidt said "there are 40,000 epilepsy sufferers in Ireland and if by talking about my family's experiences we can raise the profile of the condition, then I feel that's important."

So, who says the Six Nations can't do tries and running rugby? The sun shone brilliantly across the tournament, from Rome to Edinburgh to London, and it rained tries; 27 of them in all, as compared to just 33 over the previous four rounds.

Members of the women's 1st XVI who were also crowned Women's Six Nations Champions after their victory over Scotland. Photograph: Dan Sheridan/Inpho

Three teams with big winning margins to chase were liberated by the unique circumstance of the day. Even the three teams – Italy, Scotland and France – with nothing tangible to play joined in the party. To be honest, the argument for having scattered kick-offs was strengthened. It wouldn't have been the same had the games kicked off simultaneously.

With Wales setting the tone, Ireland following, and France deciding they'd have some fun at England's expense too, the three games yielded a faintly astonishing 211 points. And yet on a day when there were so many potentially defining moments – Leonardo Sarto's breakaway converted try for Italy with the last play of the game in the Stadio Olimpico, Noa Nakaitaci adjudged to have touched down a milli-second before his left foot touched the grass behind the dead-ball line – it was arguably the saving of a try by Jamie Heaslip which was the day's defining moment.

It came in the 76th minute, Stuart Hogg stepping inside Tommy Bowe and over the line, only for Heaslip's tackle to slip the ball from the Scottish fullback's hand just before he touched down. Had Heaslip not kept working and chasing, a converted Hogg try would have left England with the target of a 19-point win rather 26.

It felt big at the time and it was a fitting testimony to the sheer honesty of effort of this team. "As much as anything it's grit and character and determination," said Schmidt. "Jamie can make those tackles without a doubt but he could have just given up a little bit there particularly in the context [of the game]. We had a good lead but we knew that every point would be precious and his determination managed to give us a level of comfort."

As Vern Cotter said afterwards: "Every action in the game is a moment of truth." The Scottish coach was lamenting his own team's errors but his words could never have been truer. To put Ireland's 40-10 win in perspective, Schmidt reminded us that Scotland had lost their first three games by a score and had led 13-10 a week previously.

Asked what characteristics of his team he was most proud of, Schmidt said: "The resilience they showed. You could see them starting to bounce back on Thursday. I texted the players on Tuesday and just said training wasn't flash today but get a day's rest and let's start from scratch on Thursday and really launch ourselves into this last challenge. You know when you ask something of them they are going to give it their very best shot."

Expectations for the World Cup will hardly diminish now. Forecasting that England will draw more resolve from another near miss, Schmidt spoke of continuing to "stay a little bit under the radar".

"We're going to try because I just think it's going to be an incredibly tough tournament. We've never made a semi and everybody knows that that's where we've got to try to get to. That's what we'll work toward and probably the low-key approach, if we can take that into that challenge it would be great because I think you can get distracted and that's always a risk." Then three in a row? "I just need to find a beverage. Can I say that?" said Schmidt.

Never in doubt.

MARCH 24TH 2015

Henry Shefflin: Mesmerising, from beginning to end

Keith Duggan

Sixteen years at the heart of the fastest game and it has gone by in a flash. Noon tomorrow – March 25th – will find him sitting in Langton's hotel, the unchanging establishment where legions of Kilkenny hurling gods have crossed the threshold down the decades. He will explain to the public why he won't be seen wearing the black and amber again and of how he just knew it was "time".

And there will be something forlorn about the breeze in the Marble City, even if there is nothing to mourn. Henry Shefflin's hurling life with Kilkenny has been a sustained performance of endeavour mingled with genius. It has been one long ovation.

If he got a lucky break, then it was that he happened to be born in the same playing era as exceptional talents like JJ Delaney, James "Cha" Fitzpatrick, Tommy Walsh, Richie Power. Since word travelled from Noreside on a humdrum Tuesday afternoon, his almost embarrassing treasure trove of 10 All-Irelands, 11 All Stars, five national leagues, three All-Ireland clubs with Ballyhale and three times the supreme Hurler of the Year accolade – have been trotted out on the radio, on the websites and on the main evening news.

Ireland is a village, no question, but the news about Shefflin would have reached every GAA person around the world within hours and it would have felt like a significant shift, like the end of special and distinctive era in Irish sporting and cultural life. Many summers have passed since it was accepted that the tall, pale, copper-haired stickman from Kilkenny belonged to the fraternity of GAA's immortal figures. And that his persona might just overshadow all of them.

How do you declare the greatest? How to compare, say, the hurling craft and influence of a blue-eyed Corkonian named Ring born in Cloyne during the War of Independence with a publican's son born in 1979, the year of Pope John Paul and of Charles Haughey's ascent to power and of Joy Division's Unknown Pleasures; the year, in fact, when Ring's sudden death caused a cold wind to whip through Cork county and the country in general.

The most relevant comparison is that they both caught the imagination of the Irish sporting public in a way that was unprecedented. The most relevant comparison is that in front of packed houses in Thurles or in Croke Park, they had the power to grab

Kilkenny hurling great Henry Shefflin brings the curtain down on his glittering career with a formal announcement at a press conference in the city's Langton Hotel.   Photograph: Morgan Treacy / Inpho

the souls of all present, for an instant or for the hour. They weren't fazed by all eyes on them, all the time.

Maybe Shefflin had a stroke of luck too in that he was raised in Ballyhale, the place which has acquired a near-mythical status in Kilkenny's golden vale of hurling villages. He has accounted for his grounding in the game often enough: the received jolt of magic of the all-conquering Shamrocks sides of the 1980s, the simple and profound instruction given by Joe Dunphy, the local schoolmaster and then growing up in a house of uncommonly gifted hurlers.

The brothers won medals in stripes before him, remember: John in a man-of-the-match display in the minor All-Ireland in 1990 and Tommy an under-21 medal in the same year. Decades before Henry was referred to as the "King" – and it's a title that always conflicted with his views on the importance of the collective – he was regarded as an ordinary enough young prospect: a big lad mad for the game in a county teeming with such teenagers. "A

fella with a big ould arse to throw in at full forward" was his lightly disparaging verdict on his days with St Kieran's college.

The stick-craft was developed and refined in the squash court behind the family pub but it wasn't until he was out of his teens that he went supernova in a way that mystified even his closest friends and that will only be satisfactorily explained in his biography this autumn. Between 1998 and 2000 he was transformed over a couple of seasons from a fringe candidate of the county under-21 team to the on-field conscience of the new model army which Brian Cody began to assemble.

Shefflin's Kilkenny years – 1999 to 2014 – coincided with a hugely transformative period for the GAA, when it became a more expansive and slicker organisation whose games commanded huge media interest – and revenue. Shefflin was an able communicator, genial and full of common sense and always careful about his public utterances. He

Martyn Turner's take on the judgement of the electorate and Sinn Féin's stance on water charges.

came across as such a rock of common sense that he inadvertently demystified some of his most extraordinary performances.

It wasn't so much the decorative skill of John Troy or DJ Carey that set him apart, as much as the omnipotent range of his fundamental excellence. His marksmanship, his ball-winning, his passing, his tenacity, his temperament and, perhaps best of all, his instinct for delivering the plays that simultaneously steeled his Kilkenny teammates and withered the belief of opposing counties. He worked like a demon and hit hard. He made Kilkenny seem invincible.

Everyone knows that Shefflin won 10 All-Irelands with Kilkenny but now that he has left, the question will be asked. How many All-Irelands did Kilkenny win with Henry Shefflin? Those nerveless, coldly beautiful closing minutes of September 2009; the fearless assault on Galway sensibilities in the final two years later; those were just two days when it

seemed as if his force of will was as important as his pure hurling talent.

It shouldn't be forgotten how hard he fought for his obsession. A cruciate ligament injury in the All-Ireland final of 2007. A cruciate in the All-Ireland semi-final against Cork three years later – and his exit in that year's final when his departure from the field presaged the end of Kilkenny's stunning drive for a fifth consecutive All-Ireland title.

He ignored the toll on his body and worked harder and harder and kept on coming back, season after season, seemingly as impervious to age as Cody. But he is 36 now.

He has given so much. So while it is such a shock to think of him calling time and wishing the ship and crew good sailing without him, it is no surprise. All-Ireland hurling has entered its post-Shefflin existence and in the immediate few days, there is something saddening about that. But what a splendid contribution; what a pleasure and a thrill to see him play.

Even the hurlers and counties whom he crushed in those 10 crowning summers will tip their caps this week.

Mesmerising, from beginning to end

MARCH 26TH 2015

'At our school, all laughter has perished'

Suzanne Lynch

In many ways it seemed like just a normal school day in Haltern am See as students began arriving just before 7.30am Tuesday morning. Streams of teenagers walked towards the Joseph-Koenig Gymnasium, many wheeling bikes, others arriving from the nearby train station.

"We're here to make today easier, to help these children mourn," said one policewoman as she talked quietly with members of the media, who stood behind red and white cordoning tape.

As pupils arrived, they paused to look at the rows of candles that had been set up around the school.

One sign read "Yesterday we were many, today we are alone". Below the words were 16 white crosses, symbolising the 16 students who lost their lives in the Germanwings plane crash on Tuesday.

Haltern is a town left devastated by Tuesday's crash. Eighteen of its citizens – 16 teenagers and 2 young teachers – have been lost. In a statement, the town council said the town of 37,000 people was stunned at the tragedy and "frozen in mourning".

While the victims have not yet been officially named, details were emerging yesterday about those who lost their lives.

Fourteen girls and two boys, all understood to be 15, boarded Flight 4U 9525. They had begun learning Spanish this year, and a group from their Spanish partner school had spent a week in Haltern in December.

The two teachers who lost their lives in the crash were understood to be young females, one of them newly married within the past six months.

Speaking at a press conference organised by officials and the police yesterday at Haltern's town hall, school headmaster Ulrich Wessel described how, when he had heard the news, he had hoped his students had not boarded the flight.

"I was at a school principal's meeting and got a message to contact the school administration quickly, that there had been a plane crash en route from Barcelona to Düsseldorf. My first thought was – it sounds stupid – 'hopefully not the plane with our students'.

"Then it was clear: the flight number was the same, the time was the same. Sometimes there are two flights from the same airline with five minutes' difference. But after half an hour it was clear this tragedy had struck our school."

Looking drawn and upset, Wessel said that he called the parents and asked them to come to the school. The moment when he met the parents was "not something I'll need twice in my life. Someone asked me yesterday how many pupils are in my school. Instinctively I said 1,283, but it's 16 fewer than that." Germanwings had offered to fly affected families to the crash site, but no family members had decided to travel at this point, he said.

Some 50 councillors were on standby at Joseph-Koenig school yesterday to help support students.

Said Sylvia Loehrmann, the education minister of the North Rhine-Westphalia region: "I am a teacher too, so I know how terrible this is and how long it takes to get into people's heads. Students I spoke to said they cannot understand how they lost their best friends. How they can lose someone close to them."

Flags across Germany were lowered to half-mast on Wednesday, while schools across the state will hold a minute's silence today in memory of the crash victims. Overall, 72 German citizens lost their lives in the

Crash site investigators search for clues at the site where the Germanwings Airbus ploughed into the French Alps, killing all 150 people on board. Photograph: Emmanuel Foudrot/Reuters

Airbus crash, higher than earlier estimates of 67. It represents the biggest loss of life in a single incident since the Concorde plane crash in Paris 15 years ago, which claimed the lives of the 100 German passengers.

With the identity of most of the German victims of Tuesday's accident still unknown, public attention in Germany and across the world continued to focus on the Joseph- Koenig school.

Hundreds of international media representatives have descended on the tranquil town, about 50 miles north of Dusseldorf, since news of the crash broke.

Asked about the sudden influx of journalists to the town, the school's headmaster responded quietly and respectively.

"I do not consider this interest to be cheap or sensationalist at all," said Wessel. "I know that it's the feelings of your readers and your viewers drawing you all here."

The public support his school had received over the past few days had been a consolation, he added.

"People who have never had any contact with our school – people from all over the world – are expressing their sympathy." However, he added: "At our school, all laughter has perished."

Two days after the crash, the cockpit voice recorder was found and information on it suggested the co-pilot, 28-year-old Andreas Lubitz, deliberately crashed the plane into the Alps to kill himself while in the process, murdering everyone else.

Facebook snapshot, taken in San Francisco, showing Andreas Lubitz, the Germanwings co-pilot whose apparent suicide also involved the murder of all his crewmates and passengers.   Photograph: Associated Press

MARCH 28TH 2015

Graham Dwyer shakes head at guilty verdict as if baffled

Kathy Sheridan

For a few moments, in mid-afternoon, it seemed like just another confused question from a confused jury.

The seven men and five women had already been out for about seven hours.

They said earlier they wanted to be out of there by 4.30pm and Mr Justice Tony Hunt had declared there would be no weekend deliberations. Only half-an-hour before, the foreman had answered an emphatic "No" when asked if they had agreed on a verdict.

Now, just returned from a smoke break, they were back to ask for guidance on "the ingredients of murder".

Veterans of this nine-week trial, who had sat through every shocking, sordid, tragic detail and in some cases were having nightmares about it, were beginning to reconsider plans for Easter week.

Up to this point, Dwyer's surreal air of confidence and good cheer had seemed to grow by the hour. Unusually, he had been wearing the same blue and pink tie for several days running. Onlookers inferred it to be his lucky tie.

The man who was overheard during the week predicting he would be having a steak and vino on Saturday, clearly felt the omens were good. Earlier, as he left the courtroom after the usual relaxed chat with his father, Seán, he gave playful little handwaves and tipped a wink to him and his sister Mandy, the family stalwarts, sitting together a few feet away.

As Mr Justice Hunt explained the "ingredients of murder" in this particular case, Dwyer leaned forward, his face propped in his hand, listening intently. For the first time anyone could remember, a look of anxiety settled on his face.

Something in the atmosphere had shifted.

As the judge and jury departed again, his legal team gathered for discussion just beyond his hearing range. He craned forward, like a fearful schoolboy, straining to get the drift of the conversation. When they finally turned to him, he stood, hands in pocket, laughing nervously.

Only seven minutes later, the jury keeper was back. There was no knock on the door – the traditional signal of a verdict – or none we could hear. She walked up to the bench and whispered "verdict" in the ear of the registrar. Suddenly the lethargic courtroom was full again, crackling with tension and adrenaline.

The O'Hara family, led by Elaine's father Frank and his partner, Síle, took their usual seats in the second-last bench, protected on either side, as always, by volunteers from Victim Support in court.

Dwyer, alone on his roomy bench, settled with his hands tightly folded on his lap. Last to enter were Seán Dwyer and Mandy. She stood briefly beside her seat and very deliberately caught her brother's eye, giving a firm bow of her head, as if sending a signal or a reminder of some pre-arranged plan.

This was it.

Whatever the verdict, the judge said, he wanted silence in the court.

He needn't have worried. There was a barely audible exhalation along the ranks of the O'Hara family. Seán Dwyer never moved. Mandy's strong face seemed stunned for a moment, then she began to dab at her eyes with one hand, rifling through her handbag for a tissue.

Meanwhile, the man described by the prosecution as "a sadistic, brutal pervert with nothing on his mind other than murder", curled forward, puffing out his cheeks and shaking his head as if baffled by this turn of events.

He tried to catch his father's eye, but his father's eyes were unseeing.

Eventually, roused by the prison officers, he rose and scuttled out at a speed not seen in him before, leaving his father and sister desolate. As Seán Dwyer walked out of court, tears trickled down his face. On the other side, Frank O'Hara's partner Síle was weeping too.

Dwyer later issued a statement thanking his legal team, family, friends and colleagues for their "continued unwavering support".

There was no reference to Elaine O'Hara, the profoundly fragile woman who he had preyed upon for years and murdered for sexual gratification.

Later, as the media gathered in strength outside the Courts of Criminal Justice, the jury left together, unsmiling, wary and weary.

Soon after, a dozen members of the Garda Síochána, whose tenacious, inspired work on this case has been widely acclaimed, walked out two by two, also in silence.

Meanwhile, a Garda van with an R2 plate, took Graham Dwyer away.

And somewhere in Ireland, Gemma Dwyer and her two small children must begin to rebuild their shattered lives.

MARCH 28TH 2015

Vulnerable woman who had needed help since a teenager

Fiona Gartland

On the day she was murdered, the same day she was released from St Edmundsbury psychiatric hospital in Lucan, Elaine O'Hara was pictured on CCTV at her home, in Belarmine Plaza, Stepaside.

One of the clips showed her entering the lobby in the ground floor of the apartment block at 12.50pm. She had shopping bags in both hands and was carrying a pink fleece by its hood on her head, like a child.

What came across most strongly during the trial

of Graham Dwyer for the murder of O'Hara was the 36-year-old's inherent vulnerability; there was something child-like about her. Her online presence on websites such as fetlife and alt.com, and her sexual tastes and desires to be submissive, only emphasised her vulnerabilities more.

She'd spent six weeks in St Edmundsbury Hospital when she was discharged in 2012, having effectively signed herself in after telling her doctor she had prepared a noose for her own suicide.

It was not the first time she had been admitted to psychiatric care. Since the age of 16, she'd been in and out of the unit 14 times, under the care of the late Prof Anthony Clare and subsequently Dr Matt Murphy. There were references in court to concerns about her fantasies – about wanting to be restrained and tied up – from the age of 12. Once her parents discovered her self-harming behaviour in their Killiney home, they brought her for help.

She told Prof Clare about a play in her head in which she was being restrained by other people and punished by them. He feared the gradual emergence of a psychotic illness, but this never happened.

She was eventually diagnosed with depression and a borderline personality disorder. Dr Murphy explained in court this meant she registered emotions very acutely and strongly.

She had extremely low self-esteem, believed herself to be worthless and valueless, and was prone to self-harm.

In a prescient comment, Prof Clare wrote to a colleague in 2006 saying: "It is not going to be diabetes, I'm afraid, or even a straightforward depressive illness that determines the fate of Elaine."

St Edmundsbury Hospital was her safe place. It was the place she returned to when she could not cope with the outside world - part of the support structure, along with her family and most notably her father, which kept her going. The death of her mother in 2002 and of Prof Clare in 2007 set her back, triggering spells in the unit, though each time she was discharged she seemed a little stronger.

In 2005, O'Hara moved out of home and into what

was a converted garage at Rockville Crescent, off Newtown Park Avenue. She moved on to a bedsit in Ardmeen Lodge, in the same area, in 2008.

The apartment in Belarmine Plaza became her home in September 2010. She owned the property and had a mortgage on it.

She had two jobs; one in Robertson's newsagents, Blackrock, and one as an assistant at St John's School, Ballybrack. She was also studying childcare.

On July 14th, 2012, O'Hara was admitted to St Edmundsbury's after admitting to suicidal thoughts. According to Dr Murphy, she often had these. They were a part of her illness.

But, the psychiatrist said, she had made a distinct improvement over the years; maturity had helped her to manage her moods better.

When Dr Murphy discharged O'Hara on August 22nd, she was bright, cheerful and optimistic. He said he would have been surprised and disappointed if her mood had slipped back and she hadn't turned to the hospital for help.

What Dr Murphy did not know and what few people had an inkling of was her dangerous relationship with Graham Dwyer.

They met on Alt.com some time in late 2007. Video clips showing Dwyer having sex and stabbing O'Hara were shot in Rockville Crescent, and dated from 2008. The pair were also in contact in 2009, before their relationship came to an end.

Dwyer re-entered O'Hara's life after she moved to Belarmine. The opening text on March 25th, 2011, read "Hi Elaine, hope you are keeping well". She responded "Who is this?" and once she'd identified him: "I'm not into blood anymore."

Her online presence and her desire to be enslaved put her in contact with men she did not know on the internet. They came before the court, most of them startled by the exposure of their private lives.

Two of the men had actually met her – one had coffee with her in the Dundrum Shopping Centre, followed by sex in Rockville Crescent.

The second man talked of her displaying sex toys on the bed in her Ardmeen Lodge bedsit and how she'd appeared embarrassed and depressed.

Through text messages, the pattern of power-play between Dwyer and O'Hara could be seen; his initial willingness to agree to her terms – "no cutting" – followed by a period when she was completely in his thrall, allowing herself to be "punished" by master, allowing him to cut and strangle her.

In July 2011, it appeared O'Hara had taken the power back. She told him if she was ever to find someone and have children she needed to be free of stabs. Again he offered her terms, holding out the possibility of giving her a baby.

They discussed finding and murdering a woman. But while O'Hara indulged in talk about the plan, she also shied away from it, telling him she was "just not ready for it yet". There were further breaks in their relationship, as the power balance shifted from one to the other.

In June 2012, O'Hara told him to leave her alone and it looked like he might. But something happened around the time O'Hara went into hospital in July 2012, something that did not reveal itself through the messages, and by August 14th she was back in thrall to him again.

It seemed Dwyer gave her something she wanted, the master-slave relationship – someone to take control of her life and tell her what to do. She said in messages more than once she was incapable of making decisions and she was lonely.

She told Dwyer he was the best master she ever had. In a text while in hospital on the day she disappeared, O'Hara also told Dwyer she was scared of him and the hold he had on her. Yet she was not capable of resisting.

As Seán Guerin SC suggested in his closing argument, for O'Hara it appeared fighting was better than loneliness.

Dwyer directed O'Hara to Shanganagh Park on the evening of August 22nd, 2012, and across the railway bridge and "down to the shore and wait". She left her car and did as she was told, leaving her iPhone behind in her apartment and in the process ensuring, as was his plan, that she could not be traced.

No-one knows how O'Hara felt as Dwyer drove her up to the mountains and led her to the spot he'd prepared for her death. No one knows if she pleaded with him when the time came, or if she knew he intended her to die.

But for those who sat in the courtroom while the videos of Dwyer cutting O'Hara were shown, her gag-muffled sobs, her screams and cries, and her whimpering are the sounds that will be associated with the end of the life of that vulnerable woman.

APRIL 7TH 2015

Compulsory swimming in schools would benefit whole country

Brian O'Connor

Whilst trying to prevent bored children from killing each other last week, a couple of things struck me. One was when did the Easter school holidays turn into a marathon? The other was how hard would it be to insert something mundane rather than all-digitally holistic into the curriculum – like teaching primary school kids to swim.

Not in some standardised, targeted, bureaucratic hands-across-the-water exercise in red-tape production, but actual swimming, with kids winding up, say, being able to swim a length of a pool without ingesting half a gallon of chlorine.

Too simplistic? You're probably right. Swimming is compulsory in UK schools, with just such an official bar – one length of the pool – and it's a bar a depressingly large percentage still manage to gurgle their way under, no doubt becoming even more resentful of the compulsory element to it than they were in the first place.

But at least there's official recognition that swimming

is different. Even those who otherwise despise sport can recognise the value of being able to swim. It can, literally, save your life, maybe even someone else's. It's also a skill that lasts a lifetime, with all the attendant benefits that come from that. Most of all, it can be great fun.

Watching my own going 'tonto' in the pool last week, like sleek seals completely at home, it was impossible to put a value on their ease in the water, although depressingly possible to run an internal tot on how much yours truly missed out on over the years through an inability to swim.

Lucky enough once to be able to get about the world a bit, damn near all of it wound up eventually at sea-level, maybe the result of some primal water urge which still couldn't overcome an even more primal fear of the stuff.

This mottled Mick managed to get baked in Byron Bay without once getting in the sea, a notable achievement considering the whole point of Australia is water. Cape Town's penguins had the Boulders water to themselves. And who goes to the Caribbean to walk around the sights?

Learning to swim as an adult is an ordeal and it eventually took countless boring, resentful and fruitless early-morning pool trips until anger won out. It takes getting to a stage where you get so sick of not doing it that you actually wind up doing it. Pretty to watch it can't have been, but the sense of accomplishment at completing a first length of the pool was overwhelming.

However, it was never the natural process it would be if I had learned as a kid. Too much thought goes into it. Even now I can only swim with an assortment of nose-clips and goggles which, if they were put next to a racehorse's name on a race card, would look like

Four-year-old James Boyce putting a fountain to good use in the heat wave at Tullamore Town Park in Co Offaly.
Photograph: James Flynn/APX

every kind of blinker, tongue-tie, cheek-piece, and noseband in existence.

But there's a pay-off. It has opened up an avenue of exercise to a carcass battered by years of jogging and its legacy of aching joints and an attention-seeking Achilles tendon. Theoretically at least there's still an escape route from even more morbid obesity.

Since we're constantly being pounded with dire warnings of how even more unhealthy we're becoming, a painless, beneficial activity open to young and old, which has social as well as health plusses, and which provides a valuable skill, has plenty to recommend it, enough surely for an official commitment to encourage it at a young age. A cursory curriculum examination revealed an 'aquatics programme', which outlines details of teaching swimming strokes and gaining competence and confidence "in, under and on water" but is a masterpiece of vague civil service shinola in that it doesn't say whether or not it wants kids to learn how to actually swim.

Invariably some will say it should be up to parents to teach their own kids instead of passing the buck to already overloaded schools. And there's always the eternal facilities wail.

But there's a bigger picture here in terms of long-term benefits to a state from backing a healthy activity which is enjoyable enough for even non-sporty kids to embrace rather than resent – if they can swim.

It's important for primary schools to get involved, reaching children when they're young enough to teach easily, and before awful debilitating adolescent self-consciousness becomes an issue.

And it's important for the State to be fundamentally involved because sustained commitment requires sustained financial backing, not a token few weeks here at parents' expense in order to tick off the PE box.

Effectively that requires making swimming an exceptional case, on any number of levels. And that would result in protests from other sporting bodies looking after their own patches. There is also a world of pain in administering a system that would make a meaningful impression rather than turning into just another link in the bureaucratic chain.

But I would argue it is worth any amount of aggravation and investment. Learning to swim is an absolute good. It can't hurt you. It doesn't matter how old you are. Significantly, it is also something women and girls have a history of engaging in and persisting with long after they have up on other sports.

Make it compulsory if you like, introducing the intent such a move automatically entails. It would be a damn sight more relevant than some stuff that is already compulsory.

But ultimately it's not about definitions: instead it's aiming to make a tangible and positive long-term impact on people's lives. Surely that can't be beyond our collective wit.

APRIL 8TH 2015

Low-hours and zero-hours contracts give employers one-way flexibility

Laura Slattery

You have to wonder how interviews for internal promotions play out at Dunnes Stores. "Where do you see yourself in five years' time?" Confused pause. "I work for you, remember. I don't know where I'll be in five days."

When Enda Kenny told the Dáil he supported its striking workers in their "right to have clarity in their working lives" he was effectively saying: "Look, Dunnes, there seems to be some unnecessary jerking around going on here – please sort this out before someone blames me."

The attitude of Dunnes management may be hard to pin on the Government, but it is the responsibility of the Taoiseach and his colleagues to stop this particular

Cousins Padraig Fay and Mia O'Neill, who has cystic fibrosis, at the launch of Cystic Fibrosis Ireland's awareness week.
Photograph: Alan Betson

strain of exploitation from embedding itself in the culture of Irish workplaces.

In the name of one-way flexibility Dunnes employees have little clue from one week to the next how many hours' work they will get. This makes it impossible for them to plan, not just financially but for every aspect of the lives that Dunnes would prefer they didn't have. They benefit from no upside to the arrangement as, according to the Mandate union, they are under pressure to be available for work at all times.

It's the same imbalance of power that is at the heart of the "zero-hours contract" phenomenon, now an election issue in Britain. Zero-hour contracts do not guarantee workers any hours at all. They turn a slice of the labour force into the 21st century equivalent of the archetypal Depression-era man who joins the crowd outside the factory gates each day and tries to catch the foreman's eye.

Labour leader Ed Miliband describes the 1.8 million zero-hour contracts in the UK economy as an "epidemic" and promises voters he will limit their usage to a three-month period, after which the employer will be required to offer a regular contract. The outgoing coalition has already banned the "exclusivity" clauses that were used to restrict about a fifth of zero-hour contractors from accepting offers of work elsewhere to make up the shortfall in slack weeks.

Pressed by a BBC journalist, who suggested zero-hour contracts might be suitable for those who don't want full-time work, Miliband said the problem was that they were now "the primary way" that certain large companies did their hiring. Rather than maintaining a pool of casual workers to absorb natural ebbs and flows in demand, they use zero-hour contracts as their preferred method of treating their core workforce – with contempt.

The issue is not just the number of hours but the

119

unpredictability of them, Miliband explained, as emphatically as he could given it was one of those TV interviews where he was obliged to talk while travelling backwards on an election battle bus.

The Dunnes workers who embarked on industrial action last week are not on zero- hour contracts, but ones that typically guarantee 15 hours a week. Their plight is very similar, however.

They talk of the stress of hours being "cut to almost nothing" without warning and their fear of victimisation if they have the temerity to complain. There is a big difference, as their testimony of "scraping by" attests, between working 37½ hours a week and working 15.

This is why the provisions of the Organisation of Working Time Act 1997 are next to useless. They state that when employees are put out of pocket as a result of not being given the hours they were requested to work, or make themselves available to work, they must be compensated for 25 per cent of the time, or 15 hours, whichever is less. Good luck paying the bills with that.

In February, researchers at the University of Limerick's Kemmy Business School were appointed to investigate the "prevalence and impact" of zero-hour and low- hour contracts (those that guarantee eight or fewer hours a week) across both the private and public sectors. Their task includes assessing whether or not workers have sufficient protection under the law.

The Dunnes example already shows that they do not. It also demonstrates that workers don't technically have to be employed under zero-hour contracts for bosses to find a way to keep them dangling, uncomfortably, for years, in an unconvincing effort to pretend they don't need them.

An Irish version of "Red Ed" Miliband's proposal, tightly limiting the length of time that workers' hours could fluctuate so wildly for no good reason, would be more meaningful. But in any case, the number of people in Ireland who have uncertainty written into formal employment contracts is likely to be far lower than the total number who bear the brunt of toxic rostering practices.

Employers have long been accused of demanding flexibility from workers while giving little or none in return. In the depths of the recession some came to expect an even more intense combination of servitude and gratitude.

The picket lines outside Dunnes are the most visible manifestation to date of bullying behaviour that needlessly throws lives into permanent limbo.

APRIL 13TH 2015

Why Mozambique's rats are man's best friend

Mary Boland

Mourinho is late for work. A torrential downpour, typical at this time of year in western Mozambique's mountainous Manica province, has set him back at least half an hour on this Monday morning in March. Rain plays havoc with Mourinho's ability to do his highly specialised job.

When at last it eases at 6.30am, he and 11 similarly delayed co-workers fidget impatiently while travelling by jeep with their supervisors through the village of Dombe in Sussundenga district to the field where their daily assignment begins.

Within minutes, Mourinho is scampering across the landscape, straining excitedly out of his tiny harness, sniffing and scratching the dusty earth, his nose puckering, big ears twitching, and his long black whiskers rippling while two supervisors observe and take notes of his behaviour.

A quick sniff is not so significant; a prolonged bout of

Mourinho gets his reward – a banana. Photograph: Mary Boland

scratching in the soil – especially if one of his team-mates later behaves the same way in the same spot – usually indicates that explosives lie beneath.

Mourinho is one of 12 African giant pouched rats tasked with sniffing out the TNT of landmines in this incongruously idyllic setting on the edge of Chimanimani National Reserve, a vast forested area on the Zimbabwean border that boasts spectacular waterfalls and the imposing Monte Binga, Mozambique's highest peak.

For decades, this zone was a crucial battleground in two vicious and devastating wars during which landmines were sown in place of food, and where locals are still suffering the effects 23 years after hostilities ended. It was here last November, on a sleepy plain bordered by cornfields, that 18-year-old newlywed Virginia Mateus lost a leg after stepping on a landmine while making bricks to build a house.

"This is why we're here. After the accident we came to check and clear the area so that the people can get back to farming and other normal activities, and have confidence that they are safe," explains Januario Bape, a team leader with Belgian NGO Apopo, which breeds and trains the rats – they're about the size of a small domestic cat – in neighbouring Tanzania.

After nine months' intensive drilling at a rat boot-camp in Morogoro, followed by an accreditation test, young "graduate" rodents are despatched for work across the border. Since 2008, Apopo's mine-detection rats, along with their human "handlers" and manual demining teams, have helped reclaim more than 11 million sq m (1,100 hectares) of land for Mozambican communities, and destroyed more than 13,200 landmines and 1,100 bombs. The mines the rats uncover are later checked and safely disposed of by their human colleagues.

The widespread use of landmines during some 25 years of conflict – the 1964-1974 war of independence between Portugal's colonial forces and the Marxist Front for the Liberation of Mozambique (Frelimo), and the 1977-1992 civil war between Frelimo government forces and Renamo fighters – meant generations of Mozambicans who fled or were forced from their homes during wartime were later deprived of the freedom to return and rebuild their lives.

More than a million people died from fighting and famine during the civil war. The mine-strewn landscape that resulted – Mozambique was among the world's most mine-contaminated countries – continued to claim lives and maim civilians, and made development impossible.

"It's good that they're doing this work, even though it's too late for my wife," says farmer Samuel Fernando Sitoe (27), husband of landmine casualty Verginia, who is convalescing with family in a neighbouring district. "It's good for farmers to be able to work safely on the land. No one had any idea there were mines there – we had been through that area so many times without a problem."

This is one of Apopo's last projects in Mozambique. A major clearance effort launched in 1993 by the United Nations and international NGOs is finally coming to an end, and the authorities are preparing to declare the country landmine-free.

Apopo's rats – the Cricetomys gambianus, plentiful in Africa and in most countries more likely to be barbecued than put to work – are credited with playing a starring role in Mozambique's transformation. Weighing in at around 1.2kg and with a razor-sharp sense of smell, they identify TNT and landmines far more quickly than humans equipped with metal detectors, and are light enough not to set them off. On this project, explains team leader Alson Majongota, it took the rats' team nine days to clear 7,400 sq m of land; the (all-human) manual demining team, working in parallel, needed 15 days to clear just 5,440 sq m.

The idea of using rats for demining came to Apopo founder Bart Weetjens 20 years ago when he read about gerbils being trained to identify the scent of explosives. The Cricetomys's exceptional olfactory skills, intelligence, low weight and wide availability

Tiger Woods stretching his arms and back during the second round of the US Masters at Augusta, Georgia. Photograph: David Phillip/Associated Press

convinced Weetjens the rodents could make a major contribution to development efforts.

Living happily on a diet of avocados, bananas, tomatoes, peanuts and apples, the rats, who live for seven to eight years, are also far cheaper to train and maintain. It costs about €6,000 to train a mine-detection rat compared to the €23,200 ($25,000) the US-based Marshall Legacy Institute invests in training a dog to do the same job.

"Rats are easier to work with than dogs," explains Zacarias Chambe, Apopo operations officer. "They don't get attached to their owner or handler, so they can be transferred easily from one handler to another. But a dog – a dog bonds with its handler, and can't be so easily handed over to someone else to work with."

The rats are taught to associate the smell of TNT with a clicking sound and a food reward, says Chambe. One of the handlers, Victor Boquico, demonstrates the technique with "Mocadas 53" (the rats are named by their trainers in Tanzania): as soon as Mocadas scratches the ground to indicate he has sniffed TNT and then hears his handler pressing a clicker, he dashes over to Victor, stands on his hind legs and grabs the proffered half-banana in his tiny paws, his cheeks puffing as he stuffs the fruit with cartoon-like speed between long, tapping teeth.

"It makes me feel proud that, because of this work, people can move freely and live their lives," says Sartina Chivambo from the southern province of Gaza, one of some 25 women deminers working for Apopo in Mozambique. "All of these jobs were done before by men," she says, raising the protective shield of her helmet as she finishes up for the day. "This really shows that women can do anything that men do."

Her colleague, Felicidade Matsinhe, a young widow also from Gaza and mother of a nine-year-old girl, says she hopes to travel abroad to do similar work when Apopo winds down in Mozambique.

The NGO's rats have a head start on her: they're already detecting mines in Angola, and there are plans to send them soon to Cambodia, says Apopo Mozambique programme manager Ashley S

Fitzpatrick.

With the workday over, Mourinho and his rodent colleagues twirl contentedly like kittens in their cages. "After all these years, we are still dealing with the war," says Chambe. "You see the madness of war. And you see the hope."

APRIL 16TH 2015

Landmark decision rewrites evidence rulebook

Ruadhán Mac Cormaic

The Supreme Court doesn't lightly overturn its own decisions. It's particularly slow to reverse its most important judgments. But that's what happened yesterday, when, by a 4-3 majority, the court in effect repudiated a 25-year-old rule that tightly restricts the State from using evidence it obtains in breach of a constitutional right.

By any standards, it's a landmark decision. The six judgments, which together run to hundreds of pages, are by turns trenchant and delicate, passionate and precise, written with the knowledge that they will be pored over by law students and practitioners for decades to come.

"This is as significant a case on criminal law and evidence as any that have come before the court in the last twenty-five years. It affects in an important way the rights and liberties of every citizen," wrote Mr Justice Adrian Hardiman, who was in the minority.

The case arose from the trial of an individual known as JC, who was tried for robbery offences at the Circuit Criminal Court. During the trial, the judge excluded six statements made by the accused (three of which were inculpatory) because the accused, at the time when the statements were made, was unlawfully detained by the gardaí. The judge found the evidence

123

fell foul of the so-called exclusionary rule.

The trial proceeded without the prosecution offering any further evidence, and the jury was directed to bring in a verdict of not guilty.

The exclusionary rule was laid down in the 1990 case of DPP v Kenny, which in effect barred the State from using evidence obtained in breach of a constitutional right, regardless of whether or not the breach was deliberate. In this appeal to the Supreme Court, the State had invited the seven-judge court to relax the Kenny judgment.

The judges accepted the invitation, but only just. The 4-3 division reveals striking intellectual differences, which are laid bare in the individual judgments. The two key texts for the majority are those of Mr Justice Donal O'Donnell and Mr Justice Frank Clarke.

They argue that a middle way must be found between Kenny, which represents a near-absolute exclusion, and the 1965 case of The People v O'Brien, which stated that only deliberate and conscious breaches of constitutional rights could lead to the exclusion of evidence.

There was a balance to be struck between two potentially competing principles: on the one hand, that society and victims of crime were entitled to have an assessment carried out at a criminal trial of the culpability of an accused based on proper consideration of all evidence; and, on the other hand, the need to ensure that investigative and enforcement agencies (including An Garda Síochána) operated properly within the law.

"It is part of the proper function of this court to adjust its prior decisions in the light of developments in the law, experience, and analysis," Mr Justice O'Donnell wrote. "Having carefully considered the issue, I conclude, with great respect to my colleagues present and past who take or took a different view, that I do not believe that the decision in Kenny can withstand scrutiny."

The new test is set out by Mr Justice Clarke, who says it strikes the "appropriate balance". From now on, evidence obtained unconstitutionally will be admissible if the prosecution can show the breach was due to inadvertence. Chief Justice Susan Denham and Mr Justice John Mac Menamin agreed, securing a majority of four.

The judgments are replete with polite judicial euphemisms about reviewing, recalibrating and adapting Kenny, but the implication is clear: the majority believes it was incorrectly decided and it has been over-ruled.

In his 166-page minority judgment, one of his most impassioned, Mr Justice Hardiman deplores what his colleagues have done. He is "gravely apprehensive" that the majority has "cut down" Kenny, one of the "monuments" of constitutional jurisprudence, and sees the move as "a major step in the disengagement of this court from the rights-oriented jurisprudence of our predecessors."

He is "horrified" that it is proposed to make "inadvertence" a lawful excuse for State infringements of individuals' constitutional rights.

"I deeply regret to say that the experience of the courts over the past 40 years strongly suggests that 'inadvertence' will be accepted very generally as a reason to allow to be provided in evidence the fruits of deliberate and conscious violation of citizens' rights," the judge writes. "Needless to say, it is not proposed to extend any parallel laxity to ordinary citizens."

Mr Justice Hardiman recounts in detail the critical findings of tribunals of inquiry into Garda activities and recent "deeply disturbing developments" in relation to the force and its oversight. He cites Minister for Justice Frances Fitzgerald, who noted last year "the significant recent disquiet over the administration and oversight of justice in this State". He adds: "I consider it utterly unwise, to use no stronger word, to grant to the gardaí, in that context, the effective immunity from judicial oversight which this case does."

He was joined in the minority by Mr Justice John Murray and Mr Justice Liam McKechnie, who said he remained unwavering in his view that the justification for the rule in Kenny was correct.

"I feel that the modification of the rule as suggested by the majority is largely unworkable and will greatly add to the length and complexity of a trial," he said. "It will also result in great uncertainty."

It took the Supreme Court more than a year to decide the case. Its impact will be felt for much longer than that.

APRIL 19TH 2015

Numb: war journalist 'memoir' originally written as novel

Patrick Freyne and Hugh Linehan

The "memoir" of a British war correspondent who purportedly committed rape, murder and other crimes before dying last year was initially written several years ago as a novel, it has emerged.

Author Colin Carroll had described the novel in an interview more than five years ago with a local newspaper in Cork.

Using a pseudonym, Carroll appeared two weeks ago on the John Murray Show on RTÉ Radio 1 and the Sean Moncrieff Show on Newstalk to promote his book, Numb, published by Dublin-based Liberties Press.

He said it was a work of non-fiction based on the diaries of a journalist who had spent his career in conflict zones including Northern Ireland, Bosnia and Iraq.

Carroll graphically described on air how the journalist had supposedly been involved in the torture-murder of an IRA man in Belfast in 1981, and the rape of a teenage girl in Sarajevo during the Bosnian war.

Carroll was also interviewed for The Irish Times' Off Topic podcast, where he denied that the book's many implausibilities suggested it was either a fiction or a fraud.

Following that podcast, Sean O'Keeffe of Liberties Press stated that the publisher "stood over" Numb as a memoir, although he acknowledged that the publisher had not seen any of the book's source material.

Fermoy solicitor Colin Carroll in the guise of a sumo wrestler. In a separate incarnation, Carroll is Louis La Roc, ghost writer of Numb, published as the memoirs of an anonymous war correspondent.

Nor had it verified Carroll's claims to be the anonymous ghost-writer of bestselling books for international celebrities.

In a further interview with The Irish Times two days ago, O'Keeffe reiterated his belief that Liberties Press had not been misled, but also stated that, as a publisher rather than a newspaper, the company didn't have "a responsibility to report the news in an accurate way".

Carroll's interview with weekly Munster paper the Avondhu on May 27th, 2010, was discovered by Cork-based writer Donal O'Keeffe following a search of newspaper archives in Cork City Library.

In it, Carroll, described as an "adventurer, novelist and solicitor", states that he has written a novel called Numb, which is doing the rounds of various London publishers.

"The concept for the novel came to me in Dubrovnik two summers ago when I went there for a week's holidays," Carroll told the newspaper. "I was disturbed at how the war had been glossed over."

He also said he had completed "seven or eight chapters" of the book, which was about a London war journalist.

"It scares me to think that I could write such a book and about such a subject," he told the Avondhu in 2010. The version of Numb published by Liberties Press in 2015 contains scenes of lurid sexual violence, interspersed with the narrator's supposed philosophical musings about the motivations for his crimes.

Numb is still being stocked in the non-fiction sections of most Irish bookshops. Sean O'Keeffe told The Irish Times he wasn't aware of the 2010 article, had nothing to say about it, and that Liberties Press continued to stand over Numb as a memoir.

Asked whether he would consider contacting bookshops and retailers about the issue, he asked "Certainly not, Why should I?"

Questioned on whether newspapers and broadcasters should read future press releases from Liberties Press with scepticism, he replied: "The Irish Times or RTÉ or anyone can make any decision they like about anything that's sent to them. That's really not my concern."

Mr O'Keeffe rejected the suggestion that Liberties had ethical or professional questions to answer over Numb. "The publisher of a book on the Graham Dwyer case might have a case to answer for cashing in on the public's voyeuristic interest in a fairly lurid murder," he said. "But I have no problem in standing over the book and the manner in which we published." Colin Carroll did not respond to a request for comment.

APRIL 22ND 2015

Hillary Clinton lends an ear on workplace visit but no policy talk

Simon Carswell

The event is beautifully staged: the owner of the business and six employees sit around as Hillary Rodham Clinton fields questions and shares her views on what she would do if elected US president.

It is the perfect tableau for the dozens of media people who outnumber the 40 employees watching the former secretary of state at Whitney Brothers, the childrens' toy and furniture maker in the town of Keene (population 23,409) in the rural hills of southern New Hampshire.

The presidential candidate appears engaged in conversation, trying to connect with voters about what's on their minds, all in the public eye.

On Monday afternoon, in this factory, the choreographed scene resembled that time when the school inspector called upon the teacher in the classroom: everyone on their best behaviour, everyone

US Democratic Party presidential hopeful Hillary Clinton visiting workers at the Whitney Brothers toy and furniture factory in New Hampshire. Photograph: Lucas Jackson/Reuters

asking the right questions, everyone looking focused, serious and sincere.

The scene differed sharply from the lively townhall-style events at the weekend when many from the packed field of Republicans travelled to the Granite State for a candidate forum organised by the state's Republican Party. Various questions were thrown at the candidates.

The contrast captures the very different races being run in the two parties: a crowded field in one and a likely coronation in the other.

There were no sharp-edged questions in this workshop, just a smooth discussion with a Democrat that was well short on hard policies. The topics ranged from drug abuse to community college education to upskilling workers to tax relief for small businesses.

New Hampshire will be the first to hold a presidential primary and the second state after Iowa, in January, to pick party nominees on the road to the presidential election on November 8th, 2016.

"We don't really get too close to the national political leaders so that was really the first time, up close and personal, I had a chance to meet her, listen to her, talk to her. She seemed like a pretty genuine person. I was impressed," Whitney Brothers owner David Stabler told The Irish Times afterwards. He was so impressed that he said he would vote for her. He last remembers voting Republican, for John McCain in 2000.

Clinton, eight days after declaring her candidacy, is in the second state on a listening tour aimed at earning votes as a "champion for everyday Americans" and dispelling any notion she is taking anything for granted eight years after losing her first presidential bid to a better-organised rival, then senator Barack Obama of Illinois.

Last week she travelled to Iowa in a blacked-out van she has christened "Scooby". There, in January, party members will pick their candidates in caucuses heralding the start of the presidential election process. On Monday, Clinton moved on to New Hampshire. Yesterday she participated in a roundtable discussion with students and teachers at a community college in the state capital, Concord.

The northeastern state has been good to her and her husband. Bill Clinton's second-place finish in New Hampshire in 1992 rejuvenated his campaign and made him "The Comeback Kid" on his way to winning the Democratic nomination and the White House.

Hillary's victory here in 2008, the first by a woman in a presidential primary, was more of a comeback as she won in a surprise victory after losing Iowa to Obama. A repeat victory here eight years on seems assured right now in the absence of any serious challenger, as Clinton is six-to-one ahead in the polls to Massachusetts Senator Elizabeth Warren, a favourite with grassroots progressives on the far Democratic left who has said she is not running.

"I imagine some New Hampshire Democratic activists look enviously at their Republican counterparts and say, 'gee I wish we were getting the attention they will be getting over the next several months with all these candidates competing for the support of activists'," said Dante Scala, a politics professor at the University of New Hampshire.

Not all Democrats in Keene are happy with Hillary.

"I would rather that it would be Elizabeth Warren or Bernie Sanders" – the socialist independent senator from neighbouring Vermont – said Barbara Hull Richardson (92), a Keene resident standing in the cold outside Whitney Brothers waiting for a glimpse of Hillary.

"They are more progressive. Hillary has to move away from Wall Street. She is just too much into the 1 per cent versus the 99 per cent."

Inside, Clinton shifted left towards Warren's anti-Wall Street message, saying she wanted to support the "production of goods" and "real services", and to "take a hard look" at the tax benefits for the market-trading room, "which is just trading for the sake of trading".

Afterwards, she was asked by reporters about her rich benefactors, namely about revelations in an upcoming book, Clinton Cash by Peter Schweizer, a former adviser to George W Bush, which claims that US policy changed to help donors to her family's charitable foundation.

"We're back into the political scene and therefore we will be subjected to all kinds of distractions and I'm ready for it. I know that comes with the territory," Clinton said in response to the allegations.

"Republicans seem to be talking only about me," she noted, adding that she wanted to hear what concerns people in New Hampshire.

"I want people to know that I'm listening and I'm accessible, and I'm running a campaign about them," she said.

Some people the former senator and first lady met in New Hampshire have a long way to go before they make up their minds.

"I have to reserve my opinion," said Marsha DuBois (72), whose Kristin's bistro and bakery (owned with her daughter) in Keene Clinton visited to glad-hand the grassroots and pose for the customary politician-with-baby campaign photo. "We are just starting. I need to hear a little more."

APRIL 25TH 2015

Leave those dandelions alone – they're bumblebees' breakfast

Michael Viney

An annual spring communion with the polytunnel's visiting bumblebees found me in a bright-blue T-shirt, the tunnel's rising warmth having stripped me of anorak and jumper. The big fluffy queens of Bombus terrestris paused from cutting holes in the backs of broad-bean flowers, the

Dandelions by Michael Viney.

better to suck out their nectar, and came over to buzz me closely, circling like biplanes on reconnaissance in the first World War.

The attraction was my T-shirt's colour, this confirmed by the bees' exploration of the even more vivid blue of the label on a bucket of chicken manure. A bit of purple, I am told scientifically, might have offered even more promise. This streaks the bold black-and-white blossoms of the beans, and our bed of purple cranesbill geraniums will soon be thronged with bees for weeks.

How odd, then, that bright yellow is the colour of the first spring wild flowers: celandines, primroses, dandelions. Dandelions, above all, their florets oozing nectar, set the beeline for Bombus when she emerges, hungry for breakfast, from winter hibernation.

Another study, from Cambridge University, decided that flowers with colours standing out boldly from their background are the most important to foraging bumblebees, and dandelions certainly fit that bill. Conquering prejudice, I now welcome their golden glow, so early in a chilly March.

That's certainly the choice of the important All-Ireland Pollinator Plan 2015-2020, now supported by some 20 government agencies and NGOs, north and south. Allowing dandelions to grow around the farm is just one proposal in a document abounding in practical targets. These borrow international initiatives, as the human world faces up to the crisis of losing much of the abundant choice on supermarket food shelves. (Some 4,000 of Europe's vegetable varieties exist thanks to pollination by bees.)

Among the plan's model examples, all backed by scientific trials, are planting road verges with native grasses and flowers (as in the US), bringing reed-stem nest boxes into farmland (as in Germany),

129

and bringing solitary bees into urban gardens with artificial nests of bamboo or drilled wood (as in the UK). The list goes on, through the need to save or create wild-flower meadows, flowering hedgerows and field margins, and more bee-friendly strips between fields of crops and prairies of flowerless grass. The decline of honeybees in Ireland has been largely caused by the presence of the varroa parasite on imported queens, so the losses among the principal wild pollinators are even more troubling. A third of our 20 kinds of bumblebee are threatened with extinction, plus a similar share of our 76 species of solitary bee and about a fifth of our 180 hoverfly species. For the past 20 years Ireland's commercial polytunnel growers of around-the-year strawberries have been importing colonies of Bombus terrestris from Europe, bringing with them the risk of introducing new disease if they escape.

Mine, of course, flew in the tunnel door from the Wild Atlantic Way with a resonant Thallabawn buzz. They are also remote from pesticides, in particular the neonicotinoids, in widespread use to control aphids on vegetable crops and beetles on rapeseed. Ireland abstained from the EU vote in 2013 banning three of the "neonics", citing lack of Irish field research on their impacts.

The ban has yet to be made permanent, but the latest negative finding internationally, from two Scottish universities, shows that even low levels of neonicotinoids impair bee brain cells and cut numbers by half in bumblebee colonies. The new pollinator plan acknowledges the lack of Irish field research but notes an unsurprising finding by Trinity College Dublin in 2011 that Irish organic dairy farms have higher numbers of both flowers and insects.

The plan was developed by an impressively broad steering group, drawn from government agricultural departments north and south, Teagasc, environmental agencies, the National Roads Authority, schools and gardening groups, Tidy Towns, beekeepers and more – everyone, it seems, except the farming organisations, surely "key stakeholders" in such a "shared plan of action". Perhaps they will have offered some commitment before final publication, later this summer.

Meanwhile, a model of community action is offered by a group in Limerick who have enriched a derelict stretch of the city centre with a bee-friendly garden in which to sit. They have also used it for a wild-bee exhibition and workshops, and have had the National Biodiversity Centre train a score of bumblebee surveyors to monitor species and numbers across the county. (Go to limericksbuzzing.ie.)

"Homelessness", as the pollinator plan puts it, is the number one threat to bees, as the intensification of farming wipes out their natural habitats. But hunger comes next, as towns and gardens are emptied of the wild flowers we call weeds. Let's leave more dandelions in the cracks, for a start.

APRIL 27TH 2015

It's hard to accept yourself when your country doesn't

Una Mullally

On Friday the 13th of March, 2015, I walked into St James's Hospital for a test. My stomach was acting weird and the doctor I had been referred to booked me in for a colonoscopy. It's a routine procedure but my girlfriend Sarah insisted on coming with me and picking me up. We kissed each other goodbye as they called my name in the waiting room. When the nurse was taking my next of kin details and asked who was going to pick me up, I stuttered: "My g-girlfriend, my partner." I went red. I rattled off her phone number.

When the nurse left, I rolled my eyes at myself. Why, after all of these years, do I still have to act like that? Why stutter? As I undressed and got into the disposable hospital gown, I was angry and embarrassed.

Rachel McCaffrey and Nikki Kavanagh promoting the 'Merry Me Wedding Fair' at a Dublin hotel as part of Yes campaign in the Marriage Equality referendum. Photograph: Leon Farrell/Photocall

Maybe a part of me thought the nurse would react in a certain way, which she didn't. Maybe it's just years of a stigma that reveals itself a teeny tiny bit every time you have to inadvertently come out to someone. Maybe I thought I would be judged. Anyway. I stuttered.

Earlier that month, I won Journalist of the Year at the GALAS LGBT Awards in the Shelbourne Hotel. My book on the movement for marriage equality in Ireland was also nominated. I go on the radio and television to talk about gay rights. Yet I still stuttered to a nurse when I said "girlfriend". What am I like? I guess it's hard to accept yourself when your country doesn't.

After the procedure, I woke up. Sarah was sitting by my bed. I was still groggy from the sedation, so my legs wobbled as we walked down the corridor. Sarah held my hand.

I was just starting to focus when the doctor told me they found a tumour. They didn't have the biopsies yet, but straight away knew it to be cancer. The entire room started to fade away. I felt the doctor gently clasping my forearm, the type of human contact that's shorthand for bereavement. It was five days after my 32nd birthday. I heard Sarah ask how big the tumour was. "By our standards it would be considered large," came the diplomatic reply.

Sarah held me as I walked out of the hospital in the midst of a panic attack. She stood there when I screamed at the sky in the carpark. She took notes when the surgeon explained that this was very serious and they needed to move straight away to see if it had spread to my liver and my lungs. A week after Friday the 13th, the longest week of my life, the

131

surgeon sat down with Sarah and I, and told me it wasn't terminal. Sarah took more notes. I am lucky. The cancer I have is stage three. I am not going to die in the next few months.

This week is my third week of treatment. And the treatment is aggressive. I wear a chemotherapy pump that feeds an infusion through a line in my arm 24/7. I'm in hospital five days a week for radiation. I am at the beginning of a long road.

In a strange way, the referendum has been a good distraction. Every evening and weekend I can, I go canvassing with other volunteers. When radio stations ask me to go on and debate, I do. I try to ignore the hysterical noise of the No campaign. I try to smile. Truth will out.

The spirit of positivity among volunteers around the country would bring a tear to your eye, and it often has to mine. The sense of hope, camaraderie, good humour and solidarity that I've seen among those knocking on doors, putting up posters, fundraising in pubs and community centres, flyering outside matches, will stay with me forever. Most of us want an equal country but we have to get out there and vote for it. This is our time.

At every moment since I was diagnosed, Sarah has been by my side. And she will continue to be by my side as we beat this together. I used to think of myself as a private person but I can't be during a campaign where LGBT lives are being exposed, dissected, appraised and judged.

So here I am. Like any couple, myself and Sarah are not an abstract to be debated on RTÉ. We are real people. These are our real lives. Because when myself and Sarah stand next to our friends, with their boyfriends or girlfriends, or husbands or wives, we know that we are equal. And we are tired of being told that we are not. Our life together is self-evident. We are not lesser than.

In the last month, I've learned very quickly what perspective means. It's not a slogan or a soundbite. Like most people, I just want to get on with my life. But how can that life be a full one when I'm not equal, and when my relationship with my partner, as strong and loving and committed as it is, is not equal? Right now, I can only imagine that life. After May 22nd, I want to live it.

APRIL 29TH 2015

Shock and bewilderment as Karen Buckley laid to rest

Miriam Lord

In Analeentha churchyard as the funeral Mass was ending, a group of young nurses stepped from the crowd and formed two straight lines on either side of the hearse.

They waited in silence, each holding a single red rose. Though it was wet and the wind was bitter, they stood unflinchingly in short-sleeved white tunics as if, in their sorrow, they couldn't feel the cold.

Not long ago, Karen Buckley was their classmate at nursing college in Limerick. Now they are mourning her: their friend, who went on a night out with pals and never returned.

There was a Karen everywhere you looked yesterday: bright, confident, clever young women at the exciting beginning of a life full of promise and possibility.

They clung to each other in bewilderment and shock. This horrible, senseless murder – how could it happen to one of them?

A Karen everywhere, and everywhere was Karen.

She was baptised in the small church of St Michael the Archangel, from whence she would be buried. She made her First Holy Communion and Confirmation there. When she was little, she was an altar server. The parish priest from that time came back to concelebrate her requiem Mass.

Karen went to the national school next door. She

Nurses from Karen Buckley's graduation class at the University of Limerick attend her funeral at the Church of St Michael and Archangel at Mourneabbey in Cork. Photograph: Colin Keegan/Collins

played in the fields around it. She supported the local GAA club. She waitressed in the local hotel when she was in school.

Karen is that open and pleasant local girl who takes your order with a smile. She is that photo on the wall with mortarboard and parchment. She is the reassuring night-time text. The Facebook update. The daughter, sister, friend, colleague.

That this could happen. How could it happen? Every family's nightmare.

"What shall I say?" said Parish Priest Fr Joseph O'Keeffe at the beginning of his homily. "What can I say?"

It was a beautiful homily.

He spoke of time.

"Karen's death seems so totally inappropriate. It violates our sense of order . . . 24 years simply doesn't seem like the right time to die – doesn't seem to add up."

He spoke of tears.

The "indescribable hurt" when a child is taken from us. "It is an hour of heartache, a time of tears."

And finally, he spoke of faith.

"Within the scope of human reason, a tragedy such as this simply doesn't make sense. Therefore, we either despair or find our strength in faith."

Faith was strong in that church yesterday. Faith and fortitude.

Yet again, despite all they have been through and are enduring, the Buckley family made sure that the priest thanked everyone for their help and support over the last few weeks.

As Fr O'Keeffe's words were relayed by loudspeakers from the packed church to the overflowing marquee and churchyard, there was scarcely a sound.

At the church door, men in caps bowed their heads and leaned in sideways against the wall. Members of Clyda Rovers GAA club – the river Clyda flows

Ciaran Kilkenny of Dublin just managing to outpace Eoin Cadogan of Cork to take a point in the League Division 1 final at Croke Park which Dublin won 1–21 to 2–07. Photograph: Tommy Grealy/Inpho

through this lush north Cork valley – who acted as stewards for the day, stopped what they were doing and listened.

You could hear the cattle in the fields beyond and the steps of one man walking down the road to the church gate.

Representatives of the police force in Glasgow, where Karen Buckley died, came to pay their respects and they were joined by members of An Garda Síochána. Fellow students from Caledonian University, where she was studying for her master's in occupational therapy, came with bunches of flowers. The Lord Mayor of Cork was in attendance and some politicians too.

The media kept a respectful distance.

But above all, this was a community gathering. The Mass was a community effort. In the marquee, the seats came from the nearby sports hall. Up the road in the GAA club, the ladies spent their morning making sandwiches for after the funeral.

Inside the light-filled church, the choirs from Analeentha and adjoining Burnfort combined to sing for Karen. Local woman Carmel Breen was soloist.

There was a sense of the community enfolding the Buckley family, trying as best it could to support and protect them.

Local farmers moved cattle to turn their fields into car parks.

"We've never done this before. I hope we do it right and I hope, dear Jesus, I hope we'll never ever have to do this again," said one of the stewards.

The carpet at the wooden altar was gleaming. The altar itself was made from native wood by a local carpenter in time for last year's Holy Communion.

As the congregation gathered, the morning was punctuated by the school bell ringing next door. The flags there were flying at half mast.

A large floral spray from her devoted family rested on Karen's coffin. Bright, girly flowers – pink and white lilies and roses and floaty gypsophila.

Prince Harry (centre) shows President Michael D Higgins a detail on the Helles Memorial to the Allied dead of Gallipoli who have no known grave, accompanied by (left) his father Prince Charles, and the president of Turkey, Recep Tayyip Erdogan. Photograph: Chris Bellew/Fennell Photography

135

There was a large frame photograph of Karen, head inclined, vibrant, smiling out at everyone. Red rosary beads wound around it.

Her cousin Pádraig Hurley described the offertory gifts which her three brothers carried to the altar. Brendan brought up a picture of his sister's first day at school. Kieran brought her nurse's uniform.

"Karen was known for being a kind and caring nurse whose smile would light up a ward," said Pádraig.

Damien took up the dress she wore to Brendan's wedding. "As you can see from the picture, she looked beautiful."

Tears flowed.

Karen's cousins and friends read the prayers of the faithful. All young women, remembering her through their grief. Some of them could hardly speak, struggling through their words, their sobs audible in the background long after they finished.

Her parents, John and Marian, brought the bread and wine to the altar. Faith and fortitude.

The weather worsened as the service progressed. Under grey skies, the nurses took up position outside. Then the voice of Siobhán Leahy, another cousin, rang out across the churchyard. She had a poem to read.

"Small and gentle, Honest and true/Our sister Karen/ How much we will miss you . . ."

She spoke of a much cherished young woman who had dreams and plans and loved to laugh.

A smile to lift a thousand frowns/
Brown eyes shining – big and round
A country girl – big hopes, big plans
Big heart, big smile and caring hands.

It was freezing now in the churchyard. And the heavens opened, making it easier to cry.

The nurses, sodden to the marrow, stayed in their places, dabbing their eyes with disintegrating tissues.

"We love you, Karen," whispered Siobhán.

And then a haunting song swelled out from the PA. Goodnight my Angel sung by Celtic Woman.

Goodnight my angel
Time to close your eyes
And save these questions for another day . . .
Goodnight my angel, now it's time to sleep.
And still so many things I want to say
Remember all the songs you sang for me.

The guard of honour stood strong. Shivering. It was heartbreaking.

The coffin was put in the hearse. Karen's family stood behind it, grouped together and hugged, long and hard.

Karen was the youngest. The only girl.

John, her father, asked specially for that song.

She was buried alongside her grandparents a few miles along the road in Burnfort Cemetery. The yellow gorse in bloom around the boundary walls and two young cherry trees at each side of the gates, buds bursting into pink blossom.

And in a small graveyard in north Cork on the cusp of summer, they laid Karen to rest.

MAY 1ST 2015

Stories of survival grow rare as anger mounts at pace of government reaction

Clifford Coonan in Kathmandu

Sirens blaring, the ambulance revs into the courtyard of the Gorkha hospital from the nearby village of Panch Kuwa Durali, transporting a teenage boy who is one of the thousands devastated by the epic Himalayan tragedy that struck Nepal on April 25th.

Rescuers from Norway, France and Israel find Krishna Kumari Khadka alive in earthquake rubble in Kathmandu, six days after the tragedy hit Nepal. Photograph: Navesh Chitrakar/Reuters

The boy's arm is badly fractured but it will be okay, the doctors say, as a team of Indian and Swiss medics took him away for treatment.

The mighty snow-capped Ganesh Himal looks down on Gorkha, an historic capital in Nepalese history located in one of the most beautiful places on this planet, but the district was the epicentre of the 7.9-magnitude earthquake that tore Nepal apart at 11.56am last Saturday.

The city is now the focus for people from remote villages looking for help, trucks carrying supplies chug up and down its dusty streets, and a helicopter brings succour to those too remote to find it elsewhere.

Chij Maya Gureng (35), from the village of Simjung is lying on a mat outside the hospital, surrounded by her family. Her eye is red, her face badly bruised. She is clearly in pain, groaning as she lies on the pallet.

"She was sitting near the house when part of the roof fell upon her. Her seven-year-old son, her father-in-law and her brother-in-law's son of 11 all died, they were all crushed inside the house," said Dhan Maya Gureng, her daughter-in-law.

The family was stuck in their hamlet for four days before an Indian army doctor came and they were brought to the hospital by helicopter.

Her daughters Rupi (9) and Nita (10) are beside her, combing their hair.

"There was no one to help her there in the village. Her leg is immobile, she has problems with her eye, and her hands are also injured," said Gureng. "They stayed in a field for three days, with no tents, fearing the building would collapse.

Bilkha Bahadur Gurung, a neighbour who works in Saudi Arabia and was home on holiday, brings food to the women.

"There is nothing in our village now. Five people died, eight people were injured and all 20 houses in the village were destroyed.

"There is no house standing," he said. "In time we will rebuild, or maybe it will stay deserted."

The chances of finding more survivors are fading as the death toll exceeded 5,500, but the injured are still coming in for treatment from these villages, and they have been waiting for nearly a week.

It wasn't all grim news yesterday. Pema Lama (15) was pulled to safety from the ruins of a guesthouse in Kathmandu after five days trapped in the rubble, and the news gave the spirits a boost but these stories are increasingly rare.

Many people have been sleeping in the open since Saturday's earthquake. According to the United Nations, 600,000 houses have been destroyed or damaged.

There are long queues to get buses out to the provinces to see relatives, and some buses are travelling packed with people, some sitting on top of the vehicles.

Some eight million people have been affected, with at least two million in need of tents, water, food and medicines over the next three months.

At the hospital, government adviser Dr Bijan Pant is rushing back to Kathmandu for a crisis meeting with Prime Minister Sushil Koirala.

"We are assessing the situation and trying find out the most vulnerable areas in terms of casualties and buildings. I would like to know more details," said Dr Pant, who was accompanied by a number of overseas experts.

Dr Pant said the casualty number was sure to rise.

"It will go up for sure. We haven't been able to get into the centre yet, we are still at the periphery," he said.

There is much anger among local people at the slow pace of the rescue in some areas, with Nepalis accusing the government of being too slow to distribute international aid that has flooded into the country, including aid from Ireland.

Gorkha is a famously resilient part of Nepal. This is where British and Indian armies have long recruited the tough Gurkha soldiers.

Nurse Binisha Magar (28) said that most of the injuries at the hospital were head injuries, fractures.

By yesterday the hospital had seen 260 patients, of whom 11 had died and 75 had been referred to other hospitals. The doctors are Swiss and Indian.

"The patients started arriving one hour after the quake. We have enough medical supplies and international donations have been helpful, but there are not enough beds," she said, pointing at the mats on the ground.

Dr Chandan Kumar Jha is one of the Indian doctors at the hospital, a Red Cross specialist who was working closely with a team of uniformed doctors from the Indian army.

"What we are seeing is what happens when a rock falls on you. Head injuries. Chest and inter-abdominal injuries. Many were unable to escape the site for several days, young children, elderly people unable to move," said Dr Jha, who is from the state of Bihar.

""They will recover but the psychological stress, the trauma, will stay with them. It's not easy to bring everyone back to their original condition but we do our best. We have the skills and the willpower."

Other injuries include amputations because of gangrene, a problem with people who have gone untreated for longer periods.

Manu Maya Rokka, who guesses she is around 60, is working as a dishwasher in the Vision Hotel. She had 12 children, two died, nine have moved away and all she has left at home is her daughter.

"My daughter has been paralysed since she was 1½ and is 30 now. After the quake she was covered with stones and bleeding from different parts of her body, her nose, her head. My husband is mentally ill for the past five years," said Ms Rokka.

"The whole house was destroyed and I carried her from the house. Since then I have been sleeping under the sky, by the road, I don't even have a tent.

"I have to go back to the place because of my daughter. We are quite poor, so I'm hoping for help to at least build a hut," said Ms Rokka.

Kaman Singh (39), from Kasigaun, has brought his father in to have treatment for his arm, broken in the quake. He has been working in a restaurant in

Britain, but came back to his home village, Kasigaun, as visa issues are resolved.

"My house is completely finished. The town of 400 houses is destroyed. Around 50 people were injured and 10 are dead. We still haven't found everyone," he said.

"We will rebuild it, a new house. But it's difficult. There are landslides. And if you need to work in the fields, you can't build a house. Very difficult."

MAY 2ND 2015

Oh lord: next generation takes the keys to Waterford county

Patrick Freyne

I t was a pain changing the bank cards," says Lord Waterford, 9th Marquis of Waterford. He's telling me about becoming Lord Waterford back in February.

"You changed your cards?"

"Well I had to, I was the Earl of Tyrone before," he says. "So it said 'Henry Tyrone' on my credit card."

"Not 'the Earl of Tyrone?'"

"You don't fit into the boxes when you have a title."

"What does it say now? "

"'Henry Waterford'. I'll tell you, when I went into the bank manager he was fairly confused. He said normally you have to go through all these [processes]. They're worried about people money-laundering, you see, but he said 'I think this is a different situation'."

I am visiting Henry Nicholas de la Poer Beresford, the new Lord Waterford, in Curraghmore House. We are standing in a vast, deserted courtyard. Statues peer out of alcoves. The house itself looks forbiddingly gothic. It's actually a Norman keep encased in a

Lord Waterford in front of the family home, Curraghmore House in Portlaw. Photograph: Patrick Browne

Victorian mansion, surrounded by Georgian ranges, a landscaped garden and 3,000 acres of land. The de la Poer family has lived here for 800 years.

On the keep, looking down on us, is a St Hubert's Stag, a deer's head with a cross between its antlers. The stag saved the house from burning in the 1920s. "The IRA, whoever it was, had straw along the top of the house ready to set the match," says Lord Waterford. "But there was a full moon over the lake and the full moon shone onto the cross which shone onto the courtyard, and the man who was about to light the bales thought this was a sign from above so didn't light them and hence the house is still standing."

Is that true? He laughs. "I've always been told it is. Hopefully it's true before you write it down on paper."

He seems like a lord. He has an outdoorsy face, wears tweed and moleskin and has spent his life devoted

139

to polo. He is unfailingly polite but reserved. He's happiest to elaborate when he finds something amusing, like the credit card story or the IRA burning down the house story. In general he likes short sentences and "yes" and "no" and "I don't know" answers. This leads to me asking a lot of questions, which seems to take him aback. "Help me out here!" he says, at one point, to the photographer.

When I arrive I ask if there's anywhere I can plug in my phone. Unfortunately, none of the old-fashioned round sockets fit my charger, so we wander from room to room until we find a modern socket in the beautiful blue drawing-room beneath plaster ceilings and ceiling paintings by Peter de Gree. The blue drawing-room is next to the yellow drawing-room which is next to the dining-room. These are among the rooms open to the public. The tour guide is the ex-

butler of the previous Marquis. In the blue drawing-room there are paintings, a case of military medals, a large, ornate golden mirror and many obscure pieces of furniture including an oriental screen originally "from the bedroom of Marie Antoinette".

How did they get that? "I don't know," says Lord Waterford.

He became Lord Waterford in February when his father, the eighth Marquis, died. He was 81, says Lord Waterford, "but you never expect someone to die, do you?"

He and his wife Amanda are moving in and plan to open the estate more. They're participating in the Waterford Garden Trail, running a Bluebell Festival tomorrow in aid of the South East Radiotherapy Trust, hosting a Mud Run on August 22nd and building a tearoom in the courtyard.

Elaine Hughes from Lusk in Co Dublin with her Canadian sphinx cat, named Sphinx Alien Rocky Road at the 29th Supreme Cat Show of the Cat Fancy of Ireland held in Ballinteer Community School. Photograph: Aidan Crawley

"It's very challenging trying to keep this historical house standing up with a roof on it," he says. "You have to have a large income and with farming and forestry, it's hard to do. That's why we're developing more into the tourism and want more people coming here…My father didn't like too many people around." The new Lord is 57 and has spent most of his life going over and back to England where he managed farms and stables and polo teams. His oldest son is a top polo professional (he has two other children). When do people stop playing polo?

He laughs. "You're looking at one now." He pats his belly. "Too old and fat."

Growing old and fat is a luxury for the Marquises of Waterford. There's a curse.

"There was a child or something reputed to have been hung by a Marquis of Waterford and the mother or grandmother put a curse on the family that the Marquis of Waterford would die a painful death. And that probably was the case till my father died peacefully in his bed."

Previous Marquises have experienced shooting accidents, drownings and even occasional lion attacks. The current marquis first thought about the curse, he says, when his son, Lord Le Poer, now Earl of Tyrone, was born. "There wasn't a Lord le Poer for 200 years, because there was never three generations alive at the same time. So that was it. It must be over now, hopefully." He chuckles. "I'll be watching my back."

Does he take it seriously? "Oh, you don't worry about those kinds of things do you?"

He takes me out to the grounds. We pass the inner hall with its cantilever staircase and family portraits. He shows me the third Marquis, who originated the phrase "painting the town red" while on a bender in Melton Mowbray in 1837 (he literally painted the town red). "He was fairly wild," says Lord Waterford with understatement.

We go to the impressive outer hall which is part of the original 12th-century keep. There, beneath very old plasterwork, is an incredible collection of old, posh junk. It's worth itemising: a grandfather clock, a megaphone, a Victorian pushchair with wooden

horses that move up and down, a very large key, a pile of firewood, a hand-drawn family tree (I point this out and he peers at it as though for the first time), a top hat belonging to the third Marquis, a stuffed fox in a glass case killed by the third Marquis ("[it] gave him a good hunt"), antlers on the walls, three elephant feet and an elephant's trunk filled with umbrellas, golf clubs and walking sticks, some stuffed lions ("The sixth Marquis liked killing animals in Africa"), a cardboard box full of animal skulls ("Those are more recent") and a table covered with hats. He punches an ancient polo hat gently, making a dent. "It must have been useless," he says disapprovingly.

Above this there's a huge painting of an 18th century family. There are 11 people in the painting including the first Marquis, who hired James Wyatt to develop the house and gardens, and his brother John Beresford, the former revenue commissioner who brought James Gandon to design the Four Courts. At the centre is their mother, Catherine, Countess of Tyrone, the only female to inherit Curraghmore (the Beresfords married in at this stage) and the woman responsible for building the Shell House, a seashell-covered folly in the grounds.

We walk out to the Shell House. There's a smell of burning wood and there seem to be pheasants everywhere. We pass wrought-iron statues of hunting dogs, wolves and boars bought at the Paris Exhibition. "In three weeks this whole area will be blue [with bluebells]," he says. "It's beautiful. Like a sea." In a few weeks, he says, the whole garden will be "ablaze with colour".

In the Shell House shells line the wall and little stalactites of shell fall from the ceiling. In the centre stands a statue of Catherine and there's an old stone crest at the door. "It's not our crest. I don't know what it is."

Their own crest features the St Hubert's Stag. The family motto is "Nil Nise Cruce", but Lord Waterford can't remember what it means (it means "nothing but the cross" – I looked it up). We walk around the Wyatt-designed lake and see the 13th-century bridge built in anticipation of a visit from King John (he never came). In one place in the landscaped garden, the stone of the balustrade is broken by an encroaching Horse Chestnut tree. "Wyatt wouldn't be impressed," chuckles Lord Waterford.

Few people live on the estate now. "People prefer to live in a village next door to Centra," he says. "I wouldn't. I'd prefer to live in the middle of nowhere with nobody annoying me."

He loves it here, he says. "There's a tranquillity and quietness here you don't get in the English countryside."

He loves to ride across his land. Does growing up here make him feel apart from other people? "I think with my generation it changed a lot then," he says. "There's always a class divide but I don't feel that, to be honest with you. I'd be happy talking to anybody."

He says that the Beresfords were never absentee landlords. The wall around the whole estate was called "the penny wall". "People were paid a penny a day and their food," he says. "I don't think the Famine was quite as bad in this area as in others, but they were quite well looked after, I think. Or as much as they could have been."

Did he always know he was going to inherit? "I was always going to be Lord Waterford but whether I was going to inherit Curraghmore was another thing . . . My father didn't make it clear until three or four years ago . . . [but] It would be unusual for the eldest son to be disinherited unless he did something dreadful." And he didn't do anything dreadful? "No. No. Luckily, I'm an angel," he says and laughs.

So your life was set? "It was in a certain way."

There's a photograph from early in the last century in which 19 servants are standing on the terrace of Curraghmore. Does he remember that world? "Possibly the end of it," he says. "The house is very low-key now. Money ran out or labour got more expensive."

The house looks massive. How many rooms are there? "I have no idea," he says. Later I ask again. He thinks. "There are eight or nine or 10 bedrooms."

Do many people still live like this? He says he knows a few.

Before I leave I retrieve my phone and watch Lord Waterford closing the big wooden shutters in the drawing-rooms as a clock chimes and a teckel called Hector gets under our feet. The closing shutters plunge the rooms into complete darkness. His main challenge, says Lord Waterford, is keeping a roof on the place. Keeping Curraghmore is expensive and he wants to be able to hand it to his son.

"We've lived here for the past 800 years, it would be a pity if we didn't." He pauses before adding politely: "From our point of view."

MAY 11TH 2015

Portrait of war: Absolution and 'the perfect death' on the Rue du Bois

Ronan McGreevy

The Rue du Bois is a long road that runs through the heart of French Flanders. This is prosperous agricultural country, semi-rural for the most part. Behind the neat red-brick farmhouses that line the road are vast fields of wheat, potatoes, onions, sugar beet and green beans as far as the eye can see.

Here is some of the flattest terrain in Europe, leavened only by the whitewashed memorials to the first World War. At one end of Rue du Bois is one remembering nearly 5,000 Indian soldiers. At the other end is Le Touret memorial to 13,402 British soldiers who were killed in the first year of the war and have no known grave.

With so many reminders of the first World War, the unsuspecting traveller is unlikely to grasp the significance of a lay-by and council depot where

The Last General Absolution of the Munsters at Rue du Bois, the painting by Italian artist Fortunino Matania recording the blessing, given to the 800 men of the 2nd Battalion, Royal Munster Fusiliers, by army chaplain Father Francis Gleeson, on the eve of the first World War Battle of Aubers Ridge in May 1915. In the battle, 11 officers and 140 men of the 2nd died; the painting was also lost, believed destroyed during second World War bombing of London. Photograph: Illustrated London News

mounds of sand and gravel are kept behind a green gate.

This most prosaic of locations is the site of one of the most famous paintings of the first World War, and one of the most culturally significant Irish paintings of the 20th century.

Fortunino Matania was not even there when he painted The Last General Absolution of the Munsters at Rue du Bois. Neither was the novelist Jessie Louisa Rickard. But these two artists conjured up a powerful reminder of war, something that had more than verisimilitude.

The conflict was just nine months old when the 2nd battalion of the Royal Munster Fusiliers marched out to battle on the evening of May 8th, 1915. The battalion had already been decimated twice, once at Étreux on August 27th and then at nearby Festubert

before Christmas 1914.

At the head, on his horse, was the battalion's much-loved chaplain, Fr Francis Gleeson, a Jesuit priest from Co Tipperary. He was only 31, a nationalist and Irish speaker, yet he did not hesitate to accept the equivalent rank of captain in the British army when war broke out.

Despite the horrors they had already seen, the men were in good spirits. "The scenes of enthusiasm are outstanding," he wrote in his diary.

The men were resolute Catholics, and the constant presence of death made them an "army of prayers", according to one of their number. "I have seen sights, but the faith, piety, and sincerity of that congregation, each man knowing that death was staring him in the face, would make anyone in this world proud to be a Catholic," remembered Sgt James Leahy.

As they marched down the Rue du Bois towards the British trenches, Fr Gleeson spotted an exposed altar at a lay-by. There is "no stopping-place more holy than a wayside shrine", Rickard wrote in her account. It was not a wayside shrine, however, but the shattered remains of a roadside family church, the Chapel of Notre Dame de Seez, which had been hit by a shell in the early part of the war.

The men halted. Fr Gleeson walked up and down the ranks giving what comfort he could to the 900 men of the battalion, reminding them of the honour of their regiment. Then, sitting on his horse, he gave the men general absolution.

The silence was broken by the men singing Hail Glorious St Patrick, before dispersing to march 1½km to the assembly trenches, which were to the left of the Cinder Track, a lane way parallel to the Rue du Bois that led to the German lines.

The Munsters would be in the vanguard of what was then the biggest British assault of the war on the Western Front.

The Battle of Aubers Ridge was a catastrophe for the British, who suffered 11,000 casualties in a single day. "It had been a disastrous 15 hours of squandered heroism, unredeemed by the faintest glimmer of success," wrote Alan Clark, whose book The Donkeys did much to establish the reputation of the ordinary British soldiers as "lions led by donkeys".

The British commanders had gambled on a short but furious artillery bombardment softening up the German lines sufficiently for the infantry to push through and take their ultimate goal. That goal was what passed for high ground in the area: Aubers Ridge. But there weren't enough guns and the ones that were available were worn-out, inaccurate and totally unsuitable to demolishing the German defences, which were 30ft deep in places.

When the bombardment ceased, many of the frontline British infantry had already crept into no man's land. They provided a pitiful sight for the German infantry, who were forewarned about the attack.

"There could never before in war have been a more perfect target. There was only one possible order to give: 'Fire until the barrels burst'," one German officer remembered.

The Munsters were one of the few battalions to make it into the German trenches. One officer was heard shouting "come on the Munsters!" as his men breached the German parapets. He was shot down a short time afterwards.

Lieut Col Victor Rickard, the commanding officer of the battalion and Jessie Rickard's husband, was shot through the neck just after he left the trench. He died immediately. A total of 151 Munsters died at the Battle of Aubers Ridge, according to the author Jean Prendergast, who has written the definitive history of Rue du Bois. One in six of those who had lined up for general absolution the previous evening died in the battle, and 220 were injured.

Jessie Rickard, now left a widow with a two-year-old child, wrote the story of the absolution in remembrance of her late husband. Despite her grief, she was in no doubt that he had died in a good cause. It was, she wrote, "the perfect death. No one who knew him could ever doubt that he would have chosen any other end than to die leading the regiment he so loved all his life."

Her evocative words were first published in New Ireland magazine in 1915 and picked up by the Sphere magazine in 1916. The Sphere was a beautifully produced and hugely popular periodical of the time, which circulated in Britain and Ireland. It employed Matania, an illustrator of genius, to turn Rickard's words into a painting.

Inspired by Rickard's words, and using a description given to him by Sgt James Meehan, one of the few who made it into the German trenches and lived to tell the tale, Matania turned his prodigious gifts into a painting of extraordinary emotional power.

Here were Irish Catholics led by an Irish Catholic priest, but in British uniforms and fighting in France. The painting shows the complexity of Irish identity in a time before only one version of Irish history became acceptable.

For decades, the site of the absolution was lost. The chapel that replaced the original on the site was levelled to make way for a road-widening scheme. Only for the diligence of one local man, Michel Knockaert, working from old maps and historical accounts, it might never have been found.

After extensive negotiations, a memorial will be unveiled tonight on the exact site where Fr Gleeson gave his last absolution. It has been a long road for all concerned.

MAY 9TH 2015

For now, Cameron is the man who delivered the impossible

Mark Hennessy

Former British prime minister John Major once said that every general election campaign run by any political party is a shambles until the results come in. Then, the victorious ones are deemed to have been cunningly clever from the beginning.

The Major dictum is worth remembering in the wake of the Conservatives' stunned joy following the release of the BBC exit poll at 10pm yesterday that predicted that they would win 316 seats. In the end, they won even more.

Greeting the dawn, even Boris Johnson seemed, for once, lost for words, declaring that the Conservatives, then on the verge of winning a House of Commons majority, had "won in places that we never thought we would win".

"The good sense of the British people at the last minute made the difference," said Johnson, as a subsequent prediction put the Conservatives on 325 seats, which still did not the capture the full fruits of the night.

Soon, the victory will become the Conservatives' birthright. But it has ever been thus. However, the following vignette graphically illustrates that the scale of the extraordinary victory was beyond even its wildest imaginings.

Seconds after 9.55pm yesterday, an email from the Conservative Party dropped into inboxes of selected senior figures in the London media world, just

British prime minister David Cameron speaks outside his office and residence, No 10 Downing Street in London, after his Conservative Party's electoral victory in which the Labour Party was routed, returning Britain to single party government for the first time in five years. Photograph: Adrian Dennis/Agence France-Presse

minutes before the BBC exit poll. Did it predict the result? Far from it.

Instead, it put forward attack lines that the Conservatives wanted to circulate in the critical few hours before much of Britain went to bed, arguments that it believed then would be necessary to prepare for the manoeuvring for advantage in the days and week ahead.

The Conservatives, according to this email, did not even need to be the largest party in the House of Commons to have won the right to have the opening crack at forming a government. Instead, incumbency alone gave David Cameron first dibs.

Cameron can be faulted, like everyone else, for failing to predict the result accurately. However, he can argue with little fear of opposition that he owes few others in his party credit for the victory, given the criticisms the campaign suffered from within his own ranks.

The messaging was incoherent, said some. The Conservatives could not figure out what their primary target was, said others. It had failed to drive the message to voters that the economy was coming right and their future was better entrusted to the Conservatives. The list went on.

The expensively acquired Australian strategist Lynton Crosby had besmirched the Conservatives' name by sending defence secretary Michael Fallon to accuse Ed Miliband of being prepared "to stab his country in the back over Trident, in the same way that he had stabbed his brother".

Crosby and Cameron, but even more often the chancellor of the exchequer, George Osborne, had told MPs for more than a year that the Conservatives' and Labour's support would "cross over". The date for the epiphany was delayed and delayed.

However, the basic architecture of the campaign worked, even if he has sown seeds that he may one day harvest with tears, worked, particularly when it comes to safeguarding the future of the United Kingdom itself – an entity he deemed last year to be precious beyond words.

The Conservatives relentlessly targeted Liberal Democrat seats in England, particularly in the West Country, which saw Cameron even spending much of the second-last Sunday in the campaign in Norton-sub-Hamden, a beautiful Midsomer Murders-style village in Somerset.

The time management seemed madness. The Liberal Democrats holder of the seat, David Laws, enjoyed a 14,000-strong majority, and a good local reputation. In the end, Cameron was right. Law was beaten by 6,000 votes.

Equally, he ordered the portrayal of Ed Miliband as snug in former Scottish National Party leader Alex Salmond's breast-pocket, as he endeavoured to drive home the message to voters in England that they would unfairly pay for Scottish influence in Westminster.

The strategy worked in two ways. It hurt Labour in England, but it also hurt it in Scotland, where Cameron's anti-Scottish rhetoric – as it was perceived by Scots, since they could hardly hear it any other way – made many more determined to vote for the Scottish National Party.

Conscious that he was too often seen as a bruiser in the campaign, Cameron sought today, speaking outside No 10, to spread words of peace, praising Liberal Democrats' leader Nick Clegg for working so hard to make the 2010 coalition that began in No 10's Rose Garden a success.

"Elections can be bruising clashes of ideas and arguments. A lot of people who believe profoundly in public service have seen that service cut short. Ed Miliband rang me this morning to wish me luck with the new government. It was a typically generous gesture from someone who is clearly in public service for all the right reasons. The government I led did important work. It laid the foundations for a better future, and now we must build on them," he said.

For now, Cameron is the man who has delivered the impossible: a Conservative majority – the first since Major pulled his own Houdini-like escape in 1992, but Cameron has done it in an era when politics has become more fragmented than ever.

His enemies within the Conservatives had been readying to circle against him, believing that he was about to fall short. Boris Johnson looked deflated when he realised the scale of Cameron's victory. So, too, did others. The daggers will have to be sheathed for now.

MAY 11TH 2015

'A girl always remembers the first corpse she shaves'

Mark Hennessy

Caitlin Doughty misses the dead and death. "I really miss it. The dead body does mean something to me. Being able to be around death is comforting and exciting and it makes me feel alive."

In 2006, the Hawaiian-born American, then just 23, went to work in a San Francisco mortuary, where, on her first day, she learned how to shave a recently deceased man. "A girl always remembers the first corpse she shaves. It is the only event in her life more awkward than her first kiss, or the loss of her virginity," Doughty writes in the opening lines of Smoke Gets In Your Eyes, and Other Lessons from the Crematory.

Her account of her time in the family-owned mortuary is filled with such lines: some will make the reader laugh out loud; others – such as what happens to fat people in the crematories (the American term for crematorium) – will send readers under the table squirming.

However, everything is done with purpose. Doughty believes the West – some countries more than others – has pulled away too much from death and dying, damaging both our ability to grieve and to understand our own mortality.

Doughty's fascination with death began when she was five, with a pet fish called Superfly. The fish became infected with a parasite. Soon, Superfly was floating upon the surface. Her mother had prepared "the big speech" for her daughter, where she would explain the cycle of life. However, her father had a different approach. He dumped Superfly in the toilet bowl, took his daughter to the pet shop and bought a new fish. "My first lesson in death was the possibility of cheating it," writes Doughty.

Her second lesson, however, removed such illusions. She was in a shopping centre with her parents for a Halloween costume contest. Out of the corner of her eye, she saw a little girl climb up on a railing, and then fall 30ft, head first: "That thud – that noise of the girl's body hitting – would repeat in my mind, dull thud after dull thud."

Overall, Doughty's interest in death is surprisingly uplifting. She endlessly encourages others to be less fearful of it, but, most importantly, not only not to be

Author Caitlin Doughty.

fearful of the corpse but to embrace it.

In the United Kingdom, the body is immediately removed from the family's sight. The funeral takes place 10 days later, in largely empty churches or crematoriums, hidden away from the public.

If the English are distant from death, some Americans are positively remote from it, preferring to have the dead embalmed before they are returned for display with waxy, almost tanned faces.

It was not always thus. In the third century, the bodies of martyred saints were tourist attractions, drawing large crowds of worshippers who believed that the saintly spirit lurked around the corpse, dispensing miracles and holiness.

In time, the Catholic Church charged for burial spots inside churches next to saints: "If there was a nook in the church big enough for a corpse, you were sure to find a dead body in it," Doughty writes.

The practice worked better in some places than in others. Without refrigeration, the "abominable smell" of decomposition – think liquorice, mixed with citrus undertones – could not be hidden even with "incense,

myrrh and other aromatic odours".

Embalming in the United States took off during the American civil war, when families on both sides of the conflict sought to get their sons' bodies back for burial. Because of the heat, the railways quickly refused to carry them.

Embalmers took to the battlefields, competing with one another as they, literally, fought over the dead, each one promising that no body that went through their hands "would ever go black".

In some cases "arsenicals, zinc chloride, bichloride of mercury, salts of alumina, sugar of lead, and a host of salts, alkalis and acids" were used to preserve. Cheaper options included the evisceration of internal organs, and their replacement with sawdust.

Offering secrets from the world of embalming, Doughty tells of "the trocar" – a hollow-tubed stabbing implement – that is used to puncture organs, and drain them of liquids, gases and waste.

Over time, embalmers moved from simply ensuring that bodies could be transported long distances to changing the way the public viewed the dead,

Prince Charles of Britain with his wife, the Duchess of Cornwall, at Mullaghmore in Co Sligo where his great uncle, Lord Mountbatten, whom he described as "the grandfather I never had", was murdered by the IRA, along with two children, Nicholas Knatchbull and Paul Maxwell, and a 83-year-old Baroness Brabourne, in August 1979. Photograph: Eric Luke

convincing them that the body is a source of infection and danger.

In Japan, one undertaker, Shinmon Aoki, was ridiculed for preparing bodies for burial. "His family disowned him and his wife wouldn't sleep with him because he was defiled by corpses," writes Doughty. So Aoki purchased a surgical robe, mask, and gloves and began showing up to people's houses dressed in full medical garb. People began to respond differently; they bought the image he was selling and called him "doctor".

In all, the trend is towards removing people from the cycle of life, Doughty believes. In July she will open a funeral home in Los Angeles that will seek to help families bury their dead, rather than taking the duty away from them.

"We'll come in to help the family take care of the body. Then, we'll go with them to the crematorium and they can watch the body being loaded in. We'll be there to assist, rather than just take the body away and take it behind the scenes," she says.

The connection "is a reminder that you will be this one day and a reminder of how you are living your life. One hundred and fifty years ago, people were dying around you all the time. I'm not saying, 'Let's go back to a high infant mortality rate', but there are people in their 30s and 40s who have never been to a funeral, or never known anyone who has died, except if it was a young person who committed suicide."

Her own mother was 65 before she saw her first dead body. "It is easy to go through your life and not see it," she says. "My parents are my hardest customers, the baby-boomers."

A recognition by today's society that the living should spend time with the dead would help the bereaved to "understand that the person is really dead, but also that they are going to die, that they are going to be this body".

By now, Doughty is in full flow. "It is only by acknowledging that we are all afraid of death that you can figure out where the core of your being comes from.

"[Our way] does give us a sense that death is not real, that death is almost like a video game, that someone dies and the body disappears, but that is not the reality. It doesn't give us a sense either that we are animals, we are flesh. When we die we are lying there like a side of beef. We are not super-special, we are not above animals, we don't dissolve into magic and light," she says, with a beaming smile despite the graphic imagery.

"We are all little ants down here, banging into each other. We are animals and we are fallible and we will decay and we will die. When you have that humility, not getting enough 'likes' on Instagram is not going to take you down," she says.

Doughty's creed, that society should not push death into the background, operates with or without religion. She is not religious and "not very spiritual"; she draws a distinction between the two.

"I have no faith myself. I do it without that. Having this increasingly secular culture, we need touch points, we need to have rituals that we believe in, even if they are unconnected to any religion.

"Treating flesh and bone as a more sacred thing – whether or not you believe in any sort of religious belief – is an important rite of passage. It is something that is valuable and something that we hardly ever do."

Doughty looks kindly on a growing desire in the United States for wild burial, where a corpse is placed in nothing but a shroud and buried 3ft – the ideal depth for speedy decomposition – in protected lands. Cremation has its uses, but she favours alkaline hydrolysis, where a lye made with potassium carbonate and hot water is used to break down the body quickly.

"It is legal only in eight states in the US right now, but I really think it is going to be the future. It doesn't emit carbon and uses much less natural gas. It is generally better. If you give people a choice between fire and water, they usually choose water. It is a Judeo-Christian discomfort about fire."

Soon, Doughty will be back in the comfort of a Californian mortuary. "It is such an important reality check to be around the dead. As a practitioner, it makes me feel really good to be good at it, to be able to offer people comfort."

Given that she is only 30, Doughty hardly obsesses about her own mortality, even if she is comfortable talking about it. "The ideal thing to do would be to have the body laid out for animals, put out on the lawn and have the carrion that want my body come and eat it. I am not a better animal than they are. That's the ideal method of disposal. It makes me feel good to know that I am part of this universe."

MAY 12TH 2015

'We all thought you were dead. Do you want a Twix?'

Brian Boyd

Have you been taking cocaine?" I am on an operating table in St Vincent's Hospital, Dublin. It is 6am on April 14th, and a few hours ago I had a massive heart attack.

The doctor repeats the question: "Have you been taking cocaine?" I am furious. I gather what strength I have left in my fast-fading body, raise myself up and shout at him: "I Don't Do Drugs."

I am furious because, far from being on a cocaine binge the night before, I was in the gym until 11pm, playing a tough three-set tennis match against my regular partner, Daniel. Thanks to playing competitive sport in the past few years I have never been fitter. My cholesterol reading is exemplary, my body-fat ratio impressive and I have the same waist size (32 inches) in my 40s as when I was 17. I cycle. I swim. I am in good shape.

At 11.15pm I am saying goodbye to Daniel and firming up a time for our usual Wednesday night match. At 11.30pm I am brought to my knees by a massive heart attack. At 11.45pm I am doing what any self-respecting man who has just had a massive heart attack would do: taking two Solpadeine and going for a lie-down.

I toss, I turn, I take more Solpadeine. I am convinced I have bronchitis. The pillow is soaked with sweat. I drift off and wake at 5am. I ring my GP. He tells me to ring an ambulance. I don't remember anything else. I wake up to hear one doctor saying "You've had a major, major event," and the other asking me about cocaine. I pass out again for a few hours. I come around to find my sister standing beside my hospital bed. That's funny, us both being sick at the same time and in the same hospital. I hope she hasn't got the same awful bronchitis I have.

While I was passed out I had an angiogram followed by an angioplasty (a stent). Over the next few hours I learn some horrible truths: I am told I am one of the worst cases they have ever seen in the Coronary Care Unit at St Vincent's; that when I arrived two of my coronary arteries were 100 per cent blocked; that I wasn't expected to make it. As a bonus I still need another angioplasty (and soon), but for now there is a dangerous amount of fluid on my lungs.

I haven't taken any of this in. My only thought is to text Daniel to say, "The only reason you won last night is that I've just found out I was playing with two 100 per cent blocked coronary arteries." But the need to get violently sick is more pressing. There is such a thing as black vomit. It's the trauma, apparently.

But the trauma turns out to be the easy part. The disbelief, shock and self-loathing are a bit harder. It is Tuesday afternoon and I am hooked up via wires to five or six machines. I have to breathe through an oxygen mask and there are tubes running painfully into my arms. They've got the wrong person here. I have things to do today. There has been a terrible mistake.

I am in the High Dependency Unit. A fellow patient comes over to my bed and says: "We all thought you were dead. Do you want a Twix?"

Later that day I begin to feel ashamed and

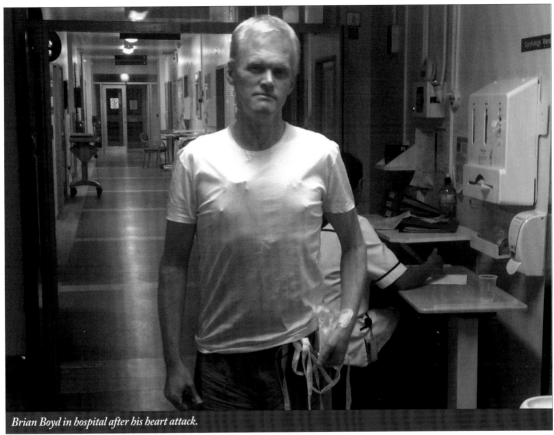

Brian Boyd in hospital after his heart attack.

embarrassed by what has happened. I resolve that only family and close friends will know the truth. Luckily, I am finishing a book, so I will tell all and sundry that I've gone away for a few weeks to wrestle down the final chapters. I don't want people to know because I don't want to be pitied.

All of this makes me less of a man. I will now be seen as weak and vulnerable. When I return to the gym, a blanket will be put over my knees and a cup of tea placed in my hand. I will be patted patronisingly on the back. Poor Brian: you wouldn't think to look at him now that he is the reigning Leinster mixed doubles semi-finalist.

The texts start to arrive: "I don't believe it; I am in shock." "You of all people!". "You're either on your bike or on the court, how can this be true?"

I smile ruefully and think of my secret.

But for now I have to tell Daniel that I can't make tomorrow's night match. The 42-word text outlining the bare details of what has happened to me takes two hours to type out because I am so convulsed with tears. Pressing "Send" on this text means my previous life is over and I will no longer be of any use to anyone on the tennis court. I weep bitter, self-pitying tears. Why me? My sporting life is over.

For the first three days and nights in the hospital, I don't get any sleep and am unable to eat. I just cry instead. At night I sob so loudly that I am convinced the other patients in the unit will sign a petition to ask for the Permanently Crying Man in Bed Six to be moved.

I experience extremes: from the young Indian nurse who sits on my bed and strokes the back of my hand and doesn't leave until I have fallen asleep, to the terrible things you see and hear in a high-dependency unit. My reaction to the distressing arrival of new, emergency patients is frighteningly childlike: I stick my fingers in my ears and close my eyes tightly.

Here's my secret: I am crying so much because deep down I know the answer to the question "Why Me?" I am carrying a malignant genetic inheritance. Ten years ago my only brother died from a massive heart attack. It runs in the family and I have been obsessed with looking after myself ever since. I want to fight my inheritance.

When it came for me that Monday night at 11.30pm, it came at me with a vengeance. As I'm repeatedly told: I'm lucky to be alive and it was only my fitness level that pulled me through.

I begin to think differently: I am alive thanks to my regular hitting partners: Daniel, Natalie and Francesco. The latter lives close by, and comes to see me within hours.

Here's what they don't tell you: when you've been through trauma and a friendly face pitches up at your bedside, you burst into tears. Poor Francesco takes a seat and stares at his shoes for five minutes while I try, and fail, to compose myself.

I tell Francesco about my shame and embarrassment and explain how I am banning the use of the phrase "heart attack" (if nothing else, it's very ageing) and how I will be using instead "the incident" to refer to what happened that Monday night.

Francesco is from Milan, and English is his second language, but that doesn't stop him going one better. "We will not say 'the incident'; we will say 'the event'," he says.

I remember the first words I heard the doctor say: "You've had a major, major event." God bless you, San Francesco.

Natalie (my brilliant mixed doubles partner) arrives later doubled over with shopping bags stuffed full of fresh food. She is full of concern and support. Crucially, she talks about a tournament in September that we should be able to play together. I sit up straight in bed and am all ears.

When Daniel arrives, I gleefully inform him that all our previous results are null and void due to my blocked arteries (I am a much, much better tennis player than Daniel but for some reason he always beats me).

He says I have just given a new and really pathetic meaning to the term "bad loser". I love being able to talk like this again.

Many, many others play their part in drying my tears and making me feel well again. Serious illness is nothing when confronted by serious friendship.

My heart, which was literally broken, is already repairing itself. I have been here 18 long days; tomorrow I go home. As I celebrate with some calf stretches, I realise that This Sporting Life has saved my life.

I got knocked down. But I got up again.

It is midnight. My phone pings with a text from Francesco. It reads: "Be strong, Brian, like you are on the court. Andiamo."

I sleep like a baby.

MAY 15TH 2015

Referendum led me to tell truth about myself

Ursula Halligan

Our lives begin to end the day we become silent about things that matter – Martin Luther King

I was a good Catholic girl, growing up in 1970s Ireland where homosexuality was an evil perversion. It was never openly talked about but I knew it was the worst thing on the face of the earth.

So when I fell in love with a girl in my class in school, I was terrified. Rummaging around in the attic a few weeks ago, an old diary brought me right back to December 20th, 1977.

"These past few months must have been the darkest and gloomiest I have ever experienced in my entire life," my 17-year-old self wrote.

Ursula Halligan by Dara Mac Donaill.

"There have been times when I have even thought about death, of escaping from this world, of sleeping untouched by no-one forever. I have been so depressed, so sad and so confused. There seems to be no one I can turn to, not even God. I've poured out my emotions, my innermost thoughts to him and get no relief or so-called spiritual grace. At times I feel I am talking to nothing, that no God exists. I've never felt like this before, so empty, so meaningless, so utterly, utterly miserable."

Because of my upbringing, I was revolted at the thought that I was in love with a member of my own sex. This contradiction within me nearly drove me crazy. These two strands of thought jostled within me pulling me in opposite directions.

I loved a girl and I knew that what wasn't right; my mind was constantly plagued with the fear that I was a lesbian. I hated myself. I felt useless and worthless and very small and stupid. I had one option, and only one option. I would be "normal", and that meant locking myself in the closet and throwing away the key.

I played the dating game. I feigned interest in men. I invented boyfriends. I listened silently to snide remarks about homosexuals. Tried to smile at mimicry of stereotypical gay behaviour.

In the 1970s, homophobia was rampant and uninhibited. Political correctness had yet to arrive. Homosexuals were faggots, queers, poofs, freaks, deviants, unclean, unnatural, mentally ill, second class and defective humans. They were society's defects. Biological errors. They were other people. I couldn't possibly be one of them.

Over the years I watched each of my siblings date, party, get engaged, get married and take for granted all the joys and privileges of their State-acknowledged relationship.

My coping strategy was to pour myself into my studies and later into my work. I didn't socialise much because I had this horrible secret that must never come out. It was a strategy that worked until I'd fall in love again with a woman and the whole emotional rollercoaster of bliss, pain, withdrawal and denial resumed. It was a pattern that would repeat itself over

A pro-Yes mural, by artist Joe Caslin, on the façade of a 15th century tower house in an undisclosed location in the west of Ireland. Photograph: David Sexton

Crowds celebrate in the Upper Yard of Dublin Castle as the result of the Marriage Equality referendum are announced: Yes 62.4%; No 37.6%. Photograph: Charles McQuillan/Getty

Martyn Turner on the church and the marriage equality referendum

the years.

And never once did I openly express my feelings. I suppressed everything and buried myself in books or work. I was careful how I talked and behaved. Nothing was allowed slip. I never knew what it was like to live spontaneously, to go with the flow, to trust my instincts . . . I certainly couldn't trust my instincts. For years I told no one because I couldn't even tell myself. It was a place I didn't want to go. It was too scary; too shameful. I couldn't cope with it. I buried it. Emotionally, I have been in a prison since the age of 17; a prison where I lived a half-life, repressing an essential part of my humanity, the expression of my deepest self; my instinct to love.

It's a part that heterosexual people take for granted, like breathing air. The world is custom-tailored for them. At every turn society assumes and confirms heterosexuality as the norm. This culminates in marriage when the happy couple is showered with an outpouring of overwhelming social approval.

For me, there was no first kiss; no engagement party; no wedding. And up until a short time ago no hope of any of these things. Now, at the age of 54, in a (hopefully) different Ireland, I wish I had broken out of my prison cell a long time ago. I feel a sense of loss and sadness for precious time spent wasted in fear and isolation.

Homophobia was so deeply embedded in my soul, I resisted facing the truth about myself, preferring to live in the safety of my prison. In the privacy of my head, I had become a roaring, self-loathing homophobe, resigned to going to my grave with my shameful secret. And I might well have done that if the referendum hadn't come along.

Now, I can't quite believe the pace of change that's sweeping across the globe in support of gay marriage. I never thought I'd see the day that a Government Minister would come out as gay and encounter almost nothing but praise for his bravery. But that day did come, and the work done down the decades by people like David Norris, Katherine Zappone, Ann-Louise Gilligan and Colm O'Gorman made me realise that possibilities existed that I'd never believed would ever exist.

I told a friend and the world didn't end. I told my mother, and the world didn't end.

Then I realised that I could leave the prison completely or stay in the social equivalent of an open prison. The second option would mean telling a handful of people but essentially go on as before, silently colluding with the prejudices that still find expression in casual social moments.

It's the easier of the two options, particularly for those close to me. Because those who love you can cope with you coming out, but they're wary of you "making an issue" of it.

The game-changer was the marriage equality referendum. It pointed me toward the first option: telling the truth to anyone who cares. And I knew if I was going to tell the truth, I had to tell the whole truth and reveal my backing for a Yes vote. For me, the two are intrinsically linked.

That means TV3 taking me off referendum coverage. The rules say they must, and when I told them my situation, they reorganised their coverage in half a day. Twenty years ago or 30 years ago, it would have taken more courage than I had to tell the truth. Today, it's still difficult but it can be done with hope – hope that most people in modern Ireland embrace diversity and would understand that I'm trying to be helpful to other gay people leading small, frightened, incomplete lives. If my story helps even one 17-year-old school girl, struggling with her sexuality, it will have been worth it.

As a person of faith and a Catholic, I believe a Yes vote is the most Christian thing to do. I believe the glory of God is the human being fully alive and that this includes people who are gay.

If Ireland votes Yes, it will be about much more than marriage. It will end institutional homophobia. It will say to gay people that they belong, that it's safe to surface and live fully human, loving lives. If it's true that 10 per cent of any population are gay, then there could be 400,000 gay people out there; many of them still living in emotional prisons. Any of them could be your son, daughter, brother, sister, mother, father or best friend. Set them free. Allow them live full lives.

MAY 29TH 2015

How Willie Walsh won over the Government and stakeholders

Barry O'Halloran and Cliff Taylor

It took longer than it ever imagined, but International Consolidated Airlines Group finally won the Government over to its €1.4 billion bid for Aer Lingus this week. It means that IAG and its Irish chief executive, Willie Walsh, now have the support of the State's 25.1 per cent stake in the airline as they set about launching a €2.55 a-share offer for the company.

Former Aer Lingus pilot and company CEO Willie Walsh in Dublin in February 2015 to speak to TDs in the hope of convincing them that the proposed takeover of the Irish airline by the British group, IAG, which he now heads, was a good idea.
Photograph: Aidan Crawley/Bloomberg

Walsh played a key role in bringing some initially sceptical politicians on board over the past five months. And while the drama might have lacked fireworks, there was, as usual, plenty going on behind the scenes .

IAG began to seriously consider making an offer last September, when a number of things were coming together. Aer Lingus's efforts to carve itself a significant slice of the transatlantic market were paying off. Crucially, the airline was finally closing on a resolution of a €750 million pension problem that once seemed intractable.

Along with that, the biggest shareholder, Ryanair, had been wrestling for a year with an order from the UK's competition regulator demanding that it cut its 29.8 per cent stake in Aer Lingus to 5 per cent. It was preparing an appeal and faced the prospect of further legal battles just to hold onto its stake if that failed. There was also a view that it had lost any real interest in its rival.

The Government was gearing up to sell its interests in the banks as one of its agencies, Nama, was offloading property-related debt to mainly multinational buyers.

To outsiders, getting the State to part with its 25.1 per cent stake might have looked straightforward.

However, Walsh knew it would be anything but, as getting agreement would involve satisfying the demands of a host of different constituencies, namely the Aer Lingus board, the Government, trade unions, Ryanair, local interests in Cork and Shannon, and politicians of every hue. All had conflicting priorities – not least the politicians, whose eyes remain fixed firmly on the next election.

One source argues that only Walsh could have pulled it off. "Can you imagine the head of Air France or Lufthansa dealing with that kind of Irish agenda?" he asks.

IAG recruited heavy-hitters, such as Deutsche Bank, into its corner and began preparing itself for battle. It set its initial sights on the airline board, after which its plan was to focus on getting Government to agree to sell the State's stake.

On December 14th, shortly after the pension resolution had cleared its final hurdle, the group made its first approach, telling the Aer Lingus board that it was prepared to pay €1.23 billion for the airline. The

Aer Lingus and British Airways jets, seeming nose to nose at Dublin Airport as the British airline's parent company, IAG, is poised to take over the Irish carrier. Photograph: Niall Carson/Press Association

board rejected this as it did a second, valued at €1.28 billion which IAG made on December 29th, when most of the world was on its Christmas holidays.

At the end of January, following a few more weeks of speculation, and not much else, IAG got its first break. After a series of meetings through the last weekend of the month, the Aer Lingus board said it was prepared to accept the group's third proposed offer of €2.55 per share, or nearly €1.4 billion. It was thought that would be enough to satisfy most institutional investors, although some were pushing for more.

IAG's offer was conditional on acceptances from the Government and Ryanair. Although there were no guarantees of this, it looked like the bid was set to roll forward. What followed instead was a sort of phoney war, with no side making any visible advance.

Within Government circles and, to a certain extent, Aer Lingus, the feeling was that IAG wasn't selling the deal. By early February, there was a sense that the momentum gained the previous month had been lost and that the opportunity itself could slide out of IAG's grasp.

Walsh flew to Dublin on February 10th and spent a few days meeting Government officials, the media and politicians. During this visit, he confirmed to the Oireachtas Committee on Transport and Communications that IAG would guarantee Aer Lingus services to Heathrow for five years, famously adding that it would be his best offer.

Despite the inevitable wall-to-wall coverage, in the wake of Walsh's visit many believed that the message had not got through politically. The corporate side quietly groaned when Paschal Donohoe, the Minister for Transport, Tourism and Sport, announced that he was referring the proposal to a cross-departmental expert group.

Most saw this as a way of postponing a decision – or even not making one at all.

If there was a breakthrough moment, it was at the end of the week of Walsh's visit, when Aer Lingus chairman Colm Barrington and chief executive Stephen Kavanagh issued a joint statement saying that the IAG offer was good for the airline, shareholders and the country as a whole.

They repeated this days later to the same Oireachtas committee that had grilled Walsh. But it was the statement itself that apparently had the most impact politically, prodding the coalition, or at least the Fine Gael side of it, to move forward.

"It was heard loud and clear by the politicians," says one observer. "This was Colm Barrington and Stephen Kavanagh saying in no uncertain terms that this was in the best long-term interests of Aer Lingus." The key point, he added, was that the message was coming from the airline's executives and board, rather than IAG, which would have just seemed self-interested if it had said anything more.

On February 24th, Donohoe issued a statement saying that the Government was not willing to sell the stake based on IAG's terms. But he also outlined the Coalition's key concerns, which were mainly the well-rehearsed points about Heathrow slots and connectivity, and made it clear that the door was still open.

It was from this point that things began to inch towards this week's conclusion. The Government's expert group included John Fearon, Assistant Secretary in the Department of Transport; Eileen Fitzpatrick, from State agency New Era; and IBI chief executive Tom Godfrey. The group began a series of meetings with IAG and its advisers. The airline group's representatives included staff from general counsel Chris Haynes's department.

According to sources, it was clear at this stage that a deal could be done and hinged on hammering out an agreement that worked for both sides. The process turned out to be exhausting, beginning with finding a way of safeguarding the Heathrow slots.

The B-share mechanism on which it is proposed to found those protections was developed comparatively late in the day. The two sides had to come up with something that was both legally enforceable and did not break EU State aid rules. As a result, a number of points had to be referred to Brussels. There was a brief scare when it looked like one EU directorate would

Golfer Rory McIlroy takes a selfie with adoring fans, members of the cast of Riverdance, ahead of the Irish Open being played at Royal County Down. Photograph: Charles McQuillan/Getty

have a problem with the B-share, but it was quickly cleared up.

If there was a crunch issue, it was the five-year guarantee that Heathrow services between Cork, Dublin and Shannon would be maintained at their current levels . The Government did attempt to get 10 years on the table, which was never going to fly, but it did get seven.

The Minister for Transport played his part in this. In February, Donohue said that five years was not enough and he was not prepared to back down. As it turned out, Donohue drove a hard bargain, which Walsh alluded to earlier this week.

Sources say the Minister turned out to be a tougher negotiator than some expected. The issue itself also turned out be tougher than expected.

By late last month, both sides had worked comprehensively through the finest detail involved in

most of the issues, but there was still a gulf between them when it came to the guarantee. If anything really had the potential to derail the talks, it was that. In the end, seven years emerged as an acceptable figure, and the compromise was effectively five-plus-two, whereby IAG is happy to extend its five-year pledge for two more years, as long as airport charges remain at an acceptable level, with an agreed formula for determining what actually is acceptable. In essence, it allows both sides to argue that they got what they wanted.

The commitments given to Shannon, Cork and, ultimately, Knock were added as the process was nearing its end. By last weekend, it was ready to go to Cabinet, but it was not added to the agenda until the last minute. This allowed backbenchers to be briefed and gave Aer Lingus' Kavanagh time to write to the unions.

159

The only remaining question mark hung over the one thing that neither side could control – Ryanair. IAG had hoped to receive a commitment from the airline to sell its shares, but in the end was happy that Ryanair simply adopted a neutral position until such time as it received an offer.

With the Government on board, the focus has shifted in that direction, as Ryanair is now in a position to make – or break – the deal. We could yet see some fireworks.

MAY 29TH 2015

Analysis: Meek regulator unable to play role of financial watchdog

Ciarán Hancock

He's sorry for how things turned out but it really wasn't his fault. In a nutshell, that's what Patrick Neary's nine-hour appearance at the Oireachtas banking inquiry boiled down to yesterday.

It was the system of light-touch regulation that was being used across Europe at the time. It was the banks and their boards of directors who took the ruinous lending decisions. It was staff shortages in its banking supervision unit due to an inability to pay top wages. And it was the Central Bank for its failure to flag the stresses and strains that were building in the economy.

Neary never saw it as his role to be intrusive. Rather, he placed far too much trust in the banks.

Here's one example. Neary never saw it as his role to challenge Anglo Irish Bank or Irish Nationwide over

Patrick Neary, retired head of the Financial Services Regulatory Authority, which he ran in the lead up to the economic and banking crisis, arriving to give evidence to the Oireachtas banking inquiry.
Photograph: Dara MacDonaill

their customer concentration.

The Nyberg report has detailed how the top 20 customers in Anglo at May 2008 had 50 per cent of the Irish loan book, which was €41.7 billion at the time. At INBS, 25 customers represented 51 per cent of the commercial loan book.

Sinn Féin's Pearse Doherty wanted to know if these startling statistics had not been of concern to him at the time.

Neary's deadpan response was that the concentrations were within legal limits and if the concentrations were a systemic threat, then that was a matter of financial stability, which was the bailiwick of the Central Bank. It's worth remembering that the Central Bank's functions were split in two by the government in 2003, with the Irish Financial Services Regulatory Authority given oversight of financial regulation and the Central Bank in charge of financial stability.

Having listened to the evidence of both Neary and John Hurley, former governor of the Central Bank, it is not clear where financial regulation ended and financial stability began. This was part of the problem. Neary also told Doherty that the contract between a lender and a borrower was their business. "It is inconceivable that the regulator can determine who or who doesn't get a credit from a bank as a customer of that bank," he said.

In September 2007, Anglo's then chief executive David Drumm asked to meet Neary.

He asked if Neary knew anything about contracts for difference (CFDs). These had been used by businessman Seán Quinn to build a large stake in Anglo, and Drumm informed Neary that rumours to that effect were going around.

Roll on to January 2008 and Quinn turned up at Neary's door unannounced seeking a meeting. The phrase that sticks in Neary's mind is of Quinn telling him that he had small CFD positions and was "now long in financials".

Remarkably, Neary never asked him what the size of his CFD position was or which bank he had taken a stake in, even though he was aware of the rumours around Anglo.

"It was his own business," was Neary's response.

Neary's evidence also makes clear that he was only on the sidelines on the night of the guarantee. His main input was to argue that a blanket guarantee would offer more certainty to the markets.

What about his assertion to Prime Time on October 2nd, 2008, that the Irish banks were in good shape? "In hindsight, that was probably optimistic," he said. Within a couple of months the State had spent €10 billion on its first wave of recapitalisation.

Neary had joined the Central Bank in 1971, working his way up the ladder before being appointed as head of financial regulation as part of an international competition that produced a shortlist of 15 candidates.

His evidence yesterday painted the picture of a nice man who was simply overpromoted. Neary was too meek to be the financial sector's watchdog.

JUNE 3RD 2015

Blatter failed to steer the ship of Fifa's reform

Ken Early

There's a scene in Fifa's astonishing movie about itself, United Passions, in which the newly elected Fifa president, Sepp Blatter (Tim Roth), warns the Fifa marketing department that things are about to change.

"The next tournament is in South Korea and Japan, far from Europe," Roth-Blatter says. "Some of you may feel that this is a good opportunity to close lucrative deals with certain lobbies. Think again. This sport is spotless. There is simply a lot more money involved in ours, which is why, from now on, we will be exemplary in all respects. The slightest breach of ethics will be severely punished."

Some delegates smirk, others protest that Blatter's predecessor, Joao Havelange, would never have dared to insult them like this. The new president fixes them with a steely stare of cold command.

"Joao Havelange presided over our family for 24 years. Did he make mistakes? Perhaps. Not for me to judge. But I am warning you. All of you. We will play by my rules now."

Maybe Sepp Blatter really did once say something like this, maybe not. Though if he did, it's hard to imagine he really believed he could stop corruption by simply telling people not to be corrupt. He was more realistic than that. Only last week he insisted:

Sepp Blatter walking from the podium having announced his resignation as Fifa president at the organisation's headquarters in Switzerland. Photograph: Veleriano di Domenico/Agence France-Presse

"You cannot ask people to behave ethically just like that."

Yesterday, in the course of the sensational announcement that he would step aside as Fifa president, he blamed others: "The executive committee includes representatives of confederations over whom we have no control, but for whose actions Fifa is held responsible."

It was never his fault. His attitude was always: "I've told them not to be corrupt, what more do you expect me to do?" Arguably his favourite saying was "there are always a few rotten apples".

In the end, he was like a farmer whose wife is going to market only to discover her whole barrel of apples has liquefied into a putrescent sludge. When she confronts him, he throws up his hands and says "What do you want me to do? A few of them must have been rotten."

Blatter's way was to let rotten apples lie, apparently oblivious that a farmer who acknowledges the existence of rotten apples must also accept responsibility for rooting them out of the barrel.

When members of his executive committee were exposed as corrupt he would suspend them and denounce corruption in general terms, but these belated, ad hoc measures never translated into a commitment to actively police Fifa from the centre.

He would issue vague rhetoric about restructuring and reform, but he always sounded more angry about critical press reports than he did about the corruption of the organisation he was supposed to be running. In the long run, his passivity made it look as though he cared less about a clean Fifa, and more about plausible deniability.

Yesterday's revelations concerning his right-hand man, Jerome Valcke, made his deniability look less plausible. Fifa had no sooner issued a statement claiming Valcke had no role in the "initiation, approval and implementation" of a scheme to transfer $10 million to an account controlled by the corrupt Concacaf president, Jack Warner, than a 2008 letter emerged showing Valcke must have known about it.

It may well be the case that Blatter couldn't be expected to be aware of every instance in which his right-hand man helped organise the payment of something that looked suspiciously like an eight-figure bribe. If so, the defence of ignorance is scarcely any less damaging to his credibility.

In his victory speech on Friday, Blatter had appealed to God for the strength to steer the ship of Fifa for four more years. He did not sound like a man who was planning to resign within four days.

Re-election proved that his global political base had stayed solid, but his personal position was weakened by successive waves of scandal that swept away key allies. The Valcke news looks the most likely reason for his abrupt announcement, but there will be speculation that perhaps something else, some new information yet to be revealed, helped to make up his mind. It was a surprise to learn that the man who had wanted to extend his time as president to 21 years had in fact always been an ardent advocate for presidential term limits, but that's what Blatter claimed in his speech yesterday. "The size of the executive committee must be reduced and its members should be elected through the Fifa Congress," Blatter said.

"The integrity checks for all executive committee members must be organised centrally through Fifa and not through the confederations. We need term limits not only for the president but for all members of the executive committee. I have fought for these changes before and, as everyone knows, my efforts have been blocked."

Blatter will leave the heavy lifting on these questions to Domenico Scala, the Swiss executive who serves as Independent Chairman of Fifa's Audit and Compliance Committee. As chairman of the ad-hoc Electoral Committee, Scala will also oversee the election of Blatter's successor.

He has much to ponder. What should the term limits be for Fifa's magnates? How will candidates for the new model ExCo be vetted? And can Fifa afford to hold its extraordinary congress in a country that has an extradition treaty with the United States? The sports administration story of the century still has a long way to run.

JUNE 5TH 2015

Hard to see how 'verbal assaults' on Murphy were in O'Brien's interests

Noel Whelan

One would assume that since he is a very wealthy man Denis O'Brien would have access to the very best public relations advice that money can buy.

Having seen and read how he has been portrayed and has portrayed himself this week, however, one can only come to the conclusion that he has got bad value for his buck of late. O'Brien has either been badly advised or is refusing to listen to good advice.

In years to come, they will teach this week's handling of Denis O'Brien's affairs as a classic example of a very bad PR strategy. Indeed "strategy" may be too grand a description for the combination of bluster and threat involved. It has been entertaining at times, chilling at others, but in no sense has it enhanced Denis O'Brien's reputation.

It is not at all clear how the verbal assaults perpetrated upon Catherine Murphy TD on various radio programmes last weekend were in Denis O'Brien's interest.

It is not clear, either, how gratuitous attacks upon parliament and politics in general can be seen as protecting or promoting Denis O'Brien's reputation. Let's assume for a minute that someone with

James Morrisey, Denis O'Brien's media advisor, at the Four Courts in Dublin during O'Brien's application for an injunction to prevent disclosure of details of his banking arrangements with IBRC. Photograph: Cyril Byrne

access to documents taken from IBRC is out to get Denis O'Brien. And let's assume that this person has concocted the suggestion that the bank gave favourable treatment to O'Brien in the handling of his loans.

If this were the case, as O'Brien suggests, then surely the wiser course would have been to confine his counter- argument to making the point, as he has with some success in the courts, that his private banking affairs should not be in the public domain, and to particularising those aspects of Deputy Murphy's utterances in the Dáil that he claims were untrue.

Instead, what O'Brien had his spokesman do was shout abuse at Catherine Murphy and other politicians over the airways.

The first principle of public relations is that when your spokesperson becomes the story you're losing.

So it is difficult to understand why O'Brien's paid

spokesman, James Morrissey, engaged in a full-blooded politicised assault upon Catherine Murphy. Morrissey suggested, among other things, that she is busily peddling falsehoods about O'Brien and IBRC for personal political gain.

The problem for Morrissey and, more importantly, his client is that such a suggestion lacks credibility. Catherine Murphy is correctly regarded by many as one of the most effective parliamentarians in the current Dáil, known for her thoughtful and careful contributions on a range of political issues.

She is no hothead. She is not prone to grandstanding. There is nothing in her form that suggests she would play fast and loose with parliamentary privilege for cheap, short- term publicity.

On the contrary, she has doggedly pursued the issues surrounding IBRC's sale of Siteserv for months through detailed parliamentary questions and Freedom of Information requests.

Martyn Turner's take on the Denis O'Brien controversy

The Government's decision finally this week to establish a commission of inquiry confirms there was something in Murphy's suggestion that these matters needed to be comprehensively and independently inquired into.

Not content with systematically seeking to dis Deputy Murphy, O'Brien and his spokesman have also felt it necessary to attack other politicians who sought to defend Murphy's use of parliamentary privilege.

Morrissey, for example, told Keelin Shanley on RTÉ radio last Friday that "to be brutally blunt about it, the Dáil is a bit of a talking club". He took the same dismissive tone in an even more robust intervention that evening with Matt Cooper on Today FM and on Sunday's This Week programme on RTÉ.

The approach has been one of casting aspersions on the motive of anyone who dares defend Catherine Murphy's right to raise the issue in the Dáil, rather than dealing with the substance of what Murphy had to say.

Even in his own piece in The Irish Times on Tuesday, Denis O'Brien accused Catherine Murphy of a "deliberate breach under Dáil privilege of a court order". Later that morning the judge who made that order confirmed that it did not and could not extend to restricting the right of a Deputy to address the matters in the Dáil or the right of the media to report those remarks.

Maybe James Morrissey and others have persuaded O'Brien, or he has come to the view himself, that there is a rich vein of public cynicism about politicians that he should tap into to bolster his own position.

O'Brien should be warned, however, that there is even greater cynicism among the public about wealthy businessmen with media interests who seek to restrain public comment about themselves.

The ultimate outcome of the legal actions and inquiries now in place is uncertain. One thing is clear, however: Denis O'Brien's reputation has been damaged rather than defended by the way he or his public relations advisers have mishandled matters this week.

JUNE 6TH 2015

Greek island gateway to EU as thousands flee homelands

Damian Mac Con Uladh

As he looked out at the five-mile stretch of blue sea separating Greece and Turkey, Eric Kempson knew he should be worried. Clearly overloaded with people, the inflatable boat, which he had been observing from a vantage point near his home on the northern shore of the Greek tourist island of Lesvos, was in difficulty. With a stiff northeasterly breeze at its back, the eight-metre vessel was veering off course and risked ending up running aground on the sharp rocks at the foot of some cliffs. But luckily for this boat's 75 passengers – who would turn out to be Somalis, Afghans and Pakistanis – help was at hand, as Spyros Kontomichalos, a well-built professional soldier, quickly dropped his plans to go spear-fishing and rushed to direct the boat towards the nearest beach.

As it approached the rocky shore, the boat's passengers leapt out into the water, delighted to finally step foot in the European Union after setting out at daybreak, almost three hours beforehand, from the Turkish coast. And with traffickers back in Turkey charging anything up to €1,000 a head for the crossing, which in better boats and more favourable conditions can take as little as 25 minutes, it's undoubtedly the most expensive journey these migrants will ever take.

"Excuse me. Is this Greece?" asked a 24-year-old

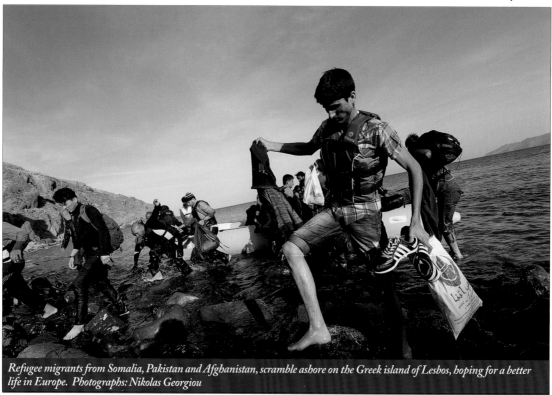

Refugee migrants from Somalia, Pakistan and Afghanistan, scramble ashore on the Greek island of Lesbos, hoping for a better life in Europe. Photographs: Nikolas Georgiou

Pakistani man, whose suit was soaked to his waist. Behind him, a group of young Somali men struggled to lift the sole woman passenger from the boat to her wheelchair, the only possession she managed to bring from the other side. Later, Riyan (30), would explain that she had been shot in the back 15 years previously. She said she was making the journey on her own, and her aim was to reach Germany where she hoped she could have an operation.

This migrant vessel was one of four to land last Tuesday morning near the beautiful town of Molyvos, with its medieval hilltop fortress that can be seen from miles around. Tourism is the lifeblood of the place and the permanent population of about 1,500 relies almost exclusively on the money they make during the summer to keep them going during the difficult winter months after the tourists have gone.

For weeks, Kempson, a British painter and sculptor who made his home in Molyvos 16 years ago, and his wife Philippa have been daily witnesses to the rapid increase in the numbers of refugees and migrants arriving from Turkey.

"It's been a nightmare for the last few weeks. We really need some help. Only a few of us have been trying to help. This story needs to get out there and Europe really needs to send some help," he says.

About 70 per cent of those arriving on the boats are Syrian refugees, including many families with young children. They are fleeing the four-year civil war that has devastated their country and, according to the United Nations, triggered the largest humanitarian crisis since the second World War.

An estimated 7.6 million people are now displaced within Syria, while almost four million have fled to neighbouring countries, mostly to Turkey, Lebanon and Jordan, where the vast majority have remained, often in appalling conditions.

Syrians in Molyvos say only Europe – by which they usually mean Germany or Sweden – can offer them and their families the safety and opportunities they desperately seek.

Last week, the head of EU border agency Frontex said 40,000 migrants had arrived on Europe's shores through Greece since the beginning of 2015, compared with 37,000 through Italy, which has been at the focus of the EU's efforts in the Mediterranean recently. Greece's eastern Aegean islands experienced a fivefold increase in migrant traffic in March and April compared with the the same period last year.

Fatma (34), who fled Damascus a month ago and arrived in Molyvos on Monday, said she paid a trafficker in Turkey €3,000 to put her, her two teenage daughters and her eight-month-old son in an inflatable boat to Greece.

She is from Yarmouk, a Palestinian suburb with the formal status of a refugee camp on the outskirts of the Syrian capital. Under siege by government forces for almost two years, parts of the district, much of which is in ruins, were overrun by by militant jihadist group Islamic State (IS) in April. She too wants to reach Germany.

During their short stay in Molyvos, the refugees generally gather in the unpaved car park at the entrance to the town, where many spend the first night sleeping out in the open. If they're lucky, a bus will take them to Mytilini, the island's capital.

There they can expect to wait with hundreds of others for days at the city's port before being admitted to a camp, processed and handed a temporary permit to remain in Greece.

That paper gives them the time to make plans to continue their journey into western Europe which, despite EU rules stating refugees must apply for asylum in the country of entry, is what thousands have already managed to do.

No bus was sent to Molyvos on Monday or Tuesday, leaving men, women and children to walk the 65km to Mytilini in daytime temperatures that reached 30 degrees. As offering any assistance to undocumented migrants is illegal in Greece, locals and tourists are reluctant to offer them lifts, although some do.

"The authorities have been putting barriers in our way and making Greeks afraid. Greeks are not like that; they are family-oriented," says Kempson.

Finding itself at the start of the tourist season and in the midst of the Greek financial crisis, Molyvos can barely cope with the surge in the numbers of refugees and undocumented migrants. There has been no official response and no humanitarian NGOs have shown up in the town, which has been without a public doctor for eight months, Kempson says.

Filling that gap is a small team of locals, among them many expats, who are struggling to offer basic assistance to the refugees, which at best includes some food every morning and evening, fruit, water, clothing, blanket, toiletries, nappies and other essential items. Others try to offer women and children a bed at least once a week.

"I'm half-Croatian, so I know what it's like to be put out of your home," said one Molyvos resident, Emma, who declined to give her surname, as she took Fatma, her children and five others home for the night.

But it's an uphill struggle. Without any outside help, the volunteers know they can't keep up with the sheer number of arrivals which, going by previous years, are expected to peak between July and September.

Many of the volunteers earn their living from tourism themselves, as Dina Adam, a hotel employee, and Hannah, owner of a children's clothes shop, explain as they make 90 sandwiches one evening for that day's arrivals. They say finding the time to help out is becoming more difficult as the season gets into full swing.

Wholly dependent on public donations, the volunteers have been heartened by the response from many tourists staying in the town, including a Dutch couple who offered the €100 that they had earmarked for a boat excursion.

"We are on holidays in Greece and see the good work you are doing for the refugees . . . Keep on helping people," the holidaymakers wrote on a note accompanying the money.

But among locals in Molyvos, there's no agreement on how best to deal with the issue. There is a fear that the considerable international publicity generated by the crisis, in particular exaggerated tabloid reports that claimed refugees were turning the island of Kos into a "disgusting hellhole" for British holidaymakers, will affect tourism.

"Yes, we get looks from some people because of what we're doing for the refugees. But we tell them we don't want them to stay here and remind them they don't want to stay here either," says one volunteer.

"I do worry about how my guests view the situation," says hotelier Dimitris Vatis, as a migrant boat comes ashore near his hotel. "Some say they've heard about it, others seem to be unaware. But in general no one knows about the refugee crisis here in Greece as all the focus is on the situation between Libya and Italy." For one of his German guests, the scene unfolding in front of her is a wake-up call, one that she and others need to see. "This is part of life. It's no longer something we see just on our TV screens."

JUNE 13TH 2015

Gender offender

Frank McNally

A female reader gave out to me a while back in the comments forum for my "use of male as normative" in part of that day's Irishman's Diary. As least, I think the reader was female – that may be presumptuous. At any rate, the user name was "Libby".

I'd been writing about "emotional inflation in the internet age", especially the tendency of people on Twitter to claim they're "incredibly excited" about this or "incredibly proud" about that. And my offence (for which I plead guilty, to spare the court unnecessary trouble) involved a sentence in which I lamented the false modesty of such exaggerations, viz: "If somebody tells you he's incredibly proud about something, he's also hinting that humility is his normal state."

Now I know perfectly well that it's no longer the done thing to follow the gender-neutral "somebody" with the gender-specific "his" – it's not as if I haven't been paying attention for the last 40 years. But the problem in general is the English language's appalling

Eddie O'Brien, team leader at Dublin Zoo's Sea Lion Cove, a new saltwater habitat, takes a close look at one of his charges.
Photograph: Eric Luke

lack of a neutral pronoun for such sentences. And my problem in particular is that I still can't bring myself to adopt the most common solution, using "they" or "their" after a singular subject.

Yes, I do it in conversation all the time; although even when spoken (as, for example, by that man who says "the mobile customer you are calling may have their unit powered off"), the usage still sometimes makes my ears bleed. But whatever about speech, I'm fiercely reluctant to use the singular "they" or "their" in print.

I realise this battle is already lost. In fact, I read of late that even the American Copy Editors Association – traditionally resistant to the usage – is edging closer to acceptance. Maybe I'm like that Japanese soldier who was still fighting the second World War in 1972. So be it – unless my commanding officer flies to this Pacific jungle in person to tell me it's over, I won't believe it.

Instead, whenever the problem arises in a sentence, I usually go back and make the subject plural, or I adopt other avoidance manoeuvres. As for the case cited above, I must have been feeling reckless that day. Perhaps I was in a rush, and when the old-fashioned somebody/his shortcut appeared ahead, beside a "no

entry" sign, I just went for it. It won't happen again, Guard, I swear.

Anyway, I was reminded of that reader's comment by the news in Britain recently that a group of Anglican women want God to be henceforth called a "she" by clergy, at least some of the time. I know that's taking us well beyond questions of grammar. But the context of their call was the increasing feminisation of their church, which in March led to the appointment of a first female bishop – a woman called "Libby" Lane.

I'm not suggesting this was the same Libby. I'm sure the new bishop has enough local sinners to deal with it without patrolling The Irish Times website trying to save wretches like me. It's just a little coincidence, no doubt. In any case I wish the Anglican women well in their struggle to make the Bible gender-neutral – they like a challenge, obviously.

But their story also set me thinking about what other canonical texts might need rewriting in these days of gender equality. Whereupon my attention quickly fell on that notorious example of female-normative bias, the 1916 Proclamation.

This was of course the work of a poet. And it's well known that in poetic circles, Ireland has always been considered a woman, usually named "Cathleen". Even so, and allowing for the passage of 99 years, the Proclamation's lack of gender balance is striking.

In its opening sentence alone – the one invoking God and Ireland's dead generations – it has a "she" followed by three "her"s. But this is as nothing compared with the longer second sentence, which has no fewer than two "she"s and six "her"s. That's 12 female references already, and Pearse still hasn't declared the Republic.

In fact, as if sensing he was overdoing it, he changes tack in paragraph three, using the first and third person plurals instead, both gender-neutral. And in the fourth paragraph, the now-declared Republic is a singular subject, taking the gender-free possessive "its".

But the female Ireland re-emerges in the document's conclusion. Meanwhile, there are only two male-normative references throughout – to Ireland's "manhood" and "the Irish Republican Brotherhood". Despite all of which, the British somehow saw fit to execute 16 leaders, all male. Miraculously, Countess Markievicz escaped with a short prison sentence.

JUNE 17TH 2015

The closure of Clerys – when the shutters come down

Kathy Sheridan

There is something magical about the combination of money and the law. When Gayle Killilea argued in a South African court that she needed the money from the €19 million sale of a Cape Town hotel to buy a €7 million property in the UK, the judge ruled against her. He decided in favour of the official assignee in her husband's Irish bankruptcy, who had applied to seize the proceeds from the sale.

It was "overwhelmingly probable", he said, that Killilea had other sources of capital since she had found the money somewhere else for a £1 million deposit as well as another quarter of a million to renovate the UK property. But ultimately, he ruled against her because he believed efforts to trace the flow of proceeds from the hotel sale would be "nigh impossible". That was due to "the ease with which funds can be transferred internationally, privacy of banking transactions and the fact that Mrs Dunne controls a network of companies registered in multiple jurisdictions".

It's how the special people roll. Seán Dunne is bankrupt on two continents, with debts of €700 million (including about €250 million to Nama). But magically, there is a wealthy spouse, with a cosmopolitan outlook. There are plenty of them.

Banking privacy, plus the marvel of redundant bankers reinvented as financial advisers to debtors of their former banks (yes, the irony is awesome), plus the laws designed to support the kind of "ease" described by the judge, combine to keep the magic flowing.

For contrast, have a look at O'Connell Street, Dublin, last Friday. At lunchtime, Clerys' staff were told the department store had been sold. Four hours later, KPMG liquidators were in the building, declaring – pfoof! – that around 460 livelihoods were up in smoke. It's business, folks. Nothing personal. The new owners of the building Natrium Ltd – D2 Private and Cheyne Capital Management, funded to an unknown degree by US-based Quadrant Real Estate Advisors – spoke to no one and have no obligation to. It's as neat an example as we will ever see of capitalism red in tooth and claw.

In 2012, Clerys was in bank receivership. Gordon Brothers, a US private equity group, bought it though a subsidiary called OCS Investment Holdings, which spawns two other companies: OCS Operations to run the store and OCS Properties to operate the lease. Together they formed the OCS group of companies. This is normal. Under Irish law, every company has its own legal personality and is treated as such by

A Clerys worker, sacked as a result of legal manoeuvres liquidating the store transferring legal ownership of the company and O'Connell Street, Dublin, property, erects protest notices. Photograph: Sam Boal/Photocall Ireland

the court. But after less than three years in business, Gordons sold the business to Natrium.

At 2.30am on Friday, Natrium buys the OCS group, hives off OCS Operations from it, transfers the shares in that company to a London-based insolvency practitioner for €1. Unhappy with the financial projections for next August, the parent company, now owned by Natrium, refuses any further loans to OCS Operations. This severs its lifeline. OCS Properties then refuses to renew OCS Operations' expired lease. The UK insolvency practitioner then asks the Irish High Court to place it in liquidation. Simple. The legalities are done and dusted in about 12 hours, all completed behind the backs of the staff, and all perfectly legal.

But the loans from the parent company – on which OCS Operations survived – are not repayable until September 2016, you say? Well, yes, but a change of ownership means that a demand for repayment can

be made by the parent company and OCS Operations is in no position to meet it. OCS Operations is snookered.

So 130 directly employed people – some of whom had given of their brain, muscle and sweat for over 40 years – and another 330 employed by concessions are left to beg for information about salary arrears, holiday pay and redundancy. We now know they will get statutory redundancy only, which means the taxpayer takes up the slack. Meanwhile, Gordon Brothers is reckoned to have made a 100 per cent profit on its investment. And Natrium has an unencumbered jewel in its claws. It's just business.

We mustn't be naive, we are told. If the new owners hadn't moved swiftly for liquidation, debtors would have been hammering down the doors. Customers owed vouchers or cash orders can go sing for it probably. Business means never having to say you're sorry. Gordon Brothers' minimal statement described

Natrium as a "real estate company". There is talk of a hotel, offices, shops, the usual. Perhaps they intend to do justice to that iconic building, opposite the GPO. Either way, there is little point in shouting rude words at them. It is their nature.

The Clerys property play is from the same freebooting system that plunged this State into a decade of misery and left us with a debt we can never pay off. The same system where companies are easy to set up, yet are granted all the enormous, attendant privileges of limited liability. The system where such companies can operate in an orderly, reputable, business-friendly environment, one fostered, suffered for, and paid for by the citizen. Yet we ask for no quid pro quos, no framework in which owners are required to commit to companies over time, no contracts with staff that are not capable of being broken.

JUNE 20TH 2015

Heartbreak in Berkeley

Simon Carswell

I only knew Nick for about a month and a half," says Gina Trombino. She is the bartender at the Sliderbar restaurant, where Nick Schuster worked as a kitchen porter for six weeks. The two grew close in that short time, socialising with workmates in Berkeley's bars outside their shifts.

Gina helped Nick with his summer list of San Francisco experiences and visits: the Golden Gate Bridge, the Ghirardelli chocolate factory, an Oakland As or San Francisco Giants baseball game, eating the best sourdough bread on a day trip to Half Moon Bay, and a trip to Pier 39 to watch the sea otters. In return, sports-mad Nick taught Gina the rules of Gaelic football.

"He was showing us that it is pretty much football mixed with soccer mixed with rugby, and how you could, like, throw it into the net or kick it over the bar," she says. "I had never seen anything like it. We were actually talking about getting a bunch of his Irish friends and my American friends together at a field, so we could play a game.

"Nick was only 21," she says, tears in her eyes. "He had his whole life ahead of him. I can only imagine how his family and his friends must be feeling right now."

Niccolai – or Nick – Schuster was from Terenure in Dublin. He was one of the six fatalities in this week's tragedy in Berkeley, California. He had been studying history and politics at University College Dublin after graduating from St Mary's College in Rathmines.

Another victim, Eoghan Culligan from Rathfarnham in Dublin, was heading into his final year studying supply-chain management and logistics at Dublin Institute of Technology.

Eimear Walsh was a graduate of Loreto College Foxrock and a third-year medical student at UCD.

Lorcán Miller, from Shankill in Co Dublin, was a graduate of St Andrew's College in Booterstown, Co Dublin. He was also studying medicine at UCD.

Olivia Burke, also a former student of Loreto in Foxrock, was months away from starting her fourth year at college, studying business entrepreneurship at Dún Laoghaire Institute of Art, Design and Technology.

Her cousin, Ashley Donohoe – at 22 a year older than the other victims – was a dual Irish-American citizen who lived in Rohnert Park, about 60km north of San Francisco.

Although they lived an ocean and a continent apart, the cousins were close. They will share a funeral Mass today at a chapel about 75km north of San Francisco before Olivia's parents bring her back to Ireland to be buried.

The five from Ireland were among an estimated 800 Irish students on J-1 summer visas in the San Francisco Bay Area this summer. Many of those 800 were roused from their sleep by phone calls in the small hours of Tuesday, as parents in Ireland tried frantically to contact their children, to see if they were safe.

That night on the US west coast – about noon in Ireland – news began to circulate of a dreadful accident at a student block in Berkeley. A fourth-floor balcony had collapsed on the Library Gardens student apartments at 2020 Kittredge Street in downtown Berkeley, and a number of students had plunged to their deaths.

"Everyone was woken up by their parents or other relatives on Tuesday, just to make sure that they were okay," one Irish student said at the vigil held for the deceased students on Wednesday in Berkeley's main public square, which was attended by several hundred people.

"It just hit me today that practically everyone here went through that experience. Parents at home – the relief they must had have. Unfortunately, other parents got different news."

"'Are you alive?' It is such a horrible question to have to be asked," said Nadia, another J-1 student from Dublin at the vigil. The 22-year-old received calls from her mother, father, brothers and aunts.

Library Gardens is a short walk from the University of California, Berkeley, and the Bart rail service into San Francisco.

In downtown San Francisco students work in the bars and restaurants of the city's tourist hot spots in North Beach, which overlook the stunning bay, with views of the derelict prison island of Alcatraz and the Golden Gate Bridge.

It was Aoife Beary's 21st birthday, and an estimated 40 people were in unit 405 of the apartment block. At about 12.41am, Warren Vercruysse, a Belgian whose apartment is on the first floor on the other side of the building from Kittredge Street, heard a loud bang, like gunfire or fireworks, and felt the building shake.

"We were asleep in our apartment that night, because we had work the next morning," says Shaday Bates,

People in San Francisco gather for a vigil of remembrance for the six Irish students who died in the Berkeley balcony collapse. Photograph: John Edelson/Getty Images

from Kilbarrack in Dublin, on her first J-1 summer, who lives a three-minute walk away.

"It was about 12.30, and we just heard a really big noise. We assumed it was a bomb, because there was a lot going on in the area that night anyways – we heard a shooting first, and then there were lots of fireworks, so we didn't know what to assume."

On hearing the bang some students rushed out of the building to see bodies and rubble strewn under the remains of the destroyed balcony.

"It is a scene that was repeated when I closed my eyes that night, and it was repeated the next day when I opened them," said one of the first emergency responders at the scene of the accident, just minutes later.

He didn't want to give his name. He had seen many emergency scenes over his years working in Berkeley, he said, but "not as horrific as this". "This is something that is embedded in my brain," he said.

He worked his way from student to student, checking for vital signs and trying to rouse them, moving on to the next person if their situation was more grave.

Initial reports indicated that a number of Irish J-1 students were among the fatalities. As the day wore on, images of the debris and drinking cups on the footpath circulated around the world.

It emerged that four Irish students and a dual Irish-American citizen had lost their lives. By day's end the death toll had risen to six; the seven injured, all Irish. Four of the victims died at the scene. Two more students succumbed to their injuries in hospital.

The seven others who fell from the balcony were brought to three hospitals. As of yesterday two of the seven – Hannah Waters and Aoife Beary – were still in a critical condition.

The five other injured remain stable. Some underwent long surgeries after the accident. Two are said to have life-changing injuries.

The dead were among the best and brightest of Ireland's youth, all but one of whom were born the year another group of Irish people travelled to the United States, to play in a World Cup that captivated a nation. This week that nation was left reeling in

sorrow at one of the worst tragedies to befall young Irish visitors abroad.

All the families in Berkeley are today, with help from the Irish consular staff in San Francisco, making final plans for the return journey. The remains of all five returning to Ireland are expected to be repatriated this weekend, months before they were due to complete the summer of a lifetime in northern California.

Tales of heroism emerged from the horror. Darragh Cogley, brother of 21-year-old Clodagh, has said on his Facebook page that his sister was doing "really well" after sustaining serious injuries and that she wanted to thank her friend Jack Halpin for "grabbing her and breaking her fall". Halpin was reported to have suffered serious back injuries and two broken legs after dropping the 12m to the pavement.

Fr Aidan McAleenan, a native of Co Down who is a based in nearby Oakland, said Jack and another of the injured, Conor Flynn, at the same hospital were doing well.

"The surgeons came down and talked to us," he said. "They said they were young and vibrant and would be able to bounce back. Some of them might need more minor surgeries but nothing life-threatening."

Some relatives were able to book flights immediately on Tuesday. Students who saw the balcony collapse from the apartment were able to call the relatives of the dead and injured quickly, enabling some to be in San Francisco, eight hours behind Ireland, by Tuesday evening.

The horror of those few minutes before emergency responders arrived, when the uninjured students at the party were left alone to tend to their friends, has not been lost on people here in Berkeley.

Speaking after laying a wreath at the memorial near the scene on Thursday evening, Minister for the Diaspora Jimmy Deenihan, shortly after arriving from Ireland on Thursday night, said that his thoughts were with those in the company of the dead that evening. "It is a traumatic time for them as well, and they need our support as well at this time," he said.

The memorial has been growing all week as family, friends and strangers have left flowers, personal

The six who died: Olivia Burke; Nick Schuster; Ashley Donohoe; Lorcan Miller; Eimear Walsh and Eoghan Culligan

mementos, notes or collages of photographs of bright and happy young faces of the dead. There are bouquets from Foxrock parish and St Mary's in Rathmines.

"Thank you for your kindness," reads one note, signed "the girl on the elevator".

"I knew this day would come but yesterday I did not know it would be today – our prayers are with you," read another message.

"Wish we could have gotten to know you over the summer," said another from a group of guys in an apartment on the floor below.

A "Berkeley Irish-American Mom" left a pot of irises, a box of tissues and a note of warm support with "a hug for each of you".

The Tricolours, Dublin GAA flag, St Andrew's College crest, packets of Meanies crisps and box of Barry's Tea made this a very Irish memorial.

Speaking to the media, both Irish and American, who have been reporting this story all week, Deenihan captured the sense of grief felt back in Ireland when the Dáil stood for a minute's silence, flags were flown at half mast across the country and President Michael D Higgins described the "greatest sadness of the terrible loss of life".

"I have never seen such an outpouring of genuine sympathy and grief from the whole country for the families of the bereaved. The six who are dead have become the children of Ireland," said Deenihan.

This summer should have been another coming of age for the six Irish students, another step into adulthood. The J-1 programme has been a rite of passage for 150,000 Irish people over more than four decades.

For the 7,000 Irish students this summer, including 2,500 in California, it is an opportunity to experience American culture, to explore, to earn money, to have fun and to make new friends.

Ireland's ties with this town date from its origins in 1878 – it named after the Co Kilkenny-born philosopher George Berkeley – right up to the present, with its Irish doctoral students at the university and the J-1ers.

Dave, a student from south Dublin, was a year behind Olivia Burke in Dún Laoghaire. He also knew Lorcán Miller "to say hello to and have a quick chat with"; they both went to St Andrew's.

Dave had been talking to Olivia two weeks earlier. They met at Pappy's, a bar on the lively Telegraph Avenue – a 15-minute walk from Library Gardens – that is popular with Irish students. "She was a bubbly girl, full of life," he said. "We were having the craic,

joking, just laughing about people in college, lecturers and stuff."

Along with Pappy's, another Berkeley bar that is popular among the J-1 students is Kip's on Durant Avenue. As they pass each other on their way to work at Fisherman's Wharf, "are you going to Pappy's tonight?" is a regular line among Berkeley's J-1ers

Nights out in Pappy's are "almost like nights" at Copper Face Jacks, on Harcourt Street in Dublin. "The same type of vibes. Everyone is there. Just a bit more country people floating around," said Dave.

Bruna, the woman tending the bar at Kip's, says this is her "third Irish summer". At the start of summer the university students finish up and the Irish arrive, she says. They tend to come in late, after midnight.

"We are happy that they're here every summer," said Bruna. "It is slow in summer, and they bring business. They like to sing soccer songs when they leave at

Photographer Peter Martin at the Anglo-Korean designed installation, Square Moon, overall winner of the Yeats 2015 Architectural Competition which was erected on the shore of Lough Gill, framing in the distance, the Lake Isle of Innisfree. Photograph: James Connolly

closing. Yeah, we like them."

There is a solidarity and natural bond among the Irish J-1ers in Berkeley. They don't need to have known each other back in Ireland for them to grow close quickly here; their bond is that they are there for the summer for work and pleasure, after college exams.

First-time J-1ers gravitate towards second- or third-year veterans for advice on the best places to search for jobs or accommodation.

Dave and Jack met Nick Schuster one night a few weeks ago. They were sitting at a table, and Nick's group came over. They all started chatting away as if they have been friends for years.

"We had no idea who they were until they sat down," said Jack.

"I was having the craic with Nick about football. We were just taking the piss out of each other – he was from Mary's and I was from Andrew's – that type of stuff, just banter," said Dave.

And, as Bruna said, soccer songs were part of the fun. Nick's group were singing the West Ham United supporters' anthem, I'm Forever Blowing Bubbles. Dave, an Arsenal fan, wouldn't let it pass.

"I was like, 'You must be West Ham fans?' And they were like, 'Nah, nah.' You can't be singing that song so," he said.

But nightlife and camaraderie are not the only factors that draw Irish students to Berkeley. The weather is sunnier here than in San Francisco, and rents are lower.

In fact the building where this group of students were renting an apartment has become a focal point of reporting in the aftermath of the accident.

Berkeley's mayor, Tom Bates, has said that the balcony collapse may be linked to water damage from inadequate waterproofing, although the investigation into the collapse is not yet complete, and he warned against jumping to conclusions about possible responses.

The San Francisco Chronicle reported this week that Segue Construction, which built Library Gardens apartments, was involved in two lawsuits in recent years involving allegations of dry rot and substandard balconies in apartments in other parts of California. Bates has said that, if shoddy workmanship turned out to be to blame for Tuesday's tragedy, he would advise the Alameda County district attorney, Nancy O'Malley, to take a criminal prosecution.

"In general it is rare that incidents involving construction defects result in criminal prosecutions," said Teresa Drenick, O'Malley's deputy.

Elliott Smith, who works at the university, says, sardonically, that Berkeley has "the most expensive slums in the world". Property is not a red-hot issue in Berkeley, he said; "it is a white-hot issue".

Some developers have built quickly here, he says, because the value of property in the area is just so high.

He says he himself has moved from an out-of-state university to Berkeley, taking a pay cut of 3 per cent. His rent here is 35 per cent higher. In his old job he rented a $650-a-month two-bedroom house. In Berkeley he has a $1,000-a-month studio.

Others controversially hinted at another cause for the accident. On Wednesday the New York Times published an article linking Tuesday's accident to previous years' incidents of "drunken partying and the wrecking of apartments" by Irish students.

One of the veterans of the J-1 exchange programme, the former president Mary McAleese, worked in San Francisco on such a visa in 1971.

She noted the fact at the end of a letter to the New York Times on Wednesday excoriating the paper. McAleese said the New York Times "should be hanging its head in shame" for using a "lazy tabloid stereotype".

The paper apologised, but not before the article was heavily shared and read online, stirring up anger in Berkeley among students still struggling to cope with Tuesday's tragedy.

First-time J-1 student Nadia, speaking at the following night's vigil, said that a response posted on social media by the sister of one of the injured summed up her feelings on that story.

"She said it was disgusting. She was on the way to the airport with her mother, crying, and they felt more hurt reading that," she said.

"The students did nothing wrong," said Jack, a J-1er from south Dublin who visited Kittredge Street on Thursday to pay his respects at the memorial and to inspect the seven broken and rotted beams, which were exposed after builders removed the rest of the destroyed balcony.

"They were standing on a balcony at a party, which pretty much everyone has done, ever. We have all been at a party, standing on a balcony with people . . . It shouldn't happen."

JUNE 26TH 2015

The power player who dealt his way to the top

Una McCaffrey

The Irish Times is being escorted to the top floor of the Northern & Shell office building in London by a hefty young man who says he "looks after" Richard Desmond. He is most pleasant, but there is something about the way he carries himself and the way his suit sits on his broad frame that suggests the "looking after" involves more protection than brewing Desmond's green tea. The notion of a bodyguard sits well with the many stories which the 63-year-old media mogul squeezes into his newly published autobiography The Real Deal. It is a caper of a book, detailing the scrapes and successes that have left the Jewish outsider from north London where he is today: the billionaire owner of OK! magazine, Express Newspapers and the Daily Star, among other assets spanning property, printing and lotteries. It also deals with some of the less complimentary rumours surrounding the man, whose succinct strategy for business meetings is "kill or be killed".

His office suite sits on the edge of the City and boasts a fine collection of cream leather sofas and a compelling view of Tower Bridge, as well as an oddly large collection of doors. At one point, Desmond jokes that one of them leads to the cupboard in which he is said to have made an executive wait after making the mistake of being late for a meeting, but quickly adds that the story isn't true. You're still left wondering though, as Desmond well knows.

"It's called colour, isn't it? I wish more people had a bit of colour."

After an initial tiny confusion between The Irish Times and the Irish Independent (an inquiry after the health of Denis O'Brien), we're off with the interview, during which Desmond becomes more and more animated. He likes to address people by name, which in this case is "Uma".

"This isn't work, Uma, what we're doing," he says, and he is almost right, because spending an hour with the disarmingly jovial, entertaining and charming Desmond who is here today is far from painful. But then one again recalls the stories in the book of trapping business associates in headlocks to get what he wants and of threatening a gangster with a broken bottle in his early teens.

There's also a curious tale about becoming embroiled with the Mafia – which Desmond says is another fabrication – before admitting that the worst side of his reputation can be useful. When his people have problems with business associates for example, they can often be diffused with a hint that "Richard can come and see you".

"I don't care. I want what I want and I won't stop until I get it," he says, smiling benignly all the while.

Until he sold Britain's Channel 5 for £463 million last year, what he wanted, it seems, was to be a billionaire. He had paid £103 million for the station four years previously, so the sale price managed to tip him over the edge of his own ambition. For the first time in his already mega-successful career, he felt financially secure.

"A billion pounds of cash is, I won't say untouchable but . . . You've seen it with the O'Reillys – it can go."

His is referring to Sir Anthony O'Reilly, with whom Desmond partnered for years in the Irish Daily Star

English media mogul Richard Desmond. Photograph: Peter Macdiarmid/Getty Images

when O'Reilly still ran Independent News & Media and whose finances are now in a parlous state. The two are not, and have never been, friends.

"I didn't like O'Reilly," he says, claiming to have never properly met the former Independent chairman beyond an encounter after hearing him deliver a speech to media-buyers in London.

"He stood up and talked about rugby and Heinz Baked Beans," he says. "He thought he was better than me."

The belief that others think they are above Desmond is a recurring theme in The Real Deal, which is littered with references to whether people are "posh" or "very posh" and shows the author puts a lot of emphasis on how his contacts are turned out. He himself likes "Savile Row, double-breasted" and reckons the dress worn today by his interviewer (possibly her best one) cost "not very much". He also reckons you can recognise posh people by their hair, even when they are dressed down, as so many tend to be these days,

much to his disapproval.

"It's the little things, isn't it?" he says, gesturing to the "posh hair" of his PR representative to demonstrate his point. As for his own attire: "I'm playing the part, aren't I?"

He has been described as "Britain's greediest billionaire" by the National Union of Journalists for choosing not to give pay rises to his Express staff, hundreds of whose jobs were culled as he set about a £14 million cost-saving plan after buying the titles in 2000.

Personnel skills aside, Desmond is very proud of the Express titles, probably to a greater extent than he is of OK!, the lifestyle title gobbled up in hair salons around the globe, the 1993 launch of which he says was the most difficult point in his career.

The Daily Express was the paper his father read and was where his father started out as a circulation manager before eventually becoming a senior executive at cinema advertising company Pearl &

Dean. And it is the Express titles that give Desmond a forum for his "crusades", the campaigns "for a fairer Britain" that he says simply reflect what the British people want. Thus, the Express titles are vehemently anti-immigration, anti-EU establishment and, currently, anti-Camelot, the operator of the UK's National Lottery.

On a typical day last week, the Daily Express led with "Outrage over lottery 'rip-off'" after the National Lottery added ten balls to the pot, with the report citing accusations of "shameless greed".

The fine line between editorial freedom and commercial gain comes in here, since Desmond is owner of the competing Health Lottery, a considerably smaller, loss-making enterprise that gives 20p of every £1 wagered to health-related good causes. He needs to stem its losses (£28 million in 2013) but to do so, he says he needs to raise the prize pot, a move prohibited unless he can sell more tickets. It's a chicken-and-egg thing – or it would be if Desmond hadn't decided that this was his next "crusade" for the people and wasn't planning to bid for the National Lottery licence next time it comes up.

"It's the poor people who are buying lottery tickets. Millionaires don't buy lottery tickets," he says, failing to add that billionaires don't buy them either, sometimes choosing to sell them instead.

The lottery approach is classic Desmond: he sees a business, likes it, takes it on and dislodges the incumbent. So it was with OK!, which he started in 1993 after a chance visit to the printer for opponent Hello!, who happened to mention that the Spanish-owned magazine beloved of minor European royalty was printing 800,000 copies. The first edition of OK!, beloved of minor UK television personalities, was launched just a few months later with a print run of 400,000. It is now available everywhere from Australia to Mongolia under licence and has the power to make, and possibly break, stars. The way Desmond tells it, for example, it was he who built the David and Victoria Beckham brand via the pages of OK!.

By the time he launched the magazine, he was already a seasoned publisher, having started out on music titles, which is probably where his heart, but not his money-making brain, still lies. His first proper career was in advertising sales where he excelled ("I turned out to be a bit of a superstar at telesales") before reaching his 16th birthday, a timing snafu that meant he was unable to legally drive the company car. However, his aptitude for eking out opportunity came to the fore even earlier, when he took a job in a pub cloakroom aged 13 and upped the game by raising the ticket price and doubling the number of coats on each hanger, without feeling the need to share his plan with the pub-owner.

"I have to confess that I didn't feel bad about doing any of this. My mother and I really needed the money," he writes in his autobiography.

This line illuminates much of what drove – and still drives – Desmond to rack up the business deals, of which there have been so many. As a teenager, he was living with his mother in a grotty flat after his parents had divorced and his father's top-notch career had collapsed around him. Cyril Desmond had become deaf in his mid-40s, when his youngest son was still very small, having contracted a bug while on business in Africa. This, coupled with his father's gambling problem, left a mark on the young Richard, making him determined to provide for his mother and leaving him (almost) eternally afraid of it all going wrong.

"I think it's because of my father. I always say I'm scared of the park bench."

Pop psychology aside, it is a fact that Desmond had set his mother up in a house he had bought for £1,000 before he even turned 20 and, with that out of the way, he was looking for the next play.

"You had to make some money. You had to look after your Mum and you had to look after yourself. That's the first thing and then the second thing is: how am I gonna do that?"

One such route came via a chance foray into the "top shelf" in the 1980s with the licence for US adult magazine Penthouse. This, and subsequent deals to publish titles including Asian Babes and Readers'

Wives, will follow Desmond to his grave, as he rejects at every turn the notion that he is a porn magnate. This is despite the fact that his company, Northern & Shell, continues to operate a number of adult television channels and still has Page Three in the Daily Star, even though the magazines are long gone. The pornographer description "irritates me", he says, suggesting "every media group has adult entertainment of some sort" and adding that his channels are fully regulated.

"I find it bizarre that they go on about Asian Babes, which sold 3,000 copies a month when you've got a magazine like OK! which could sell two million a week," he says, adding that pornography is, for him, about prostitution and shady massage parlours, not regulated television channels.

It is another window on the world, according to Desmond, who has a knack of defining things the way he thinks they should be defined and then happily moving on. He is known for similarly shifting sands when it comes to "ethics", a word that came to haunt him after a legendary 2012 appearance at Britain's Leveson Inquiry into the practices of the press. Having been asked if he was involved personally in establishing ethical standards at his newspapers, his response was vague.

"Ethical . . . I don't know what the word means, perhaps you would explain what the word means, ethical."

The ethics thing still irks Desmond.

"What a stupid question he asked me. Everybody has ethics, I'm sure Adolf Hitler had ethics. It's about what you think is right," he says. For example, in relation to Penthouse, his "ethics, or justification, or whatever you call it" came in the fact that the magazine was stocked by reputable newsagent chains such as WH Smith.

He mentions the "get on, get honest and get honourable" philosophy in his book, and it certainly chimes in part with his life, with the "honourable"

IMF managing director Christine Lagarde appears exasperated with Greece's maverick finance minister Yannis Varoufakis when the two met at a meeting of eurozone finance ministers. Photograph: Francois Lenoir/Reuters

part reflected in his considerable philanthropic efforts through children's charities, Jewish organisations (he practises Liberal Judaism), and most significantly, the funding of a centre for children at an eye hospital.

He has also spread his financial warmth over the political sector, having donated in his time to Labour, the Conservatives and, most recently, bestowing £1.3 million on Nigel Farage's UK Independence Party, which bombed at the recent UK election. The Ukip electoral performance is of little consequence, as Desmond tells it, whereas the promise of an EU exit referendum, undoubtedly hastened by the Ukip threat to the Conservative base, is important.

"I take full credit [for the referendum]. I really do," he says, quickly adding that of course he means the Express titles take full credit. I like the fact we're having an EU referendum. If I hadn't had the papers, could I have got the referendum? Probably not. And it's very important to this country."

He claims, however, to be undecided on whether the UK should part ways with its EU pals.

"I'm not sure whether we should be in it or not in it because we haven't heard all the facts," he says. He later adds: "My feeling is we need to negotiate hard . . . The Greece situation is an example. They want to keep Greece in so desperately and it's going to cost us all in Britain so much money."

And then he's off on immigration ("nothing wrong with Romanians"), EU budgetary contributions, EU laws and all the rest. He also indulges in some, ahem, light criticism of UK prime minister David Cameron, with whom Desmond and his wife, Joy Canfield, are pictured in "the book", along with, somewhat inexplicably, Simon Cowell.

"Cameron, I think, is a weak bloke. I think the trouble is, I met him when he was a PR man at Carlton Television, but he wasn't a great PR man." He expands, apparently oblivious to the presence of his own PR man only inches away: "A PR man to be the prime minister says it all, doesn't it?" He goes to apologise to said PR man, joking that his misstep is "like something Farage would do", while dismissing any political ambitions of his own.

These days, the Desmond pace is certainly less frantic as his billionaire status appears secure and his company remains profitable (£37 million operating profit in 2013). Desmond married former British Airways manager Joy, his second wife, a few years ago, and the two have a four-year-old daughter and a son born just this year. He is also due to become a grandfather, with his eldest son Robert (26) expecting his first child. He is relishing his second chance at fatherhood.

"I love it. I've actually got time now. Yesterday morning, I took her [his daughter, Angel] to school. Last week, they had a little play where they were all singing. It made my day." This compares to life when Robert was young, when his attitude was more "sports day, schmortz day".

"Even when I'd take him to the the park, he'd be on the swings and we were losing so much money on OK!, I'd be sitting there watching him but my whole mind was, 'How am I gonna sell more copies?'"

It's clear from the statistics with which Desmond sprinkles his conversation that selling copies is still on his mind, but he claims selling actual newspapers isn't at the forefront of his agenda.

"We have approaches all the time, Uma. We're a very successful newspaper group. And the digital side is growing incredibly: this month we did 160 million page views; two years ago, we were doing 50 million page views." He says online advertising revenue is growing, having climbed from £500,000 a month last year to £1 million now. He's also involved in a few media-for-equity deals through sites that might allow you to sell your house cheaply, rent it or even rate girls.

"You've gotta move with the times," he says, although, nothing if not focused, his "dream" still relates to his desire to "give the British public a fair deal on lotteries".

Despite all the bluster, he still hesitates when asked if he has finally dismissed the park bench from his nightmares, saying he only truly realised how good he was at doing deals last year when the Channel 5 sale closed. "It's been such a struggle," he says. "Up until last year, I always felt we were on the edge of going broke."

JUNE 27TH 2015

'Why would I want to date you? I'm already married to you. Would that not be a bit, I don't know, weird?'

Ross O'Carroll-Kelly

Even after 10 years of marriage, Sorcha hasn't lost her ability to surprise me. We're walking out of Donnybrook Fair, our orms laden down with bags, when she turns around to me and goes, "I think you and I should stort going out on dates again."

Naturally enough, I'm like, "Dates? What are you talking about?" I put the bags in the boot of the Lambo, then I slam it shut.

She goes, "Do you remember my friend Maolisa, spelt the Irish way – she did a Masters in HRM and organisational behaviour in the Smurfit School of Business?"

I actually do remember her. She wasn't great. She had one of those faces – looked like she'd been beaten with a bag of limes.

"Yeah, no," I go, "I remember Maolisa spelt the Irish way. What about her?"

She goes, "I bumped into her the other day in Dundrum. She's married to this amazing, amazing goy who's about to become a portner in, like, Matheson Ormsby Prentice?"

I'm like, "Fair focks."

"She told me his name but I can't remember it.

Anyway, she also has a career? And they've got, like, four children. I was like, 'Oh my God, how do you always manage to look so well!'"

"I'd be very surprised if she looked well, Babes. I always thought the girl was bet-down. I hope that doesn't come across as sexist." We both get into the cor and I stort the engine.

Sorcha goes, "Well, she looked rested then, as in, like – oh my God – so chilled out. I was like, 'What's your secret?'. And she said that one night a week she and her husband have, like, a date night?"

I'm like, "Keep going, Babes," wondering is this a trap or something. "Well," she goes, "what would you think of it? The whole idea of, like, going back to dating?"

I kill the engine. I somehow resist the temptation to hang my hand in the air for a high-five. I'm like, "Can I just say, this is muesli to my ears. I genuinely didn't think this would be your kind of thing at all."

She laughs. She's there, "Why wouldn't it be my kind of thing?"

Sorcha always got jealous when I slept with girls who weren't her.

"I'm just saying," I go, "it's very open-minded of you at last."

She's there, "A lot of married couples do it, Ross. Life is, like, so stressful, with work and family and blah blah blah. You have to take time out and think of yourselves, whether it's once a week, once a month . . ."

"Once a week," I quickly go. "Definitely once a week."

She's like, "Okay, once a week, we'll have a date night. Even if it's just dinner somewhere . . ."

"And if it leads to something else," I go, "you're totally cool with that?"

She looks at me crooked. She's there, "Of course I'm cool with it!" and she laughs. "As a matter of fact, Maolisa spelt the Irish way said that's how she and her husband have kept the actual magic in their marriage?"

I'm literally pinching myself here.

I'm there, "Yeah, no, I can see how it'd keep things definitely interesting."

Zoe Readmond and Claire Lynch from Dublin at Body and Soul in Ballinlough Castle in Westmeath.
Photograph: Allen Kiely

She goes, "I don't want us to become one of those married couples, Ross – you know, just staring at each other across a Chinese takeaway every Saturday night. We should be out, like, socialising."

I'm there, "Hey, I'm all about meeting new people, Babes. Keeping it fresh and blah blah blah."

"I was thinking we should sort of, like, ease our way into it? We should stort off by going on dates with each other's friends."

I do a quick mental inventory of all of her friends that I like. Sandrine. Amie with an ie. That bird with the long white coat who I thought was some kind of hospital consultant but actually just works in Kiehl's.

"There's definitely material to work with there," I go. "Which of my friends were you thinking in terms of?"

She goes, "What about Oisinn? Is he going out with anyone at the moment?"

She's borking up the wrong tree there. Oisinn wouldn't go near her. We played rugby together. It's called Bro Code. Deal with it.

I'm there, "You could certainly ask him. Don't be offended if he says no, though. So when are we going to do this thing?"

We're still porked outside Donnybrook Fair, by the way. I'm still wondering am I possibly dreaming this?

She goes, "Well, I was thinking in terms of this Saturday."

I'm like, "Saturday works for me."

She goes, "Do you know my friend, Medb – she's in my mindfulness class?"

I'm there, "Er, no."

She's like, "I just thought you two would definitely hit it off. You have, like, totally the same sense of humour."

"Is she hot?" I go. "Not that looks matter. But they're

obviously very, very important."

Sorcha's there, "She's one of those girls who definitely makes the best of herself."

I pull a face. That's what girls say when someone is horrendous.

I'm there, "I think I might pass on her, Sorcha. What else have you got?"

Sorcha's like, "Why is her appearance important to you, Ross?"

And – quite reasonably – I go, "I don't want to date someone who's, as you said, a bit of a mess in the old face deportment."

That's when the atmosphere between us suddenly changes.

Sorcha goes, "Date her? Ross, I'm talking about me and you going out for dinner with her and her husband, Ailill."

I'm suddenly confused. I'm there, "Okay, I'm possibly being a bit thick here. But you were the one who said we should stort dating again."

She goes, "I meant going on dates with each other."

I'm like, "But why would I want to date you? I'm already married to you. Would that not be a bit, I don't know, weird?"

The air in the cor suddenly tightens. She goes, "Excuse me?" and I suddenly realise – not for the first time in our marriage – that we're on two totally different pages.

I stort the cor again and I nearly drive head first into the path of a 46A.

"Ross," Sorcha goes, "what did you think I was talking about?"

I'm there, "Maybe we should stop talking for a while, Babes. Let me concentrate on the road here."

Tomas Liudvinavicius clutching his five Chihuahuas at Marley Park's Bark in the Park event in Rathfarnham, Dublin. Photograph: Aidan Crawley

JUNE 29TH 2015

Holidaymakers express solidarity with locals

Lara Marlowe in Sousse

Forty-eight hours after an apprentice electrician named Seifeddine Rezgui pulled a Kalashnikov assault rife from a sun umbrella and began mowing down sunbathers on the beach in Sousse, a pile of roses and lilies marks the place where they were murdered.

The bouquets are interspersed with handwritten messages asking why the atrocity happened.

An Irish Tricolour is stuck into a corner of the makeshift shrine. "Dia libh go léir" (God be with you all) and "Céin fáth?" (why?) is scrawled in ballpoint on pieces of cardboard. A copy of Francesca Brown's My Whispering Angels – "The Irish Bestseller," reads the cover – abandoned on the beach in the pandemonium last Friday, lies atop the flowers, its pages turning brown in the sun.

The flag, inscription and book are reminders that three Irish citizens – Lorna Carty from Robinstown, Co Meath, and Laurence and Martina Hayes, a husband and wife from Athlone – died in the carnage.

David Cooney, Ireland's ambassador to Tunisia, who is based in Madrid, and the head of the Madrid embassy's consular services, Caoimhe Ní Chonchúir, returned to Sousse late on Sunday to collect belongings of the slain Irish people from the Imperial Marhaba Hotel, where they were staying.

They then returned to Tunis, to try to speed formal identification and repatriation of the remains.

On arrival in Sousse, one feels one is witnessing the death of Tunisia's tourist industry, which accounts for 15 per cent of the economy. How could it ever recover from those images of sunloungers transformed into stretchers, of blood dripping into the hotel swimming pool, of sprawled corpses covered with beach towels? The gloomy, marble foyers of the luxury hotels along

Sousse's beach are empty. Even before two gunmen killed 22 tourists in the Bardo museum in Tunis in March, the low-cost, package tour model, which offers a week's sun holiday for as little as €200, was in difficulty.

A surprising number of tourists remain, despite the slaughter. Affection and loyalty to the Tunisians are one reason. Like Mrs Carty and the Hayeses, many Europeans tourists return time and again. Others stay out of defiance. "It can happen anywhere in the world," shrugged a British cement worker arriving on Sunday at nearby Enfida airport. "If I cancel my trip, the terrorists win."

Now tourists and Tunisians weep together before the memorial flowers on the beach. All day, there are little demonstrations of grief and solidarity: a 15-strong delegation from Douar Hicher, 250km away; French speakers holding hands in a circle around the marker. A mother and daughter sob in each other's arms beside the flowers. They are Chrissy (40) and Caitlin (17), the eldest of five Hamley children, from Cornwall.

On Friday, one of their Tunisian friends rang to say, "They are shooting tourists on the beach. Hide." Nine members of the Hamley family huddled in a room at the nearby Riviera hotel while the massacre took place.

"The hotel staff turned the televisions off so we couldn't see," says Chrissy. "That made it worse because we didn't know what was happening . . . People were shouting at the staff in our hotel, 'You're all terrorists', and the staff were crying.

"We went to the marina this morning, and strangers came up to us, desperately wanting us to believe they are peaceful people, which they are," Caitlin continues. "We'll come again, because you can't let a minority of evil people dictate and instil fear in you."

Volker Schumacher (59), a tax collector from Stuttgart, was sleeping with a book over his face when the shooting started. He and his wife ran to an adjacent spa building, where they hid for an hour. "I didn't see the killer," Mr Schumacher says. "I have no eyes in the back of my head. I was afraid he'd shoot me

Residents of Sousse in Tunisia lay flowers on the beach where 38 tourists were shot dead by an Islamist gunman.
Photograph: Abdeljalil Bounhar/Associated Press

in the back. I didn't turn to see other people falling."

When Mr Schumacher returned to fetch the belongings he'd abandoned, he found two bodies by the poolside and another 10 or 12 on the beach. Why didn't the Schumachers fly back to Germany? "My wife wants to go home," he admits.

"But I'm determined to stay until Friday. The people here are fantastic. They're the reason I'm staying."

JULY 6TH 2015

Slowly the map turned orange as surreal week ended with electoral earthquake

Ruadhán Mac Cormaic in Athens

Greece held its breath. So did the rest of Europe. On the stroke of 7pm on Sunday, Athens time, as polling stations across the country closed their doors, a unanimous call resounded across the television studios.

The No side had it, according to four opinion polls. But the result remained unclear, the response muted. Opinion polls are less reliable than exit polls, and they've got it wrong before. All was quiet on Syntagma Square.

But the gap didn't narrow; it widened. As the count began and the results filtered through, the map of Greece slowly but surely turned orange – the colour of No.

The figures were staggering. Corfu, with 20 per cent of boxes opened, had voted No by 70 per cent. In Kefalonia it was 65 per cent. In the working-class port town of Piraeus, 72 per cent.

With the first official projections estimating that the No vote would exceed 60 per cent, Syriza figures were jubilant. Politicians from New Democracy, the conservative opposition party that had called for a Yes, were crestfallen.

Crowds began to gather on Syntagma Square. A surreal, often bewildering week had delivered an electoral earthquake.

The stakes could scarcely have been higher. Greek banks have been closed for the past week, their cash fast running out and their customers restricted to daily withdrawals of €60. Pharmacies have reported shortages.

All week, European leaders had warned that a No vote would result in a historic rupture and could culminate in Greece leaving the euro zone.

All day, however, polling stations offered proof that a great many voters didn't see it quite that way – or were willing to run the risk.

As she prepared to vote on Adrianou Street in central Athens, 22-year-old economics student Thenia Mikalopoulou said the decision weighed heavily on her, but she was leaning towards a No. She was avowedly pro-European, proud of Greece's place in the euro zone, but wondered whether now was the time to put a stop to a cycle that had left Greece on its knees. "I want [them] to negotiate more and make a better deal," she said. "I think it's achievable".

Mikalopoulou counted herself among those who wanted Greece to retain the single currency but who "want something better" and saw a No vote as a way of forcing a change in direction. "We have to do something," she said.

For Giorgos (44), a shopkeeper whose kiosk fell victim to the crisis and had to close down, a No vote was not a judgment on Greece's place in Europe but on the austerity policies creditors were trying to force on the country.

"It's not a matter of ending negotiations. It's a stand to say: no more, we have had enough austerity," he said.

Giorgos, now studying agricultural engineering in the hope of building a new career, did not vote for Alexis Tsipras's party in January's elections, but didn't hold him responsible for the current stand-off with Greece's lenders.

Greek prime minister Alexis Tsipras gestures at the end of yet another inconclusive meeting of eurozone heads of government in Brussels. Photograph: Laurent Dubrule/EPA 1july06

"The institutions didn't give him anything. They pushed him into a corner. We said, 'we'll take 10 measures', they said, 'okay, take 30 measures.' It's not sensible."

He probably wouldn't vote for prime minister Alexis Tsipras today, "but as a citizen of this country, I want Tsipras to achieve something for the Greek people." Giorgos admitted to a certain fear about the future. Voters on both sides are afraid, he says, "but on the No side, we have the painkiller of pride."

Not everyone was willing to run the risk of a No vote, however. Stelios Tziras, who runs a small business in the city, called the referendum "a trick" played by Syriza on the Greek population for its own political ends.

"Even the question itself," he said, referring to the text¬heavy ballot paper, which referred to a lengthy document that Tziras said neither he nor anyone else has read and which the creditors said is no longer on the table.

"He who organises the referendum can ask whatever he wants. Syriza is looking for a No vote, and does whatever it can to push people towards voting No."

Tziras voted for the centrist Potami party in January and said he worried about the country's direction over the past six months.

"It's only the beginning," he says about the closure of the banks. "I'm afraid for the future. Today everyone can cope – it's not that difficult for a week. But an economy can't last like this."

As tourists peered in through the gates of the Adrianou Street polling station, in the shadow of the Acropolis, Christos Retoulas – a stout, cheerful 40¬something who works in the public sector – said he was sure his No vote would put him in the majority. He resented the creditors' offer of a "take it or leave it" deal, as if there was only one way of resolving Greece's impasse.

"It's this Augustinian dualistic worldview that doesn't allow for synthesis of opinions," he said. But there

189

was also a more practical reason for his No vote: the lenders were offering nothing at all on debt relief, and a strong message from the people of Greece might force them into a rethink.

"Greece needs a deal that includes debt. Without a debt deal, you might as well throw money into a well."

JULY 8TH 2015

A moment of terror in the sky above Dublin

Patrick Logue

It was a fitting end to the most aggravating flight I have ever been on. It was just as we were within touching distance of the tarmac in Dublin. You could see cars racing up and down the M1 and the market gardening outlets of north Co Dublin glistening in the half sun.

As we prepared ourselves for the final thud on the ground, we were suddenly thrown backwards into our seats. Ryanair flight FR6874 from Barcelona to Dublin surged back into the air. Amid the thunderous roar of the engines, you could tell the passengers were gritting their teeth and clenching their buttocks. Being in the trade, I immediately wrote a headline: "Two journalists among 150 killed in Dublin air crash."

I made funeral arrangements. No flowers, a track from Pink Floyd's Dark Side of the Moon as the coffin is wheeled out of the non-denominational service. People weeping and remembering. Eulogies, kind words, comfort for my grieving family. Soup and sandwiches in a local hotel and, of course, a rake of pints.

Back in the real world, the aircraft cut through the clouds and continued at some speed at a 45-degree angle, it seemed, towards the stars. Puzzlement and concern were palpable in the cabin as the plane banked right and levelled up while continuing the mysterious and worrying ascent. Eventually the nervous air was broken by an announcement by one of the cabin crew: "Attention, ladies and gentlemen, the captain has decided not to land the aircraft at this time."

No excrement, Sherlock, we thought to ourselves.

"This is normal procedure," came the end of the message. This was certainly not normal procedure. Normal procedure is that the big bird is put down delicately and with precision on the ground and we all toddle off through passport control.

Scenarios raced through my mind. Were we returning to Barcelona? Had one off the wheels fallen off? Or had one of the engines failed? A bird strike, perhaps? Maybe a tray table hadn't been returned to the upright position. Was the captain still in control of the aircraft? I began to regret spending the five-minute safety procedure lesson reading that excellent opinion piece by the Greek finance minister in The Irish Times. If we landed in Dublin Bay, I wouldn't know where to find my lifejacket or how to make it inflate. My nerves were shot.

But then the soothing lozenge of the captain's voice wafted out. Cool as you like. I imagined he had his feet up, aviator shades on, sipping on a pina colada. "Hello, ladies and gentlemen, this is your captain. We decided not to land just there as another aircraft was blocking the runway. We'll just go around again and be on the ground in Dublin shortly." No big deal, basically. Don't hold the front page. Cancel the funeral arrangements.

It was the best damned announcement we got during the short hop from Barcelona to Dublin. The previous ones were loud, incessant and unnecessary, and they interfered with my enjoyment of Varoufakis's article.

There was the one about taking off, seatbelts and the like. There was the one about "in the unlikely event of landing in water". Then there was the one about landing in water in Spanish. The announcement that a passenger had a severe nut allergy and could

Environment minister Alan Kelly and Helen Maguire, a tenant with Clúid, the not-for-profit affordable housing association, at the Belmayne housing development in Dublin which he opened. Photograph Stuart McNamara. 8july01

we refrain from waving our peanuts around. This announcement was not made in Spanish. Then there was the one about food being served, without nuts. The one about perfume being sold. The one about lottery scratch cards on sale. The other one about food. The one about the trolley coming through with drinks "available to purchase". The duty-free perfume on sale. The scratch cards again. Finally there was the one about the cabin crew coming to collect the infant flotation devices.

When the captain pulled up suddenly as we were about to land, it crossed my mind that perhaps the cabin crew had forgotten one of their announcements and we had to go back up for it.

When we finally made contact with terra firma, the Spanish lady sitting to my left was beginning to babble. She turned to me in relief and said, "I heard there aren't any snakes in Ireland. Is this true?" No, I said. No snakes.

"Not unless you count Irish men," the man a seat ahead of us pipes up.

"It looks warm; it's not going to rain today?" asked the Spanish lady.

"It might rain later and then it might get sunny again," I replied.

She looked puzzled. We were all puzzled.

JULY 11TH 2015

Rescued from the Med: the migrants' journey

Lorna Siggins in Valletta

It takes a little while to find the place in the Addolorata cemetery, Malta's largest, on a hill above Valletta. Two elderly officials, who are about to lock up for the evening, seem perplexed at

Refugees and migrants who look to the sea from Libya are rescued by the LE Eithne, the Naval Service vessel dispatched to the Mediterranean to help rescue people trying to get to Europe. Photographs: Irish Defence Force.

first about the request for directions. Keen to help, they offer me a lift to what's known as the common ground, close to the back gate.

We pass dozens of mausoleums and elaborate family plots as we approach the far boundary, where many small headstones compete haphazardly for space. There's no headstone dated late April 2015; it's the three empty candle holders, along with dried-out remnants of flowers and the fresh cement seals on a dozen large paving stones, that provide the clue.

Here, on this small far-southern piece of European territory, lie 24 of more than 850 people who perished in the single worst migrant drowning on the Mediterranean this year. One of them was an infant, buried in a white coffin, named Body No 132.

Even as the interfaith funeral for them took place in Valletta, a Naval Service ship several thousand kilometres north was fuelling for a very different type of patrol. Operation Pontus, as it was called, would take Lieut Cdr Pearse O'Donnell and the crew of the Naval Service flagship, LÉ Eithne, on the service's first humanitarian mission overseas.

"We had three weeks to get ready . . . but nothing would really prepare you for what we saw," says Alan Cummins, leading sick-berth attendant on the ship, which berthed in Malta this week after just over six weeks in the Mediterranean.

His ship's commander was amazed to find Bangladeshis among the 21 nationalities rescued. O'Donnell calculated that by the time they were herded into unseaworthy craft off the Libyan coast they had already travelled 7,000km.

"You can talk about figures – lots of them – but every one is a human being," says Ali Konate, a softly spoken air-conditioning engineer based in Valletta, who was one of those same boat people 13 years ago. Back then, as a 17-year-old, the Malian was among the first north African migrants to arrive in larger numbers from Libya. "There were about 300 on board. I had some peanuts and dates with me, and I had paid $1,100," he says. "The captain knew the route to Italy, and had been there three times, and had been banned from returning there. We came into the harbour here at about 3am, but no one came near us till eight o'clock. Then it was the police."

Konate spent 18 months in a detention centre. He was then moved to one of Malta's "open centres" and found work . He put himself through training courses and secured temporary status, which he must renew every year. He last saw his mother when he left home, at the age of 15. She died seven years ago. The desert transit, via Ivory Coast and Algeria to Libya, was the worst, Konate says. "We would come across these groups of bones, as if people lay down beside each other to die. I would try to bury them in the sand. You can't change the picture of that in your head."

Konate had agreed to meet me close to the Floriana district, just beyond Valletta's city walls. The people of Floriana are also known as Tal-Irish, because of a historical link between Ireland and Malta. Cardinal

Michael Logue, then primate of all Ireland, visited the island in 1895, and 10 years later the Floriana football club played a team from the Royal Dublin Fusiliers.

When the Maltese won 2-1 the Irish troops presented the victors with their jerseys, and Floriana FC players have worn green and white ever since. The district recently revived a St Patrick's Day festival, and the island's population of 425,000 takes a keen interest in "saints and celebrating", with districts competing for the best firework displays.

It's not only rich Irish businessmen who have made Malta their home; such is the level of integration that many working in the financial, pharmaceutical and information technology sectors don't register with the embassy, according to Ambassador Pádraig MacCoscair. Frequent direct flights between Dublin and Valletta mean that there are almost as many visiting Irish as British accents on the streets.

But a rich cultural heritage, as in dozens of Roman Catholic churches, presents a less welcoming environment for new arrivals of other faiths. The island's mixed bloodlines reflect its many influences, dating back to the Phoenicians, Carthaginians and Romans, but when Charles, the holy Roman emperor and king of Spain, gave the Maltese islands to crusaders in 1530, the new ruling Knights of Malta built a fortress harbour designed to keep out the "infidel".

Standing on the afterdeck of the LÉ Eithne, also berthed near Tal-Irish, crew members, who have just been congratulated by Minister for the Marine Simon Coveney, describe their experience as surreal. Every craft that helped to rescue migrants was in immediate danger, says Lieut Shane Mulcahy, a search-and-rescue co-ordinator.

Women with severe chemical burns from leaking fuel containers were among the many treated by the

A reindeer herder in Russian Siberia photographed by Lexi Novitske, Photographer of thre Year in the Irish Times amateur photography competition.

A huge bonfire burns close to Belfast homes, which had to be evacuated because of the ferocity and proximity of the blaze, it was lit by loyalists celebrating the 12th of July, the day Orangemen mark the victory, at the Battle of the Boyne in 1690, of the Protestant King William of Orange over Roman Catholic King James. Photograph: Justin Kernoghan/Photopress

four medical staff on board, two of them from the Army.

The ship's crew had acquired games, colouring books and blankets before they left Haulbowline Island. They had never anticipated that the youngest of the 137 children, out of almost 3,400 rescued in total by the ship's crew, would be a baby of just two weeks old. And "you'd get a lot of requests to be taken to Ireland", Cummins says.

The rather intimidating masks and protective suits for the ship's crew were recommended by the Italian authorities, Lieut Mulcahy says. Migrants were frisked as a precaution, he adds. "But the people we saw directing others on the boats hadn't been trained. They were just handed the tiller."

On the ship's previous rescue, in late June, it picked up almost 650 people. Cummins recalls looking out on deck in the middle of the night. The afterdeck

was carpeted, as was the forecastle, with sleeping bodies under emergency blankets. "I've done fishery protection, fought fires, I've been overseas in Liberia, but I never thought I would see anything like that," he says.

Five years ago Joe Sacco, a Malta-born graphic novelist, took events in his homeland as the focus for his journalistic essay Migra tion. At that stage Malta's tiny armed forces – due to take delivery shortly of the former Naval Service ship LÉ Aoife – was working flat out on migrant rescue.

The government's decision to assign new arrivals to detention centres for up to 18 months attracted international condemnation. In contrast with Ireland's forbidding system of direct provision, however, detainees then moved on to "open centres" were allowed to seek work.

"All of the stories these people had to tell were quite

horrible," says Dr Neil Falzon, a former representative in Malta of UNHCR, the United Nations refugee agency. "There were stories of smugglers depriving them of food and water, of sexual violence and rape, of corrupt border officials and imprisonment, and of unquantified deaths in the desert."

Migration became a hot political issue in Malta, where some among the resident population, sharing just 315sq km of island, felt swamped. But when Italy initiated its Mare Nostrum operation in late 2013, after 366 migrants drowned off the island of Lampedusa, the Italian authorities agreed to take migrants rescued from the Maltese search-and-rescue zone.

"As a result the number arriving here has fallen from some 1,800 people a year to almost nothing in the past two years," says Falzon, now director of the Aditus Foundation, a nongovernmental organisation that focuses on access to human rights. "So while we have this intense activity at sea around us there is a very tense silence on the island itself, and we are trying to take advantage of this period to ensure there are proper systems in place."

Aditus believes that the strict border controls being proposed by some EU member states, including Britain and Hungary, are not the solution. "Together with saving lives at sea, we are advocating a system within the EU of safe and legal channels, including humanitarian visas, rather than putting up barriers which will only divert migrants, and their traffickers, to taking other routes," Falzon says.

He says that the recent EU proposal to relocate 44,000 Mediterranean migrants among member states on a quota basis is a start. "Migration is going to be with us, and the numbers coming to Europe are small in comparison to what is happening in Kenya, Jordan, Lebanon and Turkey, where states are really struggling to cope." (Kenya still hosts the world's largest refugee camp.)

The UN refugee agency's current representative in Malta, Jon Hoisaeter, agrees with Falzon. UNHCR's central Mediterranean Sea initiative recommends 12 measures that would ensure EU states share responsibility equally.

Significantly, less than 30 per cent of more than 19,000 people who arrived in Malta by boat between 2002 and 2014 remain, according to the agency. Also, irregular boat arrivals in Greece have been higher over the past fortnight than those in Italy for the first time this year. Many continue their journey north to Germany, the Netherlands and Sweden.

"We fully agree that there has to be registration and screening, with individual assessments and no automatic right to stay, for all who arrive," Hoisaeter says. "But there has to be a many-faceted response to a complex problem, including identification of special needs and effective access to asylum processes, as well as voluntary return incentives for people who are not in need of protection, such as training, which can be part-funded by the EU.

"Legal alternatives to accessing protection in Europe, including through family reunification – where a settled refugee here is permitted to bring over his or her family, and is already in a position to give them support – is another option we advocate."

A regular system of family reunification would avoid the sort of horrific situation that Umayma Elamin Amer, founder and president of the Migrant Women's Association of Malta, has encountered.

Amer says she was able to travel from Sudan to Libya, and then on to Malta, by plane when she decided to find a better home for her two teenage children, a year ago. But she recently met a woman who had come by sea from Libya without her family and who now wants her two children, aged 18 and eight, to make the same journey.

"She knows how dangerous it is for them, she knows she is sending money to traffickers, but she thinks they are safer in a boat than staying where they are," Amer says.

Amer's organisation aims to support migrant women from many countries in navigating basic issues on arrival and in coping with a new culture. In spite of incidents of racism that make the national press in Malta, she says she has found it very welcoming. Integration is "not one-way", she says, as "sometimes it is the migrant who builds barriers around him or her".

Ali Konate also spends any free time he has working with NGOs, lobbying on migrant issues and contributing to awareness-raising initiatives in the wider community. "People see migrants as a problem, but they don't see the reason why we are here," he says.

"So we may not have colonialism, but now we have multinationals in Africa who are there to take resources. We have conflicts everywhere, and no governments.

"In Mali we have rich soil where we can grow our own food if we can just be left alone. Just think of it: no one in Europe has to pay $1,100 to visit my country in a small overcrowded boat by sea."

Speaking in Malta earlier this week, Simon Coveney acknowledged that although Ireland's humanitarian response has been successful so far, the EU faces a "big political challenge to try and create conditions in north Africa that can prevent that kind of mass movement of people".

Minister for Justice Frances Fitzgerald, who flew to Malta with Coveney, hinted that Ireland might double its offer to take a proportion of the 44,000 Mediterranean migrants that the EU aims to relocate. That doubling amounts to just 600 people, but she pointed out that Ireland's direct-provision system is almost full.

Like many of her political colleagues, Fitzgerald is careful to distinguish between asylum seekers and economic migrants.

"But how can you make a distinction?" asks Konate. "Who is not an economic migrant when you have no functioning government and your country is in the middle of civil war?"

JULY 11TH 2015

In the steps of St Teresa in Spain

Patsy McGarry

He was, he told us, the youngest guide in Toledo. There were about 60, he said. He, at 28, is the youngest. So proud he told us twice. A happy young man is Daniel, and enthusiastic about his city. As well he might be. Toledo is wonderful, complex, intriguing. A city of three cultures – Jewish, Christian, Muslim – with charming character. It's no surprise that it is a World Heritage City since 1986.

Toledo is on a headland, over 500 metres above sea

Falconers of the Mexican Army taking part in the Bastille Day celebrations in Paris. Photograph: Charles Platiau/Reuters.

level, and shows its Moorish influence particularly through its deliberately winding streets. "So hostile strangers get lost", we were told. It works too, as we found out.

Though not at all hostile, myself and the four companeros did indeed get lost as we made our way back to the Discalced Carmelite monastery where we were based that night for the hilarious fee of €30, B&B. I kid you not. Nice bright, comfortable, upgraded, monks' cells.

It is a living monastery too, as we discovered. Finding our way there eventually by early morning, with the help of a local girl who had some English and brought us there, we were met at the door by a Padre who had no English. He tapped his watch to indicate to us five journos in search of a soul that we were . . . late. Or LATE, as the tapping suggested. It seems we were supposed to be back by midnight. Us? As if. Yes, there was a deal of hilarity on our trip in the footsteps of St Teresa of Avila, the 500th anniversary

of whose birth takes place this year. Not least as none of us in the Irish media pack had Spanish and, as we discovered, as not many people in central Spain have English. So our experiences in restaurant were adventures in themselves as we and staff attempted to establish what was on the menu.

For instance, at the really excellent Nuevo Almacen restaurant in Toledo, in cahoots with our waiter, a law student in real life with some English, we discovered lamb was on when he uttered the words "meat . . . with wool?" In another we found beef when the enthusiastic young waitress pronounced (eventually) the word "cow" with the delight of an Einstein stumbling on the theory of relativity for the first time. Over the course of three days, courtesy of Spanish Tourism, we visited Avila, Toledo, Malagón, Beas de Segura, and Caravaca de la Cruz, just five of the 17 foundations established by the exhaustively indefatigable St Teresa. Included was the one we stayed in at Toledo.

Masked men in paramilitary garb at the funeral in Derry of Peggy O'Hara, the mother of INLA hunger striker Patsy O'Hara. Photograph: Margaret McLaughlin

James O'Donoghue of Kerry (left) with Philly McMahon of Dublin and Cillian O'Connor of Mayo at a GAA promotion of the start of the 2015 All-Ireland senior football championship.   Photograph: Brendan Moran/Sportsfile

She did it all in a 20-year period before dying at the age of 67 in 1582. No wonder she was the first woman Doctor of the Church. Well, she and St Catherine of Siena, both of whom joined that elite group of 34 super saints by decision, in their case, of Pope Paul VI in 1970.

Teresa set about reforming the Carmelite order of which she was a member, founding the Discalced (shoeless) Carmelites alone with St John of the Cross. But she is probably better known in religion circles as a mystic. In her writing she has described the ascent of the soul through mental prayer, quiet, ecstasy, to divine rapture.

Our concerns were more mundane. It was a case of "so many churches, so little time". But what churches! "Emotion in stone" wouldn't be a bad description. More accurately "exuberant Latin emotion in stone".

Nothing of the Anglo European grid, line-by-line pattern, there. Baroque, Rocco, Brilliant, ". . . isn't it mad Ted?".

Spanish Tourism is promoting a sort of St Teresa Camino, or "Footprints of Teresa" journey, whereby pilgrims travel between at least five of her 17 foundations at a time and are stamped on arrival at each, similar to what happens people doing the Camino de Santiago further north.

However, you may visit as many as you wish but, in order to get proper recognition, you must at least visit four in two regions – where local tourist offices will confirm your presence by stamp. You must also include Avila as a fifth location before being properly designated a pilgrim. This, dear reader, is not for wusses, and speaking as one.

Which is not to say I didn't enjoy the ordeal. The

relevant 17 cities are Avila, Medina del Campo, Malagón, Valladolid, Toledo, Pastrana, Salamanca, Alba de Tormes, Segovia, Beas de Segura, Seville, Caravaca de la Cruz, Villanueva de la Jara, Palencia, Soria, Granada, and Burgos.

The beauty of them is that this is in undiscovered country where most visitors to Spain are concerned. It reflects the truly magnificent cultural heritage of the real Spain.

So we arrived by Ryanair in Madrid and were taken to the lovely, well-preserved walled-town of Avila by bus, a journey of about 110 kilometres. There, where it all began. It was originally a Jewish town, as was Teresa's family before forced conversion to Christianity.

Teresa grew up in Avila and established the first foundation of the Discalced Carmelite Order at St Joseph's monastery in 1562. Her original home is now the simple St Teresa convent, remarkable for its simplicity considering the splendour to come.

We stayed and enjoyed the wonderful hospitality of the very comfortable Paradores Avila where they have a special "Carmelite menu" this year. It includes Carmelitas' convent-style custard, and paprika-flavoured potato with bacon chunks. Though the custard came first.

But for me Toledo was the icing on the cake (I was never too keen on custard) of this trip. And in Toledo the cherry on top had to be the cathedral.

Built between 1226 and 1493, its stunning Baroque altar, several storeys high, is truly breathtaking, awesome in its detail and just one feature of a building which would take an entire holiday to explore properly in its own right. Even the sacristy has original El Greco and Goya paintings.

It was in Toledo that Teresa established her fifth foundation. But be warned. It gets warm in summer time. It was 34 degrees when we were there at the end of May and can rise to the 40s in August.

From there we went to the small town of Malagón which traces its origins to the Romans. We visited St Teresa's third foundation and had one of the most remarkable conversations of our trip with Sr Anna Marie, an Australian architect from Sydney who entered the enclosed order there at the age of 23 in 1993.

We spoke to her about her simple life of prayer through a grill. She was accompanied on the other side by an elderly nun. They have little contact with the outside world.

Beas de Segura in Andalusia is a beautiful small city in striking mountainous surroundings. Our enthusiastic young guide Marie Therese escorted us up the very many steps to the convent of the Discalced Carmelites and 10th foundation of St Teresa, and the Monastery of San José del Salvador.

We also saw relics of St John of the Cross and St Teresa. We climbed to the highest point in the city, its restored bell tower, from where we felt we could see eternity.

By the time we had climbed back all down those steps, through beautiful narrow whitewashed streets with their shrines and hanging flowers, we were ready to sit on a bus for the three-hour journey to Caravaca de la Cruz.

On arrival at our monastery residence there late that night we were tired, emotional, and hungry, or typical of your more normal pilgrims after a long day's journey into the infinite.

Our monastic setting was far from Spartan. Again it is a living monastery which uses funds from accommodating pilgrims to sustain its existence.

Next morning in Caravaca an excellent guide – we were very lucky with our guides on this trip – took us to a now empty convent which had been Teresa's 12th foundation but which the nuns left in 2004 due to lack of numbers. It still contains many of the extravagant features we were becoming so familiar with.

The city is one of the few places where foundations were established by both St Teresa and St John of the Cross (hence the "de la Cruz").

Our last visit there was to the magnificent Basilica which presides over the city and where it is claimed a splinter of the true cross is housed.

We visited its small chapel and prayed before the

splinter " . . . no more churches . . . please, no more churches." Our prayers were answered too. We ate, and headed for the airport at Murcia.

JULY 17TH 2015

The trials and triumphs of a young Irish figure skater

Arminta Wallace

Sophia has neat blond plaits and a pink leather satchel. She's a bit shy. She lives in Gorey, Co Wexford, with her mum, her dad and her younger sister, Justina. She does swimming, gymnastics and Irish dancing. She is, to all intents and purposes, a normal Irish nine-year-old.

But Sophia Tkacheva is also a really talented figure skater, which makes her life very different to that of most Irish nine-year-olds. She travels to Belfast every weekend for coaching and practice. When we meet she has just come home from Minnesota, where she was the only child from outside the US to be offered a scholarship to the prestigious skating summer camp at the Shattuck-St Mary's school in Faribault.

Did she have a great time? Sophia nods vigorously, her plaits bobbing. What was the best part? "The best thing about it was that I did lots and lots of ice skating and lots and lots of ice stretching." The coaches were impressed by her programme, which is set to Irish traditional music and features a couple of Irish dance steps, but they helped her to improve it as well.

How many hours a day did she spend on the ice? "I think five." She frowns. "Or six." With all this practice, what did she learn that was new? "I can do all of my double jumps now. And I learned how to do a split jump. And loads and loads of other things." How hard is it to do a double jump? "Hard enough," she says.

Sophia was born in Dublin. Her father, Evgeny Tkachev, is Russian; her mother, Olga Harelik, is from Belarus. When Sophia was five, her dad was temporarily transferred back to Moscow for work, and that's when she took up ice skating. "We were thinking, what activities could she do?" Olga explains. "There were three ice rinks within a 20-minute drive of where we lived, so we thought we would give it a try."

Does Sophia remember her first day on the ice? The plaits bob. "It was, like, scary because I couldn't skate at all," she says. "I was always falling and I had a helmet."

For those of us who only ever see it on the telly during the Winter Olympics, figure skating conjures up visions of bodies flying through the air in gravity-defying leaps and spins, executed with apparent ease. The reality is grittier. Ice skating is hard work; practice sessions leave Sophia wet from the ice and sweaty. "She will be taking off all her clothes," says Olga, flinging her arms out with a laugh as she imitates her exasperated daughter peeling off layer after layer of clothing.

Then there are the falls. "Her left elbow can get horribly bruised," Olga says. "When she does jumps she falls on her left side most of the time."

Sophia's plaits are bobbing again. "Falls and tears are terrible," she says. "It really hurts."

By far the biggest problem in the life of an Irish ice skater, however, is simply the lack of regular access to ice. To make progress in skating demands a jaw-dropping level of commitment not just from Sophia, but from her entire family. "Friday after school we jump in the car and go to Belfast," Olga says. "We stay in a small B&B near the rink. To get the full ice you have to start very early. At 10am the public skating starts, so we have to be on the ice at 6.45am." They're both smiling at the very idea of all that ice. "From 6.15am until 10am we have the ice on our own," says Olga. "Just Sophia and her coach, Joanne Ulyett. Nobody else."

"And Justina," Sophia reminds her.

Her sister skates as well? "Yes," says Sophia. "She's a

Sophia Harelik from Gorey in Co Wexford.   Photograph: Patrick Browne

bit lazy at it," she adds.

"She's too small to practise like you do," Olga says gently. But Sophia isn't having that; the plaits are shaking indignantly from side to side. "There's a girl that is five years old, and she can do an axel. I saw her do it," she says.

This is the spirit that, in just over three years, has taken Sophia from beginner to member of the Irish development squad and winner of the Novice B category at last year's national championships. "There are times in Belfast when I will say, 'Let's go home'," Olga says. "And she will say, 'No, I want to do this spin again. I want to try this jump again.' She wants to skate because she knows that there will be no more skating for another week."

Of course, Sophia isn't the only Irish ice skater in this predicament. "Three of our national team have actually left the country to train," says Karen O'Sullivan, president of the Ice Skating Association of Ireland. Figure skating, she points out, is an "early specialisation sport". For a child as gifted as Sophia, regular coaching and practice at this young age is vital to her development.

Olga knows this all too well. When she and her husband realised the almost-six-year-old Sophia had an aptitude and brought her to a Russian skating school, they were told at first that it was too late. "She was too old. They didn't want to accept her."

Most of the business of the Ice Skating Association of Ireland is with seasonal learn-to-skate programmes for beginners around the country. Plans are afoot to get a permanent – or even semi-permanent – rink for Dublin. They're well aware, O'Sullivan says, that funds are short and that many similar minority sports are crying out for facilities. But with other sports, you can at least do something. You can't ice skate without ice.

Sophia and her family aren't complaining. Or not exactly. They love living in Ireland and especially in Gorey, which, Olga observes, is a terrific place to bring up children. Sophia attends the Educate Together primary school.

Olga cites the generosity that saw a Co Wicklow company, Sheep Wool Insulation in Rathdrum, sponsor Sophia's trip to Minsk last October. "When we came back to Ireland last summer we were thinking that we would look for something else for Sophia. We were quite relaxed about the fact that we may not go any further with the skating. But then Sophia was assigned to go and represent Ireland in Minsk, and we went. And, well, the more you get involved, the harder it is to give up."

How they keep going, heaven only knows. The weekly trips to Belfast are exhausting and expensive. "To be honest, sometimes I get these blue days when I think, why are we doing it?" says Olga.

Sophia is already dreaming of a return to Minnesota next summer, which means they have to start planning – financially and every other way – now. Meanwhile, they're heading to Minsk, where Olga's mother lives, for the summer. Will Sophia be skating every day there? The blue eyes are dancing in her head. The plaits are going crazy. It's her ideal summer holiday. She can't wait.

JULY 18TH 2015

America still reluctant to embrace Serena

Mary Hannigan

Is Serena respected enough (Part 8,536)?

The Women's Tennis Association did its very best to put a gloss on the roll of honour from this week's ESPY Awards in Los Angeles (ie the "Excellence in Sports Performance Yearly Award" presented by ESPN) declaring that her "phenomenal week got even more phenomenal on Wednesday night, as she won Best Female Tennis Player at the ESPY Awards for the seventh time in her career!"

Now, Serena winning the Best Female Tennis Player of the year award is as unexpected as a damp Irish summer, but what about the overall gong? Surely she

Serena Williams shows determination during her hard-fought match against Heather Watson at the Wimbledon championships. Photograph: Jonathan Brady/Press Association

got that too?

Well, no, she didn't, it went to UFC bantamweight champion (and actress) Ronda Rousey. UFC devotees would, of course, argue Rousey's award was richly deserved – and who the heck would argue with a UFC devotee? – but our old friend Chris Chase at USA Today crunched the numbers and wasn't impressed.

Rousey "spent a total of 30 seconds playing her sport over the past year (she had two bouts, one lasted 16 seconds, the other 14); Serena Williams won every single Grand Slam played in between ESPY shows (a 28-0 record)."

Time spent on the job isn't, need it be said, everything, if it was then the last-placed cyclist in the Tour de France would be a shoo-in for every annual award. But still, 30 seconds of sporting activity since February 22, 2014 is quite brief.

("What about Usain Bolt winning every award on offer in 2009 for 9.58 seconds' work?" Fair point. Hush now)

Ironically enough, just before Serena was overlooked for a UFC person, the New York Times had an article entitled "It's Time to Appreciate Serena Williams's Greatness".

She'll be 34 in September, but no rush. In the piece, Martina Navratilova is quoted being a touch tetchy about Williams being in Sweden this week to play in a small WTA event. "She should be on a beach somewhere with her feet up, but whatever," she said. "You've got to make hay while the sun shines, I guess." Like Williams needs advice on how to regulate her career (although if she wants

to catch up on Maria Sharapova's earnings, considerably higher despite winning

a quarter of Williams' Grand Slams, she needs

Sweden). Back in June when Williams won the French Open, making it the 20th Grand Slam title of her career, the prolific tweeter Navratilova only found time to post a message about American Pharoah's Kentucky Derby win, divil a mention or congratulations to the tennis player. Chris Evert, meanwhile, offered no congrats either to Williams on her Wimbledon triumph on the tweet machine, focussing

instead that day on praise of her punditry skills.

Tennis royalty, then, doesn't have a whole heap of time for Serena, most probably because Serena doesn't have a whole heap of time for them.

The NYT wondered if Williams would now attempt to "connect with her public

on a deeper level after some of the ambivalence and controversies of the past". "I hope so," said Martina, and you could almost hear the sigh.

Maybe it's time for the American public, in particular, to connect with Serena?

Martina, meanwhile, should know better than most about prejudice, and the

scars it leaves. "When Venus and I were walking down the stairs to our seats, people kept calling me 'nigger'," her father Richard Williams recalled of a 2001 trip to a tournament at Indian Wells, California. "I wish it was '75; we'd skin you alive," the abuser added.

All in the past? Na. Do a Twitter search for "Serena, Nigger" or "Gorilla" or "Ape" or 2Monkey" while she was winning her latest Wimbledon title, and note, too, the number of Americans shouting for her Russian (seriously) opponent in the semi-finals. If Serena is driven by a "**** you all" attitude to life, who could blame her? Her country is her family and friends, and that's the way it's always had to be – because she's got little love from America.

Back at the ESPY Awards, meanwhile, another gong that raised an eyebrow was world champion and no-stranger-to-domestic-violence Floyd Mayweather losing out to Rousey for the "Best Fighter" honour. Rousey's response? "I wonder how Floyd feels being beat by a woman for once." Actually, for that alone – and profuse apologies to the peerless Serena –

Rousey very much deserved to be named "Female Athlete of the Year".

Serena, you suspect, would say: 'Go girl!' Like Rousey, after all, she's a formidable fighter. She's had to be.

JULY 24TH 2015

A return to the colourful fishing village of Baltimore

Rosita Boland

There is a rumour that John Hinde photographers were issued with pots of fuschia bushes and rhododendrons that they drove around Ireland with in the boots of their cars. The reason for the botanical luggage was that, if needed, they could be strategically placed in postcard shots for a blast of colour, because in John Hinde postcards, the more colour the better.

The Hinde postcard "The Fishing Village of Baltimore, West Cork" is dominated by the red sail on the yellow dinghy at the water's edge.

I couldn't find out exactly when it was taken, but 1979 was mentioned a few times. Photographer D Noble took the shot: my large version (popular John Hinde cards were sometimes printed in big as well as small versions) carries the additional information that it was shot on a "4x5 Peco Junior Camera, with Ektachrome film, Symmar 180mm lens, exposure 1/125th sec".

On the day I visit Baltimore, it is pouring; bucketing. The quayside is deserted. I orient myself near the slipway and look back at the village from D Nobel's perspective. Unlike in the original scene, there is not a shred of blue sky to be seen.

The biggest and loveliest surprise about revisiting the scene of the postcard is that the oldest building in it

Baltimore in west Cork, as seen in the John Hinde post card series… and now – the harbour today.
Photographs: John Hinde Studios and Emma Jervis

has survived. Looking at the roofless stone castle at the far left of the postcard, strangled by ivy, its future seems sadly predictable. It seems like it's going to continue to vanish, stone by stone. However, Baltimore Castle, or Dún na Séad, which dates from 1215, is not only still standing, it has been beautifully restored by Bernie and Patrick McCarthy, who bought it in 1979. Since 2005, it has been their family home. It is open to the public and has a pirate-themed exhibition and an extraordinary barrel-vaulted banqueting hall that overlooks the sea. Patrick says that it was always privately owned. Photographs on the walls document the vast restoration project.

Bernie's great-aunt once owned the building that is now the Waterfront Hotel, owned by the Jacobs family. In the postcard it is to the left of the barrel-topped white building.

As we're talking, I can hear odd sounds nearby that are familiar and yet very strange. I hear words, but they're gibberish. "Bye bye." "Throw the ball." "Cheese." It's Shakespeare, their African grey parrot. Baltimore is well known for pirates, after all, so the presence of a parrot should be less unexpected and entertaining than it is (I can't stop laughing). "Shakespeare has so

Ed Sheeran at Croke Park. Photograph: Cyril Byrne.

many words, we're waiting for him to write a sonnet," says Bernie.

The boat that dominates the centre of the postcard was called The Richard. It was owned by Dermot Kennedy, who lives in the last house to the right of the postcard and who established Glenans sailing school.

The boat, which he bought in the late 1960s, was getting a new keel put on it at the time. The Richard was the "last sailing boat, with an auxiliary motor built into it, that was built by Paddy Hegarty's boat yard in Baltimore". The boatyard is still there, now run by Paddy's sons Liam and John.

Kennedy identifies the man on the ladder at the boat's keel as Steve Nolan, from Sherkin Island. "A great man for the yoga," he adds, which seems a random pastime for an Irish boat-tending islandman in the 1970s. As random as a parrot in a 13th-century castle asking for cheese. Kennedy sailed The Richard "all over the north African coast and to the Mediterranean, and to the Skelligs for birdwatching". So where is The Richard now? "Wrecked," Kennedy says sadly. "I sold it in the early 1980s. It was sailed across the Altantic and, on the way back, it hit a storm. I think it was towed to the Azores."

He is not sure who the yellow couple are. "Were they Hopkins? From Cork? I don't know."

"I think they were a couple from Cape Clear," says Dominic Casey, of Casey's Hotel in the village.

Aidan Bushe at what is now Bushe's Bar on the quay laughs when I tell him this. "They don't look like Capers to me," he says, using the local lingo for people from Cape Clear, as he indicates the mustard trousers. "I'd say they were tourists."

Bushe says that the housing scheme, Cliff Estate, now visible on the hill behind the quay-front buildings, was built a few years after the picture was taken.

The distinctive barrel-topped white building in the postcard was a chandlery at the time, and also sold coal, gas and cement. It was called Cotters then. Kieran Fuller – himself originally a Caper – bought it in 1977. "It only had an old roof on it, like you'd see on cowsheds; a corrugated iron roof."

They ran it as a chandlery until 1981, and then knocked it down and rebuilt it. "We put in a grocery shop and some hardware and chandlery on the first floor, and the rest of the first and second floor became accommodation." That was also the year he got married, and they moved in the following year. They still live there.

"The first thing I do every morning is to head to the window and see what's happening in the world," he says.

JULY 25TH 2015

'You are looking down at the club and it is shaking a little in your hands'

Paul Dunne

Before

We all had our own ways of getting to St Andrews. I know Jordan Spieth and Zach Johnson were among those who hopped on the charter flight from the John Deere Classic but my journey was quite different. I'd been playing for Ireland in the European Team Championships in Sweden and we had about a three-hour train ride down to Copenhagen, a flight to Dublin, where I had to stay for some time in the airport, and then caught another flight to Edinburgh. I arrived in Edinburgh pretty late on Sunday night and went straight to our rented house in Elie, a town about 20 miles from St Andrews. My mam, dad and Alan Murray were already there and had sent me the address. I just went straight into the house, didn't knock on the door or anything, and walked straight into someone else's house. I was nearly attacked by their dog and the people came out laughing, and then pointed me in the right direction – around the side of their house – where I needed to go. It had been a long day and I was tired and I didn't bother setting any alarm. I just slept until I woke up.

When I arrived at St Andrews on Monday, the first thing I did was to register in the clubhouse. There were a few desks with administration staff, you sit down, sign your name, give your contact details for the week, get your player's ID badge, tickets for your family and they give you a locker key. There was a good luck note in mine from Titleist, with a couple of dozen golf balls and four gloves for the week.

I hadn't organised any practice round but I met Shane Lowry at lunch and he told me he was due to play with G-Mac. Did I want to play? It couldn't have worked out any better if you'd planned it. I went to practice for a couple of hours before we headed out. Shane played the first five holes with us, along with Daniel Brooks, and then Graeme and myself played from six to 18, just the two of us and not a lot of people.

At one point, Graeme took a photo of me from behind and put it onto his Twitter account with a contest with a prize for the first person to guess who I was. In the first 30 guesses, there were 28 Jordan Spieths and two Vijay Singhs. My Irish team-mate Cormac Sharvin was actually the first to correctly get the answer.

I made a point of playing practice rounds with different players. On Tuesday, I played with Matteo Manassero – Cormac's uncle, Brian, is his caddie – and Francesco Molinari and Ben An and Danny Lee joined us. On Wednesday I was due to play with Brooks Koepka but he didn't want to play because it was raining. I went out on my own, starting on 17, and Adam Scott, who was on the 16th, asked could he play the last few holes with me. He played 17, 18 and the first and then I met up with Ollie Schniederjans. It was great to play with so many different players, to get different perspectives on how to play the course. I spoke to everyone, about where to hit it, how to avoid different bunkers, learnt different things every day. Everyone I played with was very good about it, it is not like unlocking the secrets, you want to know

where you have to hit it.

During

Thursday, July 16th –First Round

I'd gone to bed at eight o'clock the night before. I never go to bed that early. I couldn't get to sleep and it was probably half 10 before I slept. I'd a 6.43am tee time and had set seven alarms, to go off every two minutes, from 4am to 4.15m. I got up at a quarter past, and was the last one up. Everyone else in the house was up, afraid I would sleep in. I had a bowl of muesli and a yoghurt and was off the course. I was ready.

Before I go out, I give myself a number in my head. It's something I used to do years ago, playing in boys' events, but had stopped doing. I started doing it again during the NCAAs in the last round when I had a chance to win there and have continued doing since. I found that putting a number in my head focused me on shooting a score. My target was a 68.

I got off to a quick start and birdied the first two, got really good yardages which meant I could spin it a lot. I birdied the Par 5 fifth and got an unlikely birdie on the ninth, where I made a long one. Part of the gameplan I had drawn up with Alan (Murray) was to make no bogeys and I was disappointed to three-putt from the edge of the 11th. I was happy to par my way in, happy enough with 69 even though it was a shot more than I had in my head.

Afterwards, I had lunch, did some short game practice and went back to the house and slept for a couple of hours. My mam and my brother David made dinner for us – the nine of us staying in the house – and afterwards I either watched TV or went to my room, which was the only place I could get Wifi. If I wanted to go on my phone, do social media or whatever, I had to go to my room. If I wanted to watch the golf on TV, I'd go to the livingroom. It was a nice little separation.

Friday, July 17th – Second Round

I'd looked at the forecast the night before it said it would rain until 11, then the wind would drop and get back up at four. I was meant to be out at 11.43am. I literally had the perfect tee time, I couldn't believe it. But when I woke up, I saw there was a three hour delay and I was thinking: "Oh, now I am going to get the windy part of the day."

By the time I got to play, late in the afternoon, the wind direction had changed. The first day it was down off the right on the front nine and off the left on the back nine, playing really tough. It had completely flipped and the front nine was straight off the left and the back nine was straight off the right, so the whole course was playable. It didn't make any hole too long in the crosswinds. You just had to control the flight of the ball, so there were birdies on both sides. I had a number again, I thought 70 would be good.

I got off to a slow start and, on nine, I had a wedge shot in. I said to Alan, "it's about time I hit one close". I managed to hit one into about three feet and my round started. I birdied 14. On the 15th, I had a six-iron in and I noticed Tiger Woods was standing about five yards from me, waiting to play number four. "Go ahead," he said. I hadn't been nervous all day but was so nervous playing that shot, because Tiger

was watching me. It made no sense. I hit a good one and made three.

The thought of just making the cut had never entered my head going out. I knew I was hitting it well enough not to have to worry about shooting three- or four-over in a cross wind, that I wasn't going to make a heap of bogeys in a row. I shot 69 again. My first day's number had been 68, my second day 70 – so two 69s was pleasing. I was spot on.

My two playing partners, Todd Hamilton and James Hahn, both missed the cut and wished me well. James told me he hoped to see me on the PGA Tour with him some day. It was late, so we all ate at the course that night; and because play hadn't finished, I set my alarm for nine o'clock the next morning to see when I would be playing again.

Saturday, July 18th – Completion of Second Round
I slept well, knowing there was no early start for me. As it turned out, the high winds meant those completing their second rounds didn't get very far.

I didn't do much. Once I got word I wouldn't be

playing, I went out with my brother and sister and ma out to the beach and threw a rugby ball around. It wasn't like we were tackling each other. So, it was either throwing the ball or just resting for most of the day.

About five o'clock, I went up to the course and did some work just to stay loose really, more a matter of maintenance. I spent two hours there, hit balls for about 45 minutes, chipped for 20 minutes and putted for the rest of the time. When we were in college in UAB, Alan always set up putting games and chipping games for us. We just did that, set up some games, see how many you could make out of a certain amount from around the hole, then just went back and had some dinner.

We were joined by Shane Lowry, Neil Manchip, his wife Aideen and son Hugo – their house was about 150 yards away from ours – and we were just having a general chat.

The text with the tee times came about 10 and I saw I was playing with Louis Oosthuizen, which was cool. Once I had my tee time it was just normal, just get ready for another round of golf.

Sunday, July 19th – Third Round

That morning, my brother made some of these protein pancakes that he loves, which are great with some berries. I had them for breakfast and went back to sleep. The courtesy car was due to pick us up at half 11 and the drive in from Elie was quite scenic. We didn't get any traffic until we reached St Andrews and we were waved through by the police.

A lot more support had arrived from home, which was brilliant. I was nervous. You're looking down at the club and it is shaking a little bit in your hands but I got off to a really settled start. I hit a my second shot into the first really close and made (birdie) three, a low one with a couple of bounces and a little spin. I got lucky on four, blocked my tee shot but it just sneaked pass the bunker. I had eight iron and hit it to 25 feet and made it.

I started hitting our targets, playing for no bogeys and to let the birdies come. I made a mistake on seven, where I hit my tee shot a little close to the green. I

couldn't get any spin, tried to run it up, didn't get it up and it came back down. I'd a really tough putt, up and over some ridges and then downhill downwind, and I wasn't even trying to make it, just trying to two-putt, and it went in.

All the way around, every shot I hit, even the mediocre ones, got a huge roar. I shot a 66 and had given myself good looks at other birdies. I didn't know I was leading until I got in afterwards. I had to do the BBC, Radio 5, The Golf Channel, ESPN, more radio, go live on Japanese TV and then the sit-down press conference in the media centre.

All that took a while, so we all had a late dinner at the course, went back to the house. I didn't know how crazy everything had got back home. The social media was going nuts, so I turned the notifications off, turned my phone off and went to sleep.

Monday, July 20th – Fourth Round

Every day Alan went up to the course first, walked the course, looked at the pins and scoped out any interesting details or things we needed to note. He was gone by eight. I got the courtesy car at half 11, the same time as Sunday, with my brother and his two friends, Andrew Ford and John Coakley. The three of them are a bit mental, very funny and very sarcastic, so I'd just stay quiet, be an observant listener, and let the three of them joke around.

At the course, I signed autographs, maybe a couple of hundred, and I felt just the same as I did on Sunday. I didn't feel any more pressure, any more nerves. One thing was on my mind: the forecast was for quite a bit of rain. I don't mind wind. When it rains, I struggle a little bit with my grip because I kind of hang my right arm down and let it sit on the club from the side. That was maybe on my mind a little bit when I was warming up.

I remember thinking it was pretty cool to walk onto the putting green – near the first tee – and there was just Louis, Spieth and Jason Day, just the four of us. I remember staying up late when I was playing the Brabazon Trophy to watch the US Open and we were watching Lowry to see how he would do and all of those guys were in contention.

I didn't get off to a settled start. I hit my tee shot down the left on the first, which was actually a good angle in. I'd 145 yards in, with the wind off the left, and I was trying to step on a wedge. I just hit it fat. It was a shot I hadn't seen before. I have never duffed a wedge, it is usually the best part of my game. Maybe I just tried to hit it too hard and caught it heavy.

Then, on the second, the club just slipped a little bit on the downswing. It went off the planet right. I was lucky to find it. That drive on the second, I hadn't hit a shot like that in a long, long time and the shot on the first I had never hit. Those two shots rattled me a little bit in the way I had seen shots I didn't think were in my locker. It kind of throws your mind because you don't know if you are going to do it again.

But I settled back into it, made a really nice birdie on three to a tough pin, birdied the Par 5 fifth and got back to level. The difference to other days was I gave myself good looks on six, seven, eight and nine but didn't make any of them. I knew I was in trouble because the back nine was playing so difficult. Then, I had a shot into 10, from the middle of the fairway, and hit it heavy with a wedge. To do it a second time in a day really startled me. That's when I got a little let down, that it had slipped away. I tried on every shot but once you had that goal in your head (of the Claret Jug) and you knew it was gone, it was hard to get up for the last few holes like I needed to. I didn't even think of the Silver Medal.

After

Jordan Spieth came up to me outside the recorder's area. He shook my hand and said: "Nice playing this week, be very proud of yourself."

I saw him again in the lockerroom and we had another chat. The players were really nice. Justin Rose came up to me. Adam Scott. Rickie Fowler, Geoff Ogilvy. David Howell. Harrington. G-Mac. I got some nice messages from Lowry, so it was nice to have the support and feel respected by players that are that good in the game.

By Tuesday, I was back with the Walker Cup squad in Lytham for a gathering, to look at the course. It was strange on the first tee, just three people watching us

hit off. They were joking. "On the tee from Greystones . . . Paul Dunne. " It was a lot different to Monday when there were 20,000 people shouting as I hit off. But it was good. I've great friends on the golf scene and it was good to see them again.

AUGUST 7TH 2015

'It was incredible how quickly it went down. over in a matter of 30 seconds'

Paddy Agnew

It was all over in a matter of 30 seconds. It was incredible how quickly it went down – it just shows how overcrowded the vessel was and how unseaworthy too."

Cdr Ken Minihan of the Naval Service was speaking on the harbour in Palermo, just after the LÉ Niamh docked with 367 survivors from Wednesday's tragedy in the Mediterranean when an overcrowded fishing vessel carrying migrants capsized. They had paid a trafficker to take them from Libya to Europe, a route followed by thousands of migrants this year.

The LÉ Niamh also brought 25 bodies into Palermo. The number who drowned, 110km north-west of Tripoli, is not known, but may exceed 200.

For a man who had spent the previous day pulling bodies out of the water as he watched others drown, Cdr Minihan was impressively lucid as he recalled the rescue operation. The migrants' vessel capsized in sight of the LÉ Niamh which had dispatched two Ribs [rigid inflatable boats] towards it.

"As we approached the vessel . . . we noticed that individuals were moving about, making the vessel extremely unstable. All of that movement was

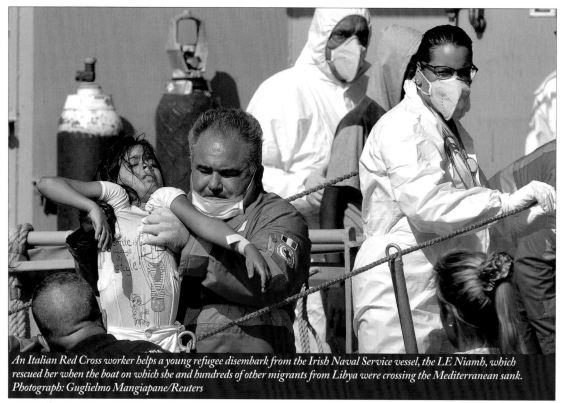

An Italian Red Cross worker helps a young refugee disembark from the Irish Naval Service vessel, the LE Niamh, which rescued her when the boat on which she and hundreds of other migrants from Libya were crossing the Mediterranean sank. Photograph: Guglielmo Mangiapane/Reuters

too much ...

"When the vessel capsized and there were lots of people in the water, our [smaller] boats moved off from the Niamh, these are boats which normally carry lots of life jackets with them.

"Normally we would hand these out to people once in the boats but what we had to do yesterday was to sail around them, trying to stay away from the big groups of people and try to throw life jackets at them because we didn't want them to get caught on the propellers of our rescue boats ...

"In the meantime, the captain ordered the release of four extra life rafts that we were carrying on board ...

"In an emergency, those life rafts can carry about 200-250 people so as we handed out the life jackets we were telling the people to swim to the life rafts because it was important that our boats did not get swamped with people because that would have stopped us handing out the life jackets.

"So we told people to swim to the life rafts and this is what they did, allowing us in the meantime to hand out life jackets to nearly every person in the water so that they could remain afloat. Obviously not all of them did ... that is unfortunate"

Even if they recounted their operation with military reserve, both Cdr Minihan and his deputy Lieut Cdr Daniel Wall acknowledged this had been a very "different" experience.

While they managed to resuscitate one child, there were other situations where the LÉ Niamh crew found themselves trying to comfort parents who had managed to physically hold onto their child but who had not been able to save the child from drowning in the chaos of the sinking.

"We're a professional search and rescue operation, that's what we do in Ireland but this was a different event on a much bigger scale ...", said Cdr Minihan. Given the traumatic nature of the events witnessed by the crew, the Naval Service will this week be sending professional counsellors out to the ship.

However, the mission goes on with the LÉ Niamh not due to return to Ireland for the time being.

Reflecting on the fate of survivors – Syrians, Palestinians, Bangladeshi and others – Cdr Minihan had no doubts about who were the culprits behind this most recent tragedy.

"The people who caused this sinking are the smugglers, there should never have been so many people on the boat . . . this was a boat which at the maximum, should carry 50 people".

AUGUST 8TH 2015

Ibrahim Halawa – an ordinary Irish schoolboy

Ruadhán Mac Cormaic

It was a Friday in mid-August, a time of year when Dublin shifts into a slower gear and the long days blend into one. Politicians were on holiday. CAO college offers were due in two days. The front pages carried a scientist's warning that temperatures in Ireland would rise to dangerous levels, but the sky over the city was a benign, familiar shade of grey.

That Friday – August 16th, 2013 – Egypt was ablaze. In Firhouse, south Dublin, where she was tending to her two young children, Nosayba Halawa kept an anxious eye on the rolling TV coverage of demonstrations that were convulsing the country of her birth. Nosayba's sisters Somaia (27), Fatima (23) and Omaima (21), and her brother Ibrahim (17), had departed for Egypt in late June.

Since they had arrived, the removal of the elected president, Mohamed Morsi of the Muslim Brotherhood, had set off a cycle of violent clashes between the newly installed government and the deposed leader's supporters.

Friday was to be a "Day of Rage", called by the Brotherhood on Cairo's Ramses Square in response to the demolition by security forces of a protest encampment in Rabaa al-Adawiya Square, which Human Rights Watch said left at least 817 people dead.

As Nosayba, the eldest of the seven Halawa children, watched the footage of Ramses Square, she could see plumes of tear gas rising above the crowds, the sound of gunshots echoing in the background.

By late afternoon, increasingly concerned about her siblings, Nosayba got into her car and drove to her father's house 10 minutes' drive away in Firhouse.

Sheikh Hussein Halawa was watching the unfolding chaos from his livingroom, waiting for another call from his children in Cairo. Earlier, Nosayba says, he had advised them to seek refuge in the al-Fateh mosque.

They were now in the mosque, and communications were patchy. The TV screen showed police, soldiers and vigilantes surround the building. "We were watching, thinking, 'what can we do'," says Nosayba. Acting on a friend's suggestion, she called the Department of Foreign Affairs, where a duty officer took the details of the four Irish citizens. "We'll do everything we can," she recalls him saying.

Night had fallen in Cairo when Seán Norton's got a call from the department in Dublin. It was his second month as Irish consul in Egypt. He was about to be drawn into one of the most complex and delicate consular cases ever handled by the department.

Ibrahim Halawa, the youngest in the family, was born in 1995 at Dublin's Coombe Hospital. He went to Holy Rosary primary school in Ballycullen, had a close group of friends, and by all accounts spent his spare time doing the sort of thing that every suburban teenager does: playing football, listening to music, sitting around on walls.

At home, Ibrahim tended to leave the room when the news came on. "The boy is basically not political at all," says one Irish official. "He's an Irish schoolboy. He likes sport, music. He writes rap music. He speaks with an ordinary Irish accent. Lovely fella."

Ibrahim's parents were born in Egypt, and their

extended families live there. So it was common for Ibrahim and his siblings to travel there in summer to spend time with their cousins. Ibrahim had just finished his Leaving Cert when he and his three sisters flew to Cairo in late June. He would later say that he had wanted to go on a post-Leaving Cert holiday to Spain with his friends, but he was asked to accompany his sisters to Egypt. "I wish I'd gone to Spain," Ibrahim told a visitor last year.

They touched down in a country in turmoil. Security forces and pro-Morsi demonstrators were clashing every day, and a state of emergency had been declared. According to Somaia, the siblings were out of the political loop when they landed. She had just finished her Montessori studies and was hoping to gain some teaching experience in Egypt that summer; another sister had applied for a place on an art course. "All of a sudden, the coup happened," Somaia recalls, "and we felt, this is not right."

The Halawas are a religious family; Sheikh Hussein, the imam of Dublin's Clonskeagh mosque, is the most prominent Muslim cleric in Ireland.

The sense of liberation that followed the ousting of Hosni Mubarak in 2011 had been intoxicating, Somaia says. "In Egypt, for once in your life, you had a voice. In Mubarak's regime, when we went for a holiday, you were not allowed to talk about any politics. Everything was okay. Mubarak was fantastic. No poor people. The economy was perfect.

"And then you go to Egypt and all of a sudden everyone is talking about politics, everyone is talking about Morsi, everyone is giving out in the media. You felt this freedom."

Somaia says she and her siblings didn't agree with everything Morsi did, but they were sufficiently angry about his removal to join the Islamist sit-in at Rabaa. On Facebook on July 28th, Omaima Halawa wrote: "I'm still [in Rabaa] and will be until our democracy is back, until our religion is no longer attacked . . . because we only fear Allah not bullets."

A YouTube video shows the Halawa siblings addressing the Rabaa crowd against a banner reading

Ibrahim Halawa by artist Brian Gallagher.

214

"Egyptians Abroad for Democracy", a lobby group set up by young Egyptian expatriates opposed to Morsi's ousting and the subsequent crackdown on his supporters.

Almost 900 people were killed when security forces launched a deadly assault at Rabaa on August 14th. A subsequent Human Rights Watch investigation found that, in addition to hundreds of protesters who threw rocks and Molotov cocktails at police once the assault began, demonstrators fired on police in at least a few instances.

The report added, however, that the protesters' violence in no way justified the "deliberate and indiscriminate killings of protesters largely by police, in coordination with army forces".

At Rabaa, Fatima Halawa was hit by a rubber bullet. Two days later, the Halawa siblings made their way to Ramses Square for the demonstration called by the Brotherhood as a show of defiance after the Rabaa killings.

The Egyptian ambassador to Ireland, Soha Gendi, calls the Halawas siblings "activists" who "knew exactly what they were doing" by joining what she says were violent protests at Rabaa and Ramses. "It's not like [Ibrahim] was a lost child and he got entangled in this. He and his sisters were there."

When they reached Ramses Square, Somaia says, they found the scene had already turned ugly: the crowd had thinned out and shots were being fired. "Then we just decided we'll head home, because there is no point being in a place like this; it's dangerous."

By that time, however, a 7pm curfew had begun, leaving them liable for arrest if they attempted the walk to their uncle's house. "As we were talking, the army kept coming towards us and shooting," she says. "We just ran towards the mosque, went inside and closed the door. We stayed there, wondering what was going to happen."

It was 3am when news of the stand-off reached Isolde Moylan, who was then Ireland's ambassador to Egypt. She spoke by phone to Omaima, who told her "thugs" were surrounding the mosque and were

Sisters of Ibrahim Halawa, Omaima (left), Fatima and Somaia, at home in Dublin with a poster featuring their brother.

215

Special Olympian Sean Coleman from Youghal at Dublin Airport with his silver medal for swimming won at the World Games in Los Angeles.   Photograph: Cyril Byrne

in a live interview on Al-Jazeera from inside the mosque.)

Witnesses described chaos and panic as security forces opened fire and shots were returned from the mosque's external minaret. "They have us surrounded in the mosque to kill us," Ibrahim said in a video recorded inside. "Everyone is willing to give themselves to the last bullet."

The ambassador advised the siblings to stay together. "I'll do what I can to get you out safely," she said. Irish officials also suggested that the Halawas not draw attention to themselves by giving any more interviews.

Working her contacts through the early hours of Saturday morning, Moylan eventually reached a brigadier who ran the international cooperation section at the interior ministry.

Moylan says she and the Irish Government were looking for the Halawas to be guaranteed safe passage out of the mosque. The officer asked if the Halawas wanted to leave; through Moylan they confirmed

minutes later. "That's settled," he said.

What happened next remains in dispute two years on. Irish officials say safe passage was guaranteed to the ambassador and the Irish government, and that it would have been guaranteed to the Halawas in person. Under the arrangement, the siblings would be taken from the scene, searched, have their records checked and then be released.

Irish officials say two groups had already left the mosque and that the deal was explained to the Halawas, but that their phone kept ringing out when the brigadier tried to call them to arrange their exit.

However, the family says there was no such thing as safe passage, given the confusion at the scene and the fact that the mosque was surrounded by police and angry local residents.

"We said, the army is outside and they're pointing to us, saying, if you leave the mosque we will kill you," says Somaia. "So we said to them, can anyone from the embassy come and take us? They said, it's not safe for us. So we replied, if you don't think it's safe for you, how would you think it's safe for us?"

Amnesty International, which has declared Ibrahim a prisoner of conscience, says it agrees safe passage was not an option and that it is "understandable" from "the video evidence and the teargas coming into the mosque as well as the sound of gunfire outside, that people would fear for their own lives if they were to come out of the mosque at this point."

The Government insists safe passage was an option. "I have no doubt that the safe passage would have been observed," says one Dublin-based official, who suggests the siblings may have come under pressure from others inside the mosque not to accept the offer. The official says that at no point was the ambassador asked to come to the mosque as part of the arrangement.

At about 2pm the next day, security forces entered the mosque and remaining protesters were escorted out. The Halawas, with several hundred others, had been inside for 17 hours. The siblings were split into two groups and put in police vans.

At the family home in Firhouse, an Egyptian number appeared on Hussein Halawa's phone. It was Fatima. She spoke briefly before the line was cut.

For the Irish Government, the arrest of four citizens presented a major challenge. From early on, the strategy was two-pronged: first, to press to have them released; and second, to provide as much consular care and assistance as possible during their detention. The three Halawa sisters were held at a women's prison for three months before they were released on bail and returned to Ireland in November 2013. Ibrahim remains in prison; the two-year anniversary of his arrest falls later this month.

He was first sent to an overcrowded, unsanitary detention centre adjacent to the notorious Tora prison. Later he was transferred to Al Salam, a military detention centre where conditions were no better and, according to one source, overcrowding was so chronic that it was difficult to lie down.

After an intervention on his behalf by the Irish authorities, Ibrahim was moved to Al Marg, a low-security prison for inmates serving the final stage of their sentences. He was there between November 2013 and August 2014, when he was transferred to Tora in advance of his trial.

Ibrahim's family say conditions at Tora were appalling. "He was one of 15 people in a room. August. It was blazing heat. No air conditioning. No beds. The toilets were blocked and stinking," says one visitor. Amnesty says Halawa was shot in the hand as he left the mosque, and Nosayba says he still cannot fully open it.

Irish authorities again intervened when Ibrahim reported that men in balaclavas had entered his cell at Tora and beaten him with chains. The Egyptians agreed to move him to what was known as the "VIP wing" at Tora, where one of his cellmates was the Australian Al-Jazeera journalist Peter Greste.

Ibrahim and Greste hit if off immediately. "Peter took him under his wing," says one visitor. "They spoke English. He lent his books to Ibrahim, and he read them all." When Greste was released last February, he said Ibrahim was a "real character" who "brought a real energy to the cell and a real sense of humour".

After Greste and others left, Ibrahim grew despondent. Asked to describe his state of mind at the time, a source who met him says: "Absolutely lifeless."

Officials from the Irish embassy visit Ibrahim regularly; as of this week, there have been 43 visits. Early on he struck up a good rapport with Moylan, the ambassador, and her staff. For her part, Nosayba Halawa, who was the family's contact point with the Government for the first nine months, says the department was "brilliant" during that time.

As time went on, however, relations grew increasingly strained. The Government and the Halawa family began to disagree on strategy.

Irish officials believed the Halawas' media campaign was counter-productive and that open condemnation of Egypt was "weakening our capacity to intervene, when intervention becomes feasible," as one official puts it.

The family felt media coverage was an important tool, and last year it went public with the claim that the Government wasn't doing enough to press the Egyptians – a criticism that was picked up by opposition parties, turning the case into a domestic political row.

In March, Sinn Féin MEP Lynn Boylan put words to a question that critics of the Government's stance had previously implied: Would the Irish Government be doing more if Ibrahim's name was Paddy Murphy? Behind the scenes, Irish authorities were meeting more problems than they acknowledged in public. One of the channels of influence Ireland uses in sensitive cases such as this is its membership in the European Union. After the ousting of Morsi and the crackdown against his supporters, however, the EU was badly divided on how to react.

A number of southern European states resisted moves for the bloc to strongly condemn the military's action, resulting in public statements that merely noted the EU's "regret" at events and stopped short of using the word "coup" to describe Morsi's overthrow by the military.

Senior EU figures have raised Halawa's case with the Egyptians, but the divisions within the bloc diluted its influence on the ground, according to one European source who was involved in the discussions. The chief focus, then, has been on bilateral lines of communication.

Ireland's ministers for foreign affairs during this period, Eamon Gilmore and now Charlie Flanagan, have raised the case regularly with their Egyptian counterparts. The two states' embassies, in Dublin and Cairo, have also been closely involved.

"I would say there is no consular case that is receiving even a quarter of the care and attention the case of Ibrahim Halawa is receiving," says a high-ranking official.

From the beginning, Egypt's understanding of the case, and the Halawas' place within it, was at odds with Dublin's. While Cairo allowed Halawa consular visits, it was also adamant that, under Egyptian law, anyone with Egyptian parents was automatically an Egyptian national until he or she formally renounced it.

The Egyptian regime also claimed there were links between the Halawa family and the Muslim Brotherhood. The family denies this.

"The whole family is part of the Muslim Brotherhood, whether they deny it or not," says Soha Gendi, the Egyptian ambassador. "Usually, the kids, they are born within this ideology. So they defend that ideology. If the father and mother believe in the ideology of the Muslim Brotherhood, automatically the kids believe in that."

A US embassy cable from 2006, published by Wikileaks, refers to suspicions about such connections based on Sheikh Halawa's position as secretary of a body called the European Council for Fatwa and Research, which gives religious opinions on issues relevant to Muslims in Europe. The council is an offshoot of the Brussels-based Federation of Islamic Organisations in Europe, an umbrella group of various branches and affiliates of the Muslim Brotherhood in Europe.

Nosayba Halawa responds that, in Egypt today, the claim of Brotherhood membership is levelled at anyone who disapproved of the military's actions in 2013.

"Let's be honest," she says. "The Brotherhood is a political group like any political group. They have the right to express themselves as long as they express themselves in a peaceful way. In Egypt now, either you are with me or, if you're against me, you're Brotherhood.

"My brother Ibrahim didn't know anything about the Brotherhood until he went to Egypt. He has learned more about it in prison than he learned his whole life."

While a political decision was made form the outset to break with Department of Foreign Affairs policy by speaking publicly about efforts on Halawa's behalf, the Irish authorities have drawn a red line at public criticism of Egypt.

According to six well-placed officials, there was unanimity in Government on the need to avoid any sign of hostility towards Cairo, and that line has held for the past two years.

Former second World War pilot Ted Veal and his friend Ann Colfer try the rollercoaster at the Tayto Park in Meath.
Photograph: Nich Bradshaw

It was no secret that Ireland had concerns about Egypt's legal system in general. In its submission during the UN's Universal Periodic Review of Egypt in November 2014, the Government said Ireland was "greatly concerned by judicial and detention policies in Egypt, including the use of capital punishment and mass trials, that threaten the rule of law and fall short of international standards on due process".

At the same time, however, Ireland has good diplomatic relations with Egypt, and Dublin remains convinced it is in Ibrahim's best interests that they be maintained. That has meant that while discussions in private can be direct, public comment are to be measured.

"We had serious problems with many of the things that were happening in Egypt," says one Irish source. "It's awkward. But there are ways of dealing with it. Megaphone diplomacy doesn't work. The more of that you do, the less they'll do" for you.

This put the Government in conflict with the family, their lawyers and human rights groups that demanded stronger action. Doughty Street Chambers, a London-based law firm that has taken up the case, says there are a number of unexplored legal avenues. It says, for example, that Ireland could put Egypt on notice of potential legal action for breach of its obligations at the International Court of Justice.

The lawyers argue that a decree issued by Egypt's president, Abdel Fattah el-Sisi, in November 2014, and used to repatriate the Al-Jazeera's Greste to Australia, could be used to free Ibrahim. Using the slogan "Pick up the phone, Enda", Opposition politicians have called on the Taoiseach to contact Sisi directly and demand Halawa's release.

The Government initially believed the presidential decree held promise for Ibrahim, and formally supported an application by his lawyer to have the teenager returned to Ireland under the terms of the new law.

At a meeting with the prosecutor general in Cairo in February, however, the Irish authorities were told the law would not be applied where an individual was in

Niamh Donnelly of Leopardstown in Dublin is congratulated on her Leaving Certificate results by her mother Marion at Coláiste Íosagáin in Stillorgan. Photograph: Eric Luke

the course of a trial process.

Since summer 2014, Ibrahim has been under a trial judge's jurisdiction. This tallies with what happened in other cases where the decree was successfully applied. "Peter Greste's initial trial had concluded and his retrial had not begun so, strictly speaking, he was not in the course of a trial process when he was returned," Flanagan told the Oireachtas foreign affairs committee last month.

The position is reiterated by Gendi, the Egyptian ambassador: "Once it has been transferred to the judicial authority, we have separation of powers. We can't just intervene. We cannot, until the case is done." At the Oireachtas committee meeting, Flanagan described as "overly simplistic" the claim that if senior politicians lifted the telephone that "Ibrahim would be immediately sprung from prison".

The Minister said he shared concerns about the length of time Halawa had spent in prison and continues to raise these concerns "at the highest level"

with the Egyptian authorities.

"Concerted and targeted work is ongoing behind the scenes with a view to ensuring that we are best placed to take advantage of any opportunity that arises to achieve progress towards a positive outcome for Ibrahim Halawa," he said.

The most benign scenario, the Government believes, is that Ibrahim is acquitted or receives a relatively light sentence that accords with the period he has already spent in prison.

The worst-case scenario is a long sentence, in which case the Government believes it would have a 60-day window to intervene and press for Ibrahim's return.

Gendi signals as much, saying there would be "room" for talks between the two governments after the trial. She adds, however, that it may depend on the outcome.

"It's a very serious case," she says. "It's not something to be taken lightly. I doubt very much that if it was the same case here, and an Egyptian citizen got entangled in this … that the Irish court system would just hand him freely to the Egyptian government."

Gendi says that Halawa has not been beaten, has been treated "in a very, very respectable way", and that she has done her utmost to facilitate the Irish authorities. "I am 100 per cent satisfied that he will have a fair trial," she adds.

For any political intervention to work, one official says, it is essential to maintain "credit in the bank". After all, calling the Egyptian president now would be to play Ireland's last diplomatic card.

"At the right time, in the right circumstances, the Taoiseach will make that intervention," the official adds. "Even the US had to wait until the case had gone through the courts," says another high-ranking official, referring to the case of Mohamed Soltan, a US citizen who was released last May after receiving a life sentence.

The Halawa family believe the strategy is misguided. "It's not enough," Nosayba says. "I don't think any of them would be able to allow his son to be in my brother's situation for two years, saying 'we can't interfere in the legal process'. The Government has spent two years using the same strategy, and it's not working."

There has also been criticism from within. "I know this is something that is being pushed, but there are certain things you can say if you're not a Government minister," former minister for justice Alan Shatter said in March during an appearance on The Late Late Show with the Halawa sisters.

"We have very good diplomatic relations with Egypt," Shatter said. "I think now this has reached a point where we should question the nature of our diplomatic relations if this continues on indefinitely."

Amnesty International has campaigned for Halawa's immediate and unconditional release. It says it understands that Egypt's assertion that Ibrahim is an Egyptian national presents "particular difficulties" in diplomatic efforts to secure his release.

"We also note that in the case of the Al-Jazeera journalists, efforts to secure their release were only successful post-conviction – and that two of them still face the threat of jail," says Colm O'Gorman, executive director of Amnesty International Ireland.

"However, Ibrahim has been detained awaiting trial, and facing a manifestly unfair mass trial, for almost two years. It is critical that Ireland continues to make strong representation on his case. It is also important that the EU focus its attention on securing his immediate and unconditional release without further delay."

At a separate meeting of the Oireachtas foreign affairs committee last month, O'Gorman said he had "enormous sympathy" with the Halawa family's view that if Ibrahim was ethnically Irish there might have been a different response to his case.

He also said that some of the xenophobic and Islamophobic comments posted online about Ibrahim were "of grave concern".

Another frustration for supporters has been the challenge of building a mass campaign. While Ibrahim's teachers have given warm and affectionate public testimony about him and his schoolfriends have made online videos to raise awareness of his situation, "it's still difficult to get Irish people truly excited" about the case, says one campaigner.

Dublin has discussed the Halawa case at length with senior officials from Canada, Australia and the US State Department. Their analysis broadly tallies with that of the Department of Foreign Affairs, according to multiple sources. At the root of that analysis is a belief that the president, Sisi, cannot intervene without burning up some of his own political capital. "Sisi is a product of the Mubarak-era system, but not in the way that the judiciary was," says a well-placed source from one of the states Ireland has consulted with. "The judiciary is its own power centre. It has its own interests. It has its own political motives, its own political culture – which is vehemently anti-Muslim Brotherhood."

The president must weigh international and domestic pressures, the source argues. From Sisi's perspective, the international pressure is relatively blunt. For all the criticism on human rights, the US will not stop sending military supplies and the EU will not cut off its financial aid. For both, not least given the crises in Syria and Libya, Sisi is strategically too important to abandon. "They can't turn off the taps, and Sisi knows that."

In Egypt, however, there is a political cost to intervening while the case is in judicial hands. "If he starts sticking his finger in the judiciary, it's going to cost him political capital and domestic support . . . The domestic pressure on him to hold the line against the Brotherhood is really quite intense."

An Irish official summarises it as follows: "We see Ibrahim as an Irish citizen and a consular case. They see this as a Muslim Brotherhood case, and in their view the Muslim Brotherhood are terrorists. That's why it's all the more important that we maintain a good bilateral relationship. We could be asking them to do us a political favour in an area that is for them very sensitive and problematic."

That view is echoed by Dr HA Hellyer, an Arab affairs specialist at the Brookings Centre for Middle East Policy in Washington and RUSI in London.

Hellyer says that while the Egyptian government has the ability to influence the judiciary, "it appears to have calculated that the cost of using that ability is more costly than it is worth."

When tensions arise between executive and judiciary, he says, "the presidency intervenes very delicately, as in the cases around Al-Jazeera and Mohammed Soltan show".

None of that gives much consolation to Ibrahim Halawa, whose trial was again adjourned last Sunday for another two months. Charges against the 420 co-accused range from murder and attempted murder to taking part in a banned protest. It is understood that Halawa falls into the least serious category, though his family say they have not received official confirmation of that.

According to Doughty Street Chambers, the teenager's case file contains no evidence to link him to any of the crimes he is alleged to have committed. He is said to be refusing prison food, taking only the meals that his mother, Amina, queues for several hours in searing heat to deliver. Otherwise he takes

"six or seven dates with some milk", Somaia says.

The experience has taken a toll on Amina, who has "got very old" the last two years and now struggles to walk without a stick, according to Nosayba.

On August 17th, Ibrahim will have spent two years in prison. In that time, Nelson Mandela died, human cloning became a reality, the world's population grew by 150 million, a terror group named Isis was formed, Nasa found water on Mars, "selfie" entered common usage. and the Smartwatch was born.

Ibrahim is now 19. His schoolfriends are about to start their third year of college.

He has told the family that his bedroom better be just as he left it, and jokes that his accumulated monthly pocket money must now amount to a small fortune.

"He says things like, 'I miss the feeling of getting a clean shower, I miss the cold of Ireland,'" Nosayba says, laughing. "I'm like, okaaay."

One day, a visitor tried to perk him up by offering to cook whatever he wanted on his first night of freedom. He opted for fish and chips. "Yeah," he told them. "I'd love some fish and chips."

On December 17th, 2010, a 26-year-old Tunisian market trader named Mohamed Bouazizi flicked a lighter and set himself, and the Middle East, alight.

Bouazizi's death was the catalyst for a wave of nationwide protests against the rule of the dictator Zine al-Abidine Ben Ali, who for more than two decades had presided over an autocratic and corrupt regime. The demonstrations continued for more than a month and eventually forced Ben Ali to flee the country.

That sent tremors rippling across the Arab world. Within days, protesters had gathered on Tahrir Square in Cairo to demand that president Hosni Mubarak release his 30-year grip on power and clear the way for democratic elections. A real revolution was brewing.

As the protests grew in strength, the Mubarak regime resorted to increasingly violent tactics to quell the challenge to its authority. Hundreds were killed and injured. Mubarak's attempts to placate the demonstrators with concessions cut little ice.

Poster hoarding art by Peter Kennard and Cat Philipps at Dismaland, a "Bemusement Park" created by graffiti artist Banksy in the English seaside town of Weston-Super-Mare.   Photograph: Yui Mok/Press Association

On February 11th, 2011, vice-president Omar Suleiman announced that Mubarak was stepping down. The crowds on Tahrir Square were euphoric.

When Egypt's first post-Mubarak elections took place in June 2012, the big winner was the Muslim Brotherhood, which had been banned for three decades. In Mohamed Morsi, an engineering professor and former political prisoner, the Brotherhood had its man in the presidential palace.

The victory was a remarkable turnaround for the Brotherhood, a grassroots organisation that, since its founding in Egypt in 1928, has grown to become the world's most influential transnational Islamist movement.

The euphoria of Tahrir Square soon gave way to discontent. Critics began to complain of an anti-democratic drift under Morsi. He alienated secularists and moderates by stuffing ministries with Brotherhood stalwarts. The economy stalled.

Morsi awarded himself sweeping powers to push through a controversial new constitution. The opposition said he was paving the way for an Islamic state. The crisis reinvigorated the opposition, and crowds came back onto the streets.

When youth activists of the Tamarud movement called for nationwide protests on June 30th, 2013, the first anniversary of Morsi's inauguration, Egyptians turned out in their millions to call on him to step down. (Counter-demonstrations drew a few hundred thousand people.)

On taking power, Morsi's new head of the army was a devout Muslim and career infantry office, Gen Abdel Fattah el-Sisi. But relations between Morsi and the military deteriorated fast.

The day after the June 30th protests, Sisi issued a 48-hour ultimatum to Morsi: either yield to the protesters' demands that he share power with the opposition, or make way for the military to impose a solution. Morsi rebuffed the ultimatum.

On July 3rd, he was placed in detention and the military took control. The removal of this democratically elected leader prompted a wave of pro-Morsi demonstrations such as the one the Halawa siblings joined.

Muslim Brotherhood leaders were arrested, and in September a court outlawed the group. Sisi became a central figure in the army-backed post- Morsi government. In May 2014 he won a two-candidate presidential election.

AUGUST 10TH 2015

Lowry stays true to his word to provide something special

Philip Reid

Nerves of steel? Make it titanium. Shane Lowry – showing fortitude, demonstrating terrific shot-making and, on the odd occasion, riding his luck – followed in Rory McIlroy's footsteps as the winner of the WGC-Bridgestone Invitational with a final round 66 for an 11-under-par total of 269 that gave him a two-strokes winning margin over Bubba Watson.

Lowry finished with the unlikeliest of birdies on the Par 4 18th, where, after driving into the trees down the left, his ball finished in a hole. Undeterred, he took his 52 degree lob wedge from his caddie Dermot Byrne and fashioned a remarkable recovery that went up and through trees, clipping a branch, and finishing on the green.

"I couldn't believe when I seen the ball coming down on the green. Just trying to lag it down and it dropped in the front door," said Lowry, who became the third Irish player – joining Darren Clarke and Rory McIlroy – as the winner of a WGC title.

A two-time winner on the European Tour – where he had previously won the Irish Open (2009) and the Portugal Masters (2012) – Lowry's breakthrough PGA Tour win has given him elevated status in a life-changing victory and momentum ahead of this week's USPGA at Whistling Straits.

Lowry's work with strength and conditioning coach Robbie Cannon has led to the player adding extra yardage to his drives, which was apparent from the off with a number of huge drives of over 300 yards. On the Par 5 second, Lowry claimed his first birdie, holing from 15 feet, and, then, on the eighth, after a drive of 368 yards, he hit a wedge approach to ten feet and sank the putt.

With overnight leaders Jim Furyk and Justin Rose struggling, Lowry's front nine of 33 moved him into the lead on his own. A loose tee-shot on the 10th seemed to have him in trouble, where he pulled his drive into left rough and was blocked out by trees. It was at that moment, though, that Lowry produced a quite remarkable recovery shot hitting a wedge up and over the trees, kicking off the greenside rough and rolling to within one foot of the hole for a tap-in birdie that moved him two strokes clear.

With two-time US Masters champion Watson assuming the role of chief pursuer down the stretch, Lowry's ability to grind as well as fashion birdies proved vital. On the 11th, he followed up his miracle shot of the previous hole with a great sand save from a greenside bunker and, on the 14th, after driving into a fairway bunker and pitching back to the fairway, he saved par with a 20-footer than brought a number of fist pumps into the air in demonstrating the significance of the putt which kept him two clear of Watson.

And Watson showed his own fighting qualities, with an unlikely birdie on the 17th where, after pulling his drive to the right and blocked out by trees, he hit a great approach to eight feet and rolled in the putt to close to within one of Lowry. But Watson's failure to birdie the 18th meant it was all in Lowry's own hands as he headed into the final two holes.

On the 17th, Lowry's approach finished up against the collar of greenside rough and, again, he demonstrated terrific resolve. His pitch finished five feet from the hole, but, coolly and calmly, he rolled in the par save to retain his lead.

But Lowry's drive on the 18th was pulled way left, into the trees, and he was left with a 141 yards approach

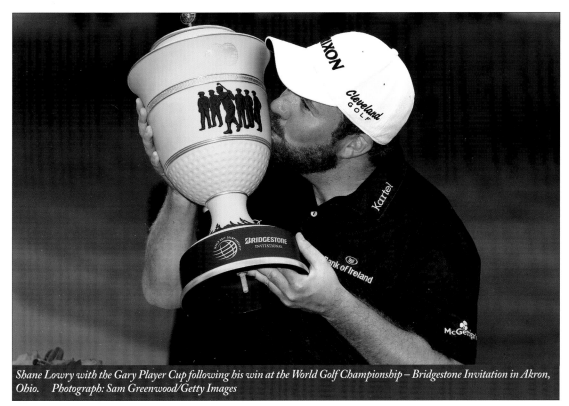

Shane Lowry with the Gary Player Cup following his win at the World Golf Championship – Bridgestone Invitation in Akron, Ohio. Photograph: Sam Greenwood/Getty Images

- through and over trees - to the green. "Front right edge?" asked Lowry of his caddie Dermot Byrne. The resultant high-five from player to caddie told its own story as much as the roars from greenside came back down to tell him that the ball had not only found the green but had finished 12 feet from the pin. His work wasn't yet finished, and Lowry rolled in the birdie putt to claim the title.

Ahead of his final round, Lowry had said: "My game has been good for a couple of years now. I feel like I'm driving the ball quite well, long and straight enough. I'm thinking, if I can hole a few putts, I can do something special. I just need to go out and do my own thing." He proved true to his word, with a bogey-free round that

Graeme McDowell entered the final round hoping to make a charge, but could only sign for a 73 for 279 to drop to 17th.

Pádraig Harrington, troubled by a knee injury picked up in a knockabout game of tennis with his children

a fortnight ago, finished with a 76 for 290 in 70th but more concerned about getting treatment ahead of this week's PGA championship.

AUGUST 15TH 2015

'Why don't you just tell Denis O'Brien's solicitor that you'll stop having Denis O'Brien Hair?'

Ross O'Carroll-Kelly

So I'm in bed on Tuesday afternoon, re-watching Ireland against Wales, with my famous tactics book open in front of me, writing out the names of the players I'd bring to the World Cup if I was Joe Schmidt and I had to choose my squad right now. And that's when my phone all-of-a-sudden rings and

'The old man' with that wig...

it ends up being Helen – as in, my old man's second wife?

"Ross," she goes, "it's about your father."

I'm there, "I hope you've finally wised up and left the knob," because she's way out of his league. I actually said it the day they got married – in my best-man speech. But that's when I hear the tears in her voice and I go, "Helen, what's wrong?"

She's there, "It's the wig!" because I think I told you

that Denis O'Brien is threatening to sue him for having Denis O'Brien Hair. "Ross, I don't think I could bear the stress of a court case."

I actually laugh? I'm there, "There won't be a court case, Helen. This is actual Denis O'Brien we're talking about. The old man will cave."

"He won't," she goes. "The power has gone to his head. Ross, he's talking about countersuing."

I'm there, "Denis's lawyers will make mincemeat of him in the High Court. It'll be funny. A day out for us."

She's like, "I need you to talk to him . . . please."

I try to go, "I'm kind of working here, Helen. There's a World Cup coming up."

Except all I can hear is, like, sobbing on the other end of the phone? She's not a fan of the game. How could she possibly understand? So I end up having to get dressed, then I drive on over there.

The old man is in the study with Hennessy. "I'm just having a legal consult with your godfather," he goes when I arrive. Hennessy, I notice, is scribbling notes on a yellow legal pad. "I've thought of another one," the old man goes, at the same time, running his fingers through his big grey mane.

"I was filling the Kompressor in one of those Topazes of his – the one at Newlands Cross, if you don't mind! – and the pump was a little on the urgent side. Ended up with half a bloody well pint of super unleaded down the front of my trousers, then had to endure a day of incontinence jokes from the chaps at the Kildare Hotel and Golf Club – yourself included, Hennessy!"

Hennessy goes, "We'll claim €500 for the trousers and €500m for emotional distress."

"Make it a good letter," the old man goes. "One of your specials. Lots of forthwiths and hereafters and whatnots. That should wipe the bloody well smile off his face."

He wanders over to the window and looks out. "Another one," he suddenly goes. "The water meter that his crowd installed. The new concrete they laid doesn't match the old concrete. It's a totally different shade, for heaven sakes!"

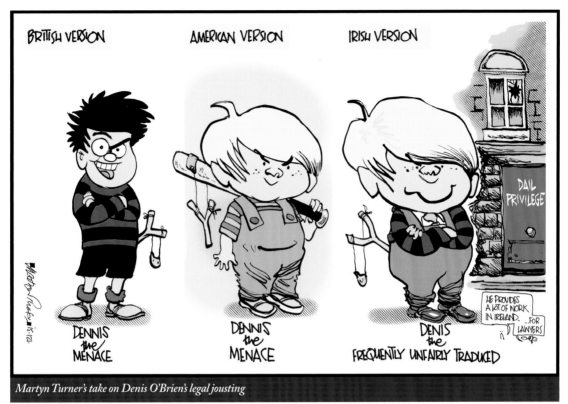

Martyn Turner's take on Denis O'Brien's legal jousting

Hennessy goes, "We could argue that it's taken – what? – €3 million off the value of the house, then claim another €30 million for mental anguish."

He's there, "Write it up, old chap."

"Stop!" I hear myself suddenly go. "Just stop!"

They both look up at me.

I'm there, "Why don't you just tell Denis O'Brien's solicitor that you'll stop having Denis O'Brien Hair?"

He looks at me in total disgust. He's like, "Where the hell is this coming from?"

I'm there, "You've been on some crazy power trip ever since you put that wig on your head. Your wife is upset. And her upset is affecting my World Cup preparations."

He stares at me, his face turning quickly red, then he shouts, "Helen!" and he storms out of the study and down to the kitchen, with Hennessy following close behind. I go after them.

Helen is cooking dinner. The old man opens up on her. He's there, "How dare you go behind my back

like that!"

She's like, "Charles, we could lose our home. We could lose everything we own!"

The old man goes, "Hennessy, send this woman a letter."

Helen actually laughs in, like, a bitter way? She's there, "Oh, you're going to sue me now, are you?"

The old man goes, "Save your breath to cool your porridge – you're getting a letter! Instructing you to cease and also desist from going behind my back."

Hennessy actually storts writing. He must be coining it with all the fees.

"Malicious slander," the old man goes. "Breach of wifely duties. Psychological torment..."

Helen bursts into tears and I suddenly can't listen to any more of this. The woman is right. The old man has become a monster and he has to be stopped.

My hand reaches out – sort of, like, instinctively? – and makes a grab for the wig. I give it a serious yank. He must be using some pretty heavy-duty adhesive because I end up pulling off half his scalp with it. He screams.

They've got one of those, like, American-style gorbage disposal units next to the sink and I think, yeah, no, I'll stick it in there, then switch it on and it will be a case of – literally – good riddance to bad rubbish.

The old man's watching all of this in slow motion, going, "Noooooo!!!"

I dance around the table – a throwback to the glory days when I use to do the same to the Senior Cup defences – and I stretch out my hand, getting ready to dump that wig once and for all.

And that's when I feel the breath leave my body and I find myself suddenly falling to the floor. The old man – no slouch himself back in the, whatever, 1950s – has tackled me around the waist.

I hit the deck and I drop the wig. If you were being technical, you'd call it a knock-on. It's lying on the floor a few feet away. We both scramble for it, but I'm still winded, and he reaches it before I do. He puts it back on his head, then stands up, shaping it with his fingers, so that the old volume quickly returns.

"Ross," he goes, "you'll be hearing from my solicitor."

AUGUST 17TH 2015

Summer finally serves up an epic to savour

Malachy Clerkin

Oh hurling, how could we doubt you? We worthless curs, we ignorant daws. We've spent the summer grumbling at the lack of a decent game and instead of fobbing us off with something mildly presentable, Galway and Tipperary lifted the cloche and served up an epic.

A crowd of 58,495 saw Anthony Cunningham's side, abrasive and elusive in equal measure, bounce their way to a stunning 0-26 to 3-16 victory. Truly, we are not worthy.

The end was deathless and erratic, entirely in keeping with what had gone before. Only a fantasist would magic up Galway's match-winner in the shape of a 22-year-old substitute playing his first ever championship match. Shane Moloney hadn't made Galway's league panel back in the spring because Cunningham deemed him not fit enough. He only got a toe back in the door to make up numbers for a challenge match against Wexford.

Here, he came off the bench with a minute left of the 70 and managed to get on the ball in space to shoot not once but twice. The first one, he made an almighty mess of, skittering a loose effort out towards the corner flag for Tipp goalkeeper Darren Gleeson

Kerry's James O'Donoghue jumps for joy at his county's All-Ireland GAA senior football semi-final win over Tyrone.   Photograph: Cathal Noonan/Inpho

to pick up at his ease.

But for the second, he scudded out on to a gorgeous 70-yard pass from Joe Canning, rounded the unfortunate Conor O'Brien whose footing betrayed him at just the wrong moment, and nailed Galway's 26th point with 10 seconds left on the clock. Bedlam in the big house.

"It's huge," smiled Cunningham afterwards. "It's worth two or three years of development work. You can work in the gym and in the winter and summer, but you don't get that experience until you're out there and it's a draw match going into injury-time and you have to get the last ball to win it."

Had Galway not found the spare point to win it in the end, we'd have walked out of the place shaking our heads at the senseless way they'd left it behind them. They were the better side here but kept Tipp in the game by leaving poor Pádraig Mannion on a rampant Seamie Callanan long after it was humane to do so.

The Tipp full-forward had 3-8 against his name by the time Galway finally made a switch, 3-4 of it from play. Outside of him, the rest of the Munster champions could only muster a paltry seven points between them. On a day when their usually iridescent attack was dulled for once, Callanan was their only route to goal and virtually the sole threat to Galway's passage to an All-Ireland final.

He had a goal on the board inside 39 seconds. He ended with three but we'll only describe the one, since they were all the same. High ball in, Callanan left alone with rookie defender Mannion at the edge of the square. Catch, turn, shot, goal. Lather, rinse, repeat in the 40th minute and the 53rd.

But though Tipp's ace was strong, it was just one card and in the face of Galway's array of kings, it could only carry so much weight. With Cathal Mannion and Jason Flynn to the fore, Galway inched their way back to lead at the break. After Callanan's second goal, they scored the next two points within a minute; after his third, they scored the next four.

Nip and tuck, tuck and nip. Bonner Maher and Bubbles O'Dwyer had goal chances but hit them weakly and Colm Callanan saved. Lar Corbett and Seamie Callanan both connected better with theirs – Callanan's a late penalty – but the Galway goalkeeper was equal to them too.

Canning had a half-blocked shot batted away by Gleeson at the other end. Everywhere you looked, drama was bubbling.

Snapshots. Noel McGrath came in off the bench and the whole stadium – maroon jerseys as well as blue – rose to cheer him on to the pitch. When he snagged the point that looked the winner, we all got lumps in our throats.

Cathal Mannion speared a point off a Johnny Glynn hook, Flynn whipped over another to equalise. We presumed we were headed for a replay until Moloney brought Tipp's year to an abrupt end.

And with it, the managerial reign of Eamon O'Shea. He was always leaving whenever the year was done but this was earlier than he or anybody had imagined. "In one sense I feel emotional, obviously losing is huge," he said. "But it's theirs, it's the players' game. Me leaving is only a footnote. It will be only a footnote. What's really important is that we continue and we push and we try to go on and be better.

"It's about for them moving on and trying to be better. That's what high-level sport is. It's a beautiful thing but it's a brutal thing and it's both at the same time. That's the essence of what happened today."

AUGUST 21ST 2015

Could you be the most beautiful bulls in the world?

Conor Pope

'I'm here to meet Jim Dockery about the bull grooming," I tell the first friendly-looking woman who crosses my path at Ossory Agricultural Show, in Co Laois.

She looks at me suspiciously. "What breed?"

It's my turn to look suspicious. Well, more confused, really. I make a noncommittal face.

She tries again. "What colour?"

"I've no idea," I say, looking at all the farmers milling around in the muddy fields around me. "He's white, I suppose."

"Not the man," she sighs. "His cattle."

Oh. Right. I've no idea, so I wander away sheepishly. Never having been to an agricultural show, I'd assumed finding the man who'd volunteered to school me in bull grooming would be easy. I mean, how many men shampooing cattle can you fit in a Midlands field on a rainy Sunday morning?

Loads, it turns out. There are hundreds of cattle tethered to railings in makeshift gazebos and they're all being brushed and polished by teams of farming folk. There are also countless sheep bleating and pigs giving out about a spontaneous donkey threesome happening in a pen beside the cattle shower. It's bedlam.

I find another farmer. "I'm looking for Jim Dockery," I say.

"There he is, over there with all those black lads," he tells me. And so he is. He's washing down his black Angus bulls and he greets me with a smile and a bottle of shampoo.

Before I start work, he tells me about his show times. Today is his season debut and he's likely to bring animals to 10 or more agricultural shows across the country before summer's end. His six young children and his wife, Tara, always travel with him. The rosettes that billow in the breeze by his gazebo suggest he's a man to beat.

He's been preparing for months. Potential winners are identified almost as soon as they're born. Beasts with "smart heads" and muscular torsos are watched closely. Once an animal shows show potential, it's whisked away from its less attractive peers and sent to bovine boot camp to be introduced to tethers and people.

Two weeks out, they're given a scrub and a haircut. "It's important to give them a trim well before the show to allow the hair time to settle down," Dockery says.

They get another wash two days before the event but the real grooming takes place on the big day.

This is where I come in. First of all I'll have to shampoo Dockery's three bulls and the cow, all of which have had dung-related episodes on their short journey from farm to field. They'll have to be rinsed with a high-pressure hose, blow-dried and brushed. There'll be baby oil and the bull equivalent of fake tan.

"Careful now," he warns as I take up a ridiculous position behind the biggest bull's back legs. "He kicks quite hard so it's probably best not to stand there," he says with the patience of a parent talking to a small, not very bright child. I move to the front and the bull catches sight of me. He doesn't like what he sees and starts bucking wildly before lurching to my side and headbutting me just above the waist.

As my day as a bull whisperer progresses, I learn I know virtually nothing about their world. I ask where my bull's horns are and am told not all bulls have horns. I ask if the cow is the baby bull's mammy. Dockery laughs and tells me she's a heifer. I nod wisely and try and remember what a heifer is (it's a cow that hasn't had a calf).

As we talk, my bull rears again. Dockery gently steers the high-pressure blow-drier I'm using away from the beast's head. "Sometimes they don't like it in their ears," he tells me. Fair enough.

"I am going to be showing one of the bulls," his son Ronan (9) tells me.

"We have a box of rosettes at home," he adds, his chest swelling with pride. Dockery tells me he enters the shows mainly for his children. "They love it. You wouldn't be doing it for the prize money anyway." A top prize in a category is €50.

He breeds Shorthorn and Angus cattle, and both are getting good prices at the factories. With all the preening, it's easy to forget the abattoir is their ultimate destination. Forgetting is easier when you hear their names. Rachel is the Shorthorn heifer. Ronan is a Shorthorn too. Louis is the big black Angus and Munchkin is a smaller version of him.

We take the Angus bulls to be weighed. Louis is 404kg and Munchkin is 342kg. These numbers matter. If they measure up they'll both enter the Aldi Class competition. It's reserved for beasts that have put on no more than 1.7kg each day from when they were born. "It stops people saying their animals are three months younger than they are to get a size advantage," says Dockery. "It cuts out the nonsense."

Pat Sheedy from Roscrea gets his cattle ready in the neighbouring pen. He points to his prize animal. "That's Merrybell. She has a beautiful head, a good top line and a nice back. She's a stylish, traditional Shorthorn colour," he says. I nod wisely like I know a good cow when I see one.

By now Rachel the heifer's hairdo is looking very fluffy, like she's been wired to a plug socket. Her style isn't enough to impress the judges, though. She comes third, as does Munchkin.

The two Ronans are up. Before judging takes place, a bull makes a break for it and barrels up one of the grassy aisles leading from the ring. This is no Spanish bull run and there's no panic. The farmers know exactly what to do. Most step calmly to one side as the half-ton beast thunders past. He turns a few corners before being placated.

The excitement over, the judging takes place. The Ronans finish second.

Imelda Middleton judged him. "I'm looking for sweetness, power, tidy heads and a great walk," she tells me. "Ronan is a smart, powerful bull for April and in time he'll finish first."

Last up is Louis, my bull. We coat him in Megashine – a kind of hairspray for bulls – and I massage baby oil into his head and rub a black cream into his hooves to make them shine. In a borrowed lab coat, I lead Louis into the ring.

He's not a raging bull until he senses that I think I'm in charge. To put manners on me he leaps from side to side as I walk in front of the judges. Dockery steadies Louis's nerves and mine. He tells me Louis is being disturbed by the PA announcements for the start of the "most suitably dressed gentleman" competition. Louis finishes second. I'm not even placed in the "most suitably dressed gentleman" competition.

Four rosettes but no winner. But there's still time. The Aldi Classes comes next. Munchkin and Louis have passed the weight tests. Both win first prize and the right to enter the Aldi-sponsored Angus bull calf competition at the Iverk Show in Kilkenny on August 22nd. It is the richest bull calf competition in Europe.

There is much excitement among the Dockery clan. I'm feeling pretty pleased with myself too. I walk up to give Louis a congratulatory pat. He pins me to some railings before stomping off with a snort. There's gratitude for you.

AUGUST 28TH 2015

Room to roam: children's lives are restricted by modern world

Anthea McTeirnan

Children's "freedom to roam" has completely changed over the years. They are now more supervised than ever before and their timetables and activities are much more planned by parents worried about potential danger all around, whether it be "stranger danger" or busy traffic.

Their worlds have shrunk. They are no longer allowed to ramble as far from home as their parents took for granted, and far fewer of them play in the street, according to various studies. Instead, they are taken to playgrounds and increasingly to purpose-built indoor facilities.

Deirdre Whitfield, who is responsible for Wicklow County Council's playgrounds, was concerned when a survey by the National Heritage Council found a huge increase in the number of children playing in indoor activity centres. The 2011 study also found a smaller percentage of children than before were playing in the "wild" and a higher percentage were going to outdoor playgrounds.

Children are "more supervised by their parents than ever", according to Dr John Sharry, psychotherapist and parenting columnist for The Irish Times.

"There is far less cultural acceptance for a child to be out wandering," he says.

For many middle-class children, he says, life has become more restricted, with play dates scheduled, events organised, activities timetabled – and children driven to them.

When Wicklow County Council started to look at its play policy 10 years ago, people were asked to think about their favourite places to play when they were children. No one mentioned playgrounds, says Whitfield. "Some people mentioned stealing apples from orchards. However, everyone loved wandering free."

A recent North-South study observed that "children's ability to travel and move about in their communities – to walk or cycle to school, the shops, friends' houses and recreational facilities – is indicative of the value our society places on children". This "independent mobility" had declined, it found.

There are a number of reasons for this closing-in of children's worlds. The increase in traffic is often cited. "There is a good justification for parents being worried about traffic," says Sharry. "Although if you look at it, children are much less likely to be killed crossing a road than as a passenger in a parent's car."

Whitfield is aware that children are far less likely nowadays to know their neighbours.

"This is important for children's play. We have to build up community capital to break down that lack of trust."

Sharry says: "It changes children's experience of life. Families are smaller now and parents are striving to be 'attentive' parents, but there is more judgment about what a child should be allowed to do."

Local authorities are aware that communities want spaces in which children can play. Whitfield says:

"We need unsupervised public spaces that are as safe as we can make them without making it 'over safe'."

Sharry agrees. "It is important to introduce adventure into your child's life," he says.

So what can parents do to expand their child's world? "Make their life more physical and introduce them to nature and the outdoors. Supervise them, but let them roam in safety," says Sharry.

Whitfield fears more restricted horizons and more limited opportunities for play are making children "less independent and disconnecting them from the natural environment".

In Co Wicklow, "we felt it was important that rather than regulating play we deregulated play and made it accessible," she says.

AUGUST 31ST 2015

Surrender is a very different matter from just giving up

Una Mullally

That's it then. Over for another year. The summer started out with a referendum hailing great social change, but as it has progressed there have been almost too many sad stories, most of all the ongoing helplessness and death of desperate people trying to scramble their way out of Syria and various African countries to us.

Their destination is the promised land of Europe, where we live in privilege and watch them die trying to get here. I'm sorry, I feel like saying to them. I'm sorry this is happening to you. You didn't do anything wrong. What the plight of not "migrants" but "people" gives us is perspective.

Arthur Gardin (centre, left), grandson of silent movie era comedian Charlie Chaplin, with Chaplin impersonator Diago Spanó, at the Waterville Charlie Chaplin Comedy Film Festival.   Photograph: Alan Landers

Perspective is a funny thing, because you can only really get it when confronted with an entirely different version of life from your own. My summer has been spent trying to deal with this bloody cancer that I have, an incredibly surreal situation. There's a common belief that you learn a lot from tough times. We can wish we wouldn't be confronted with such a lesson, but the cliche is true. I've learned a lot, mostly to do with perspective. One of my favourite films this summer was Pixar's Inside Out. At one point the character Fear says: "Alright, we did not die today! I'd call that an unqualified success." I've learned to enjoy the rare absences of catastrophe.

When your body is trying to survive, it demands you listen to it. I never really paid much attention to what my body was telling me. If I felt tired I wouldn't rest. If I felt ill, I'd pass on medication. If I felt busy I'd just go faster. But when you experience shock, or acute stress reaction, your body steers you towards certain things it demands. "Go to a beach! Now!" it says. "Spend two weeks making a jigsaw!" Hmm, alright then. "Stop listening to the radio!" But I like the radio. "Tough! You need prolonged periods of silence!"

Okay. I've learned to listen to what my body is saying. I've learned that we are very good at absorbing and reacting to terrible things, but not so much the good things. A psychiatrist in hospital told me that even if you get good news, it can be difficult to respond to or digest it. The initial "kick" of the bad news is so hard, that very few things can override it. Although striving to be happy is a general goal for us all, negativity can be more tempting a state.

The language of negativity is more colourful, bursts of outrage seem to give us something of an adrenaline rush, and being mean about others a false sense of superiority. But there's a difference between bad news and negativity. It has become impossible to listen to people being negative when their lives are perfectly fine. All those people whining on the radio or bitching in the letters pages or being grumpy on Facebook? I've learned to mute the constant soundtrack of people sweating the small stuff.

But the greatest slab of perspective is realising that you are not in control. The two biggest things in life – love and death – happen to you no matter what you do.

When I was lying in hospital one night, sick from morphine, in a delusional state and with a substantial amount of pain after major abdominal surgery, I unconsciously reached for my phone and put on Brian Eno's 1978 album Ambient 1: Music For Airports. As the music infiltrated my dreams, I woke up at dawn remembering a talk I attended in New York two summers previously.

In a small room to a handful of people, Eno discussed the type of music he makes. There is a video of it online.

"What one does as an artist can stimulate one or the other of the nervous systems that we have, the sympathetic or the parasympathetic," Eno said. The sympathetic deals with fight and flight, the parasympathetic deals with activities when the body is at rest. Eno believes his work addresses the parasympathetic, the "rest-and-digest" things.

"It's part of our being that we actually don't address very much," Eno continued, "particularly in urban environments. In urban environments, we're mostly living off the sympathetic nervous system, because we're mostly in situations that require speed, alertness, quick decisions, possibly they're dangerous, there are cars flying around and people with knives, policemen and drug dealers, so we have to be paying attention all the time."

He said that what happens with his music, is that it allows you to stop trying to be in control of things so you can allow yourself to surrender. "Now, I use this word 'surrender' quite a lot," Eno said, "It doesn't immediately have the right connotation, but there isn't another word for it. What I mean by surrender is an active choice not to take control. An active choice to be part of the flow of something."

More and more we are geared towards being competitive, working relentlessly, being hyper-alert and existing in an environment where stress is a default rather than a rarity. I find it almost amusing that experiencing something so stressful has in fact been liberating. I've learned to surrender, which is very different from giving up. That's perspective, I guess.

SEPTEMBER 2ND 2015

Nobody emerges from this enquiry in a good light

Fiach Kelly

The argument from Government in the coming days will be that the only question worth dealing with is whether Taoiseach Enda Kenny attempted to sack, or did sack, former Garda commissioner Martin Callinan.

The interim report of the Fennelly Commission gives succour to those who seek to reduce the issue to such absolutes, yet it would be wrong to do so.

The commission accepts that "the Taoiseach did not intend to put pressure on the Garda commissioner to retire" and concludes there was never a question of a proposal being put to the Cabinet that Callinan be removed from office.

Yet, in its entirety, what the report presents is a string of incompetencies layered with dysfunctionality, made worse by the heat of political controversy.

At this stage, despite a threat from Fianna Fáil that it may table a motion of no confidence in the Dáil, there is no danger to Mr Kenny's position.

While it once seemed the retirement of Martin Callinan could have been a threat to Mr Kenny, even his most strident enemies in Fine Gael say Fennelly's conclusions mean any outstanding issues are now closed.

But it is not that simple. Nobody emerges from the interim report in a good light. It is riddled with conflicts of evidence and contradictions.

The clearest conclusion that can be reached is that not everyone interviewed by the commission left their agendas at the door.

The conclusions basically lay out a he-said, she-said approach. Callinan, Fennelly finds, "interpreted the message delivered to him" by then Department of Justice secretary-general Brian Purcell, sent by Kenny

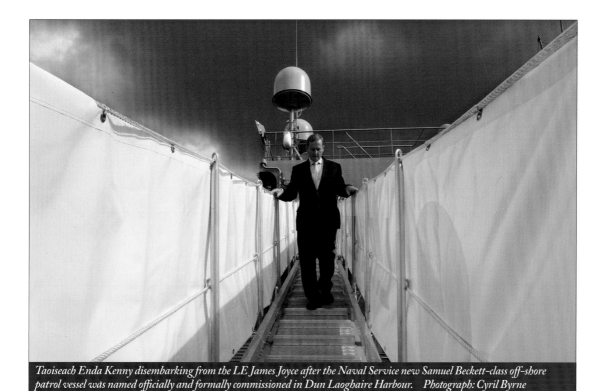

Taoiseach Enda Kenny disembarking from the LE James Joyce after the Naval Service new Samuel Beckett-class off-shore patrol vessel was named officially and formally commissioned in Dun Laoghaire Harbour. Photograph: Cyril Byrne

to the commissioner's home, "with all its attendant circumstances, as an indication that he should consider his position".

"In the view of the commission, that was a reasonable conclusion for the commissioner to reach. The commissioner decided to retire; he could have decided otherwise, but he did not wish to become embroiled in legal or other conflict with the Government."

The report says that Purcell felt uncomfortable being sent out to Callinan's home at 11pm at night to tell him of the Taoiseach's concern about the taping of telephone calls at Garda stations.

What it points to is Government by hints and innuendo. If the Taoiseach did not want Mr Callinan to resign, he should have said so.

If he instructed Mr Purcell to tell Mr Callinan that he felt the commissioner may not have survived the following day's Cabinet meeting, that arguably would also have been acceptable.

Purcell says that is the case, as does Callinan, yet Mr Kenny denies such a message was meant

to be conveyed.

Even so, Martin Fraser, the secretary-general to the Government, said it did not escape him that one of the "outcomes of Mr Purcell's visit to the commissioner was that the commissioner might choose to retire".

Purcell says he was "shocked and concerned at what he was being asked to do".

"He told the meeting on more than one occasion that it was wrong," the report adds.

It should not be forgotten in all of this that Callinan was a political liability at the time. He had mishandled a number of crucial issues, not least picking fights with the Garda Síochána Ombudsman Commission (GSOC) and describing the Garda whistleblowers as "disgusting".

Then minister for transport Leo Varadkar had described the whistleblowers as "distinguished", undermining Callinan, and the Labour Party was limbering up to follow suit.

Callinan's position was clearly under threat, and the taping issue - seemingly overplayed by Attorney

General Máire Whelan - arrived in the middle of it all.

After Callinan announced his resignation, Kenny, according to the report, told then tánaiste Eamon Gilmore that "if he were asked in the House if he had confidence in the Garda commissioner, he would not be able to say that he had".

It is seemingly clear that Kenny had problems with Callinan's position. If he had, he could have credibly told Callinan it was unlikely he would survive that week's Cabinet meeting.

In such a scenario, with a number of his ministers now pressurising Callinan, he would have been doing the commissioner a favour.

Resign or retire with dignity, or face the ignominy of having the Government publicly strip you of office, effectively.

Yet such a message was never communicated, even if the evidence points to the Coalition losing confidence in the commissioner.

Instead, the void was filled with assumptions and misunderstanding.

The report has shown the contradictions that emerge in such a scenario and while there may not be a silver bullet in Mr Justice Nial Fennelly's report, almost all participants emerge diminished from its pages.

SEPTEMBER 6TH 2015

My pet forest

Paddy Woodworth

'It's cheaper than a cocaine habit," Germaine Greer says of her current consuming passion, the restoration of a Queensland rainforest long degraded by agricultural clearances. "It's more fun than a world cruise. It's the most uplifting freedom I've known."

At 76, Greer remains almost as outrageously outspoken, and frequently as wickedly funny, as she was when she changed millions of lives with her feminist classic, The Female Eunuch, in 1970.

But there is a new hint of diffidence in her manner, sometimes a surprising tenderness in her tone. Her personal struggle to reanimate an ancient forest may have, in some ways, humbled her.

Just before our meet she had given a remarkable introductory address to an international conference of the Society for Ecological Restoration, in Manchester. She had started off by saying that she felt like "an amateur exceeding her brief" but then, typically, launched into a series of provocative speculations about a subject she has never studied academically: the monarch butterfly. Her remarks were airily free of scientific caution.

She wondered whether monarchs, famed for migrating from Canada to Mexico, are truly migrants at all or are simply bounced around North America by atmospheric pressure. She noted with displeasure their recent arrival in Australia, and admits to "disliking them for the same reasons I can't drink Coca-Cola".

But she also talked a deal of sense. She argued that ecological restoration must be paid for, like any other professional service, if society is serious about reversing the damage we have done to the global environment. She derided the dependence on volunteers of many conservation initiatives, using phrases that only someone with her feminist pedigree could get away with:

"We need professionals on the job," she said. "You can't be mean to middle-aged ladies who doesn't understand how to use a secateurs and think restoration work is a half-day outdoors followed by a barbecue."

This comment hit a raw nerve among her audience, some of whom were volunteers themselves. And volunteers do make a big contribution to conservation, if proper scientific supervision is involved. But many listeners recognised more than a grain of truth in her caricature, and it became a talking point for the rest of the conference.

When I ask for an interview Greer says that she has imposed "a blanket ban on print media" but "will

Germaine Greer hugging a tree at Cave Creek in Australia, an area of rainforest she has helped return to its natural state.
Photograph: Newspix/REX shutterstock

make an exception on this occasion." I still have no idea why.

We make our way across the road to her hotel, her arthritis troubling her every painful step of the way. She asks for a Bloody Mary – it is 10am – and settles into a sofa. How, I wonder, did she first become involved in restoration? Was she a nature lover from childhood?

"No, I grew up in the suburbs; I made daisy chains but knew nothing about native plants," she says. "I read Heidi and dreamed of being in the Alps with gentians."

But her younger sister Jane became a professional botanist, and Greer caught her enthusiasm on flower-hunting holidays, although they were not always exactly in tune with each other.

These trips are the source of some of the most beautiful writing in Greer's recent book about her rainforest restoration, White Beech. But both there and in our interview, timelines and motivations are often vague and contradictory.

I ask whether her work with Buglife, the insect NGO for which she notoriously appeared on Celebrity Big Brother, a show she had previously eviscerated, predated her interest in restoring the rainforest. There is a silence, and then: "I honestly don't know. I don't think about myself that much. I'm a classic of the unexamined life."

At first, she says her sister had nothing to do with her current project. But she clearly owes much of her remarkable botanic knowledge to their encounters. "I listened and tried to learn everything she told me, but I was naughty. I always jump to the next idea instead of doing it the hard way," Greer says.

She returns repeatedly and lyrically to their travels together, but it is always with a hint of pain. "In Western Australia we realised that after a burn the orchids come out of the ground – bang! – like feathers out of a toy revolver. So every time we saw a burnt bit we stopped the car and crawled through the

Mary Lou McDonald of Sinn Féin looks at her party leader Gerry Adams during a press briefing at the party's 'think-in' in Gormanstown in Co Meath.   Photograph: Alan Betson.

blackened undergrowth, and saw amazing things . . . But the last time we botanised together didn't work quite so well."

Greer was "crazy about finding a tiny little carnivorous sundew" that grew on her sister's street. "Jane was utterly bored by it. But that's all right. Then I bought a property in Queensland, so we would have a project to work on together, but that didn't really work, because she wasn't interested. But it's okay . . ." She tails off very quietly.

That property seems to have become the dominant relationship in her life, one she feels very personally indeed. But it wasn't love at first sight. "At the beginning I thought, 'Not for me'. I thought, 'It's horrible, buggered'. But then – I don't know why – I came back in the evening. I still think it was the forest that called me back. I just wanted to hear it when it was waking up, and the busiest time for your nocturnal animals is twilight, so I came and sat in the twilight. And then the bird came out and danced for me."

The dancer was a regent bowerbird, a canopy-dwelling species that Greer still sees unusually close to ground level around her house. She is convinced it welcomed her into the forest community. It's a typical Greer contradiction, the same rigorous academic mind that will argue about the minutiae of taxonomy embracing an irrational personal relationship with nature. How seriously does she mean this?

"Well, I have a joke with the forest that when it gets fed up with me, it will kill me," she says. "I'll just be walking and a bough will come down and I'll know nothing about it. It will be merciful. It will be better than living in a home."

Age, memory loss – "a pain in the arse" – and infirmity crop up repeatedly. She is trying to divest herself of possessions accumulated over a lifetime – "tchotchkes from all over the world. What's the point of them?" –

and of her English home and library.

"I want to get right down to, I'm saying a single room, but I don't really mean that," she says. "Well, if I end up in a facility I will be in a single room."

So will she move to her house in Cave Creek forest permanently? Her rational pragmatism suddenly reasserts itself. "No, it's too hard, too hard to live there," she says. "I could get hurt, bitten by a rough-scale snake, or break my ankle, and couldn't get to the landline. There's no mobile coverage. No, the forest is not for living in, except by the creatures who live there."

It might be easy to dismiss her as a dilettante in conservation were it not so evident that she has put a huge amount of time, resources, passion and sheer sweat into her project, and that her Gondwana rainforest foundation encourages other private landowners to do something similar.

Greer is vague about the scientific advice she has sought, however, and seems unfamiliar with some cutting-edge Australian restoration work. She says she sacked her first scientific adviser and "instigated the first planting myself".

She admits freely that her trial-and-error approach, which risks reinventing several ecological wheels at best, does not always work. "We got everything wrong. We made plenty of mistakes."

She now works with "very skilled tree people", and it seems that they are at least temporarily winning the battle to liberate the rainforest species from the invasive alien plants and grasses that were suffocating the local biodiversity. She clearly loves the work.

"I'm a little-plant person. The boys are all tree people; they can't be bothered with the little stuff," she says. "I bother about the little stuff all the time. I can be found splitting a clump of native violets, and planting them out on a tray till they establish, and then cutting them out and putting them in the ground, and they go mad. "Then the pademelons" – scrub wallabies – "come with their babies, and teach them to eat the violets. I've got photos of them picking them and giving them to their joeys."

But might not all this just be a very adventurous form of gardening? What is her scientific template for maintaining the forest into the future, as it faces the challenges of climate change and ever-increasing numbers of invasive alien species?

"We let the forest dictate who lives and who dies – that's why it's not gardening," she says. "The forest itself is the template. It covers everything in its vegetable fur, and keeps it cool, keeps it warm, and things keep coming back again, so fast you can't believe it."

Greer has encountered many critics, literary and political, in her long professional life. In choosing this rainforest as her legacy project she has submitted herself to nature and time, the toughest critics of all.

SEPTEMBER 7TH 2015

Clinical Kilkenny retain All-Ireland hurling title

Seán Moran

Kilkenny 1-22 Galway 1-18

It started with the promise of a memorable contest but by the final whistle Kilkenny had proved beyond quibble their enduring supremacy in current hurling.

Despite looking vulnerable in a first half when the movement and brio of Galway exerted considerable pressure, the champions closed ranks in the second half to limit space and corral their opponents into tight and unprofitable positions.

It wasn't an easy match in which to identify key contributors. TJ Reid, not man marked and shifting around the attack, wasn't spectacular but that also reflects the average expected of him. He still managed 1-7, only one score of which was from play but that was significant - the goal that kept Galway within

239

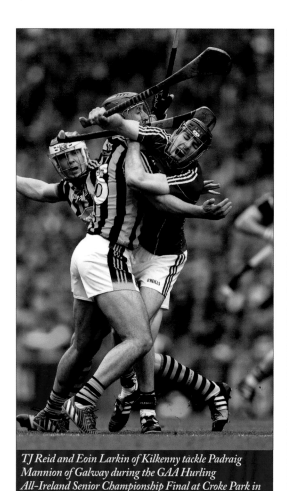

TJ Reid and Eoin Larkin of Kilkenny tackle Pádraig Mannion of Galway during the GAA Hurling All-Ireland Senior Championship Final at Croke Park in Dublin which Kilkenny won.
Photograph: Cathal Noonan/Inpho

reach during the first half and remains on course for the Hurler of the Year award.

His predecessor - if that is the case - Richie Hogan wasn't prominent but looked less than 100 per cent in the wake of quad injury speculation and was well marked by Daithi Burke. He still managed to conjure a couple of points to pay his way until being replaced on the hour.

Another injury concern, the veteran Eoin Larkin, belied fears that a broken thumb would inhibit him by playing a very consistent role lying deep and winning hard ball as well as shooting a couple of useful points. The defence wasn't as assured as usual and was under pressure in the first half but once they tightened up

after the break they relentlessly kept the play bunched in the middle and away from the wings that Galway had effectively exploited in the first 35 minutes.

They also had their successes: Paul Murphy shut out Cathal Mannion and captain Joey Holden rounded off a first season as the team's new full back by riding out a first half during which Joe Canning was leading the charge with three points from play plus a handful of frees and benefiting from the defence's tighter structure in the second period.

Canning relived the nightmare from 2012 and became largely anonymous apart from a goal scored from a free in injury-time by which stage it was purely a statistical detail.

Pádraig Walsh and especially Cillian Buckley have had more compelling displays but Walsh played effectively on Jonathan Glynn and polished off a loose clearance to put Kilkenny five ahead in the final five minutes.

As a collective their improved display turned the match and although Galway's response was profoundly disappointing for their revved-up supporters, already celebrating after the minor victory, Kilkenny take a share of the credit for so successfully redefining the terms of engagement.

When the match was a contest Galway were impressive. Physically assertive and calm in the face of the adversity of the 13th-minute goal - when the otherwise steady John Hanbury missed a ball and Walter Walsh slipped past him to set up Reid - they pressed and pressed.

If the shooting from play wasn't impeccable they did convert all of their frees between Canning's four and three huge strikes from distances of over 80 metres by Jason Flynn.

Their liveliness in play also brought scores from Conor Whelan, Flynn and Canning. Kilkenny looked flat and Walsh under-hit a straightforward chance into Colm Callanan.

Galway had a brush with serious adversity when Johnny Coen - the most jittery of the defence, who had hit a couple of clearances straight back to Kilkenny players and then had the misfortune to spoon a dropping ball over his own bar - swung Colin Fennelly to the ground by the neck.

Referee James Owens showed a yellow card but there could have been no complaints about red.

The second half began with Kilkenny three behind but they had that remedied within eight minutes with points from Conor Fogarty and a couple of placed balls by Reid. An indication of how toothless the Galway threat rapidly became was that their forwards managed one point from play.

Replacement wing back David Collins, having come on for Aidan Harte who was being troubled in the air shot two from play.

Kilkenny continued to turn the screw. Their appetite for the fray was seen in a succession of rucks and skirmishes, which they invariably won. They were also clinical with chances - just two wides in the second half and scores from play by seven of their front eight. Galway lost shape and their play became aimless. Hit-and-hope deliveries fell harmlessly for waiting defenders and only the teenager Conor Whelan up front took the fight to Kilkenny. He was rewarded with a point, confirmed by Hawk-Eye, but too often he was surrounded and un-supported on the ball.

David Burke at centrefield worked hard and used the ball well but the disintegration of the team's high-tempo play left him isolated in the face of Kilkenny's integrated patterns and the complementary play of their pairing in the middle, the increasingly influential Michael Fennelly and his gate-keeper partner Conor Fogarty.

Any chance Galway might generate late excitement evaporated with a succession of wides, starting with a Canning free - that could have reduced the margin to two in the 62nd minute but instead was immediately followed by a Colin Fennelly point for a two-point turnaround - after which Whelan, Greg Lally and Conor Cooney also missed.

Richie Power made a welcome re-appearance after a year out and showed a couple of touches of quality.

Ultimately though it was business as usual for the most successful collective in the history of the game. Implaccable and unstoppable.

My father's famous last words

MICK HEANEY

In his book Without Feathers Woody Allen has a line that has become one of his most famous quips: "It's not that I'm afraid to die, I just don't want to be there when it happens." Like all the best humour, the joke is accompanied by a sense of recognition.

It is almost an article of faith for people to say that, far from fearing death, they are reconciled to it. But Allen's joke hits on an uncomfortable truth. Death is rarely a straightforward business. For all we know that we must depart this life, we rarely contemplate the way in which we might go.

For Allen, on the other hand, it's not just the possibility of oblivion that worries him. He implicitly acknowledges that, before we go, we may have to experience moments – or perhaps years – that are deeply unpleasant, distressing or painful.

Allen has spent much of his career talking about death, or at least joking about it. The rest of us avoid talking about the prospect and process of dying until it is unavoidable. Our natural inclination is to focus on the positive, in conversation at least. Going by my own experience of bereavement, we are not keen to talk openly about dying.

This is where literature normally comes in. The written word, like any great art, can allow us to process complex or difficult subjects, illuminating truths in a way no other field of endeavour can do. As Noam Chomsky has said, we can "learn more about human life and personality from novels than from scientific psychology". You could say the same about poetry, autobiography or, possibly, the short phrase that essentially constituted the last words of my father, Seamus Heaney.

As I know from his case, when writers are confronted

Seamus Heaney by Felix Clay/eyevine

with the probability of death they can come up with a memorable valediction. In his instance it was two words in Latin, Noli timere, which translate as "Don't be afraid".

A week before my father wrote the phrase it was unthinkable that he would be in such a position. Far from being poorly, he had been out for dinner with a close friend, only to stumble on steps as he left the restaurant. He hit his head and was taken to hospital, where he was kept for observation. When his temperature remained stubbornly high the doctors decided that he should stay on while they figured out what was wrong.

There was no hint of what was to come. When I first visited him at St Vincent's hospital, in Dublin, he was in good form, catching up on his reading and chatting with nurses and doctors. If he was uneasy he didn't say it to me. Nor I to him.

But I was more worried than I admitted, even to myself. That night I woke up with a jolt after dreaming that I had received a phone call with bad news. I don't believe that this was an omen, but it brought my anxiety into sharp relief.

Until then the body of literature dealing with the experience of death had held little interest for me. But I was aware of a small but high-profile body of work on the subject, most notably Joan Didion's two heart-rending volumes of memoir: The Year of Magical Thinking, from 2005, about the death of her husband, John Gregory Dunne; and Blue Nights, her unwanted companion volume from 2011, about the passing of her daughter, Quintana.

Both books were acclaimed, and both were bestsellers; The Year of Magical Thinking was even turned into a Broadway play.

In the developed world, modern medicine has allowed us live longer, and has also given us more time to die. As the writer and surgeon Atul Gawande notes in his brilliant but uncomfortable book Being Mortal, "dying was typically a more precipitous process" in the past.

Today, longer end-of-life scenarios have also given rise to another subgenre, which can be crudely termed the terminal-illness memoir. These often remarkable pieces of testament carry the force of first-hand experience. In their writings about having cancer, the journalists John Diamond and Christopher Hitchens deal with the fact of their mortality even as their lives go into a tailspin.

After being diagnosed with throat cancer in 1997, Diamond began a candid newspaper diary about his illness, which he continued long after he had lost the power of speech – nearly until his death, in 2001. The uncertain but deeply human tone of his writing is summed up by the subtitle of his book on the subject, C: Because Cowards Get Cancer Too.

The habitually pugnacious Hitchens was, unsurprisingly, more robust in raging against the dying of the light. In his posthumous volume Mortality he is unwavering in his atheism, frank about his suffering and blackly comic in his observations: "When you fall ill, people send you CDs. Very often these are by Leonard Cohen."

Although Hitchens approaches his death with characteristic defiance, the portrait he paints is not a hopeful one. Still, like Diamond's, his account has an unvarnished quality that reminds us that we have to deal with the inescapable fact of death as best we can. For better or worse, Hitchens and Diamond had the time to reflect on their fate. My father, on the other hand, learned the seriousness of his condition only two days before his death. After being told that the doctors had detected a "split aorta", we didn't discuss the implications at any great length. But Dad soberly admitted that the diagnosis was "quite serious".

When it became clear that he'd have to undergo a risky operation I still danced around using the word "death" when talking to him, much less muse on the possibility that he might not survive.

On my last evening with him, just before he was transferred to Blackrock Clinic, I spoke to him about pretty much anything except what was about to happen, making lame jokes to distract from the almost unreal air that prevailed. I hugged him as I left – not our usual farewell – but tried not to think about the possible finality of the gesture.

If we avoid such thoughts it may be down to losing our sense of death as the one certain fact of life. Since Edward Jenner discovered vaccination our attitude to death has slowly changed. Once an ever-present, seemingly random threat, it is now regarded almost as a preventable accident. Its presence in our culture, at least as a fact of everyday life, has lessened.

In fact, one of the best books to deal with death as a natural event is for children. In EB White's classic Charlotte's Web the eponymous spider helps a pig escape the abattoir even as her own life cycle draws to a close. As a way of gently introducing children to the concept of loss Charlotte's Web is without parallel.

But for a novel with an unflinching eye for how we now die Philip Roth's 2006 novel Everyman stands out. Roth follows his nameless protagonist's brushes with death down the years, which inevitably grow closer and more frequent with the passage of time. His is a bleak outlook. As his ailments grow everything else is dwarfed, as "eluding death seemed to have become the central business of his life and bodily decay his entire story".

Roth's descriptions of getting older have a bracing honesty, as does his dread of dying. Ultimately, however, the tone is one of irredeemable despair. As an example of the artist's duty to be true to oneself Everyman is peerless. Those seeking solace at a difficult time might want to look elsewhere, however. Roth discounts the sense that death is anything other than a void to be feared. But while death is obviously not something that writers embrace any more than anyone else does, its imminence can concentrate the mind, with remarkable results.

When the gifted English historian Tony Judt was struck with amyotrophic lateral sclerosis, in 2008, it left him a quadriplegic, but, if anything, sharpened his formidable intellect.

Unable to move, Judt spent his sleepless nights scrolling through his life and ideas as a survival method, composing startling essays that he memorised using the titular mnemonic device of his posthumous collection, The Memory Chalet.

Judt is forthright about what he is enduring and about what will soon follow. "Loss is loss, and nothing is gained by calling it by a nicer name. My nights are intriguing; but I could do without them."

Writing about his fate with such candour only adds to the impact, however. Producing such astonishing work in such grim circumstances is, almost despite itself, a life-affirming action.

Similarly, the Australian writer and broadcaster Clive James has been slowly dying from serious illness for the past five years. Rather than fade away James has been determined to go out in a spectacular blaze, writing at a prodigious rate.

It is in his poetry, James's first love, that he has most evocatively dealt with his slow demise. His verse on the theme, collected in Sentenced to Life, are elegiac while bluntly acknowledging that his time is nearly up.

His haunting poem Japanese Maple was an internet sensation after it was published in the New Yorker. Counterpointing the vibrancy of the tree's colours with James's own waning energy, it is full of longing for "a world that shone / So brightly at the last, and then was gone". It is heartbreakingly honest while avoiding Roth's forlorn tone.

This is the kind of wisdom that we look to writers for. And I still wonder what my father might have written had he more time to contemplate his fate.

Instead the end was quick. On the morning of the operation my father sent a text to my mother that ended with the instruction Noli timere. This wasn't as portentous as it seems: he frequently used Latin as conversational shorthand. My mother forwarded me the text when she received it; I only spotted it when she phoned to tell me to get to the hospital. He had died on his way to surgery, shortly after composing the message.

We were devastated, but we seized on his final words as a kind of lifebuoy. It seemed to us that he had encapsulated the swirl of emotion, uncertainty and fear he was facing at the end, and articulated it in a restrained yet inspiring way.

These last words went viral after I read them at the funeral. In the weeks that followed they were parsed in articles and used as a shorthand for hope, most notably in Maser's giant graffito, in English, on South Richmond Street in Dublin.

My father had done what writers do best: boiled down our anxieties and fears in a way that makes sense. His words have certainly helped me since his death.

Likewise, Judt, James and Didion are shot through with the element that defines great art: they speak truths that the rest of us recognise but are unable to articulate.

As for whether even the greatest art can ever really equip us for our own death, we cannot know the answer until too late. But at least these writers have left us a glimpse of what may lie ahead.

SEPTEMBER 12TH 2015

An unwritten experience

Róisín Ingle

If people say one thing and ask one question about the personal column I've been writing in these pages for nearly 15 years it is this: "You are so honest but is there anything you would never write about?"

When they ask me, I tell them the truth. Of course there is. There are Somethings I wouldn't write about. Plenty of Things. Numerous and various Experiences. But it's the same one Experience that always comes to my mind when anyone asks that question. And instead of being honest about the Experience, I tell them "I have my secrets" and flash what I hope is an enigmatic smile. In terms of shutting down this particular line of enquiry, I've found it works a treat.

Róisín Ingle at a meeting of the new Irish Times woman's podcast team. *Photograph: Brenda Fitzsimons*

Many times over the years I've stopped myself writing about this Experience. And every time I've asked myself why. Was I ashamed of it? No. Was I embarrassed? Not at all. Did I feel I'd done something wrong? Quite the opposite. What I had done was the right decision for me.

I was stopping myself from writing about the Experience because of what other people might think. Which, when I thought about it, was completely against the spirit of my column.

When I came to write the introduction to my new book of columns, I found myself wanting to write about the thing I've never written about. This unwritten Experience. I thought long and hard about it and I felt it was the right thing to do.

My Experience is not something strange or unique or uncommon. It is something many other women in Ireland and around the world can relate to: I had an abortion. I am glad I did.

You might want to ask why I would write about it, why now, and that is a good question for a few reasons. There are people who are violently opposed to this service ever being available to women in Ireland so you don't have to be a social scientist to know that when I write about my abortion, certain people will post letters and scriptures and pictures to me with the express purpose of hurting me or making me feel ashamed of myself. They will get in touch telling me how I and other women should live our lives and what choices we should make and what we should do with our wombs. So I want to say something to those people, just in case any of them are reading: I have done nothing wrong and you cannot hurt me and you cannot touch me. Ever. Like tens of thousands of women in Ireland and like hundreds of thousands of women around the world I am glad and relieved and not at all ashamed that I once had an abortion.

***

I had told my pro-choice mother about the abortion years earlier. When I told her that I planned to write about it now, she was very concerned that I would alienate people. She is supportive of me in my writing and in everything I do – I could not have written my column without her blessing over the years – but after

245

she read a first draft of this she said:

"I am worried. I worry that people who like you and like your column won't like you when you tell them you had an abortion."

I was upset about this at first. I didn't like the idea of censoring myself because I would risk losing readers. On the other hand, I could see where she was coming from. And it was something I had to consider.

Wherever you stand on the issue, I want to make it clear that I am not suggesting that what I did is the right course of action for every woman who finds themselves pregnant and doesn't want to be. I just passionately believe every woman in Ireland should be free to make that choice.

My abortion is part of my story, part of who I am. But it is just one part of my life: I was divorced. I have two children. I am messy and domestically challenged. I have a tendency to lose things. I like chips. (Probably too much.) I cry easily.

I had an abortion.

* * *

Back to that question. Why write about it now? Well. There are more than 100,000 reasons. Since 1980, more than 150,000 women have left Ireland, mostly for England, to get abortions. I feel a sense of solidarity with these women, a feeling that began building up many years before my own Experience, a feeling that is stronger than ever now. I think it's wrong that these women were not able to access abortion in their own country. It is estimated that 12 women leave Ireland every day to get terminations in other countries. I want to stand up in solidarity with them and be counted.

I was a very late developer when it came to solidarity with women who had abortions. It took me a good while to catch on. In my defence I was only 12 when the Eighth Amendment to the Constitution was introduced in 1983.

Abortion was already illegal, and had been since 1861, but this change meant that "the right to life of the unborn would be equal" to a mother's right to life. I look back now to try and figure out what I was at when I was 12. I see that Red, Red, Wine by UB40

was number one when the referendum was passed. I remember every word of that song. But I don't remember anything about the referendum.

By the age of 20, I was living in a squat in Birmingham, England and not at all engaged with the X Case, where a 14-year-old girl who had been raped and was suicidal was dragged through the courts to get access to an abortion. They eventually ruled that she could have one as her life was threatened. The girl went on to have a miscarriage.

It wasn't until I was in my 20s and married and back in Ireland that I started to understand and form a definite view on abortion: I was pro-choice. At that point, I didn't know what it would feel like to be pregnant when you didn't want to be. I just knew I could never judge another woman for her choice.

Around 15 years ago, when I was in my late 20s, I became one of those women when I got pregnant and didn't want to be.

It happened before I started writing my column. It happened before I met the man who would become the father of my children. It happened after my previous relationship, a five-year marriage, had broken up.

I was flailing around in self-loathing mode. Going out too much. Drinking too much. It happened one night. I should have been more careful. He should have been more careful. I didn't think it would ever happen to me. And then it did.

I took a pregnancy test. It gave me the wrong answer. The one I didn't want to see. I was not in a relationship. I did not want a baby but I did know exactly what I wanted to do. I knew my own mind. I knew what was good for me. Even if my country doesn't think women know their own minds or think we know what is best for ourselves. We trust ourselves even if that trust is not reciprocated by the laws of the land.

I rang my friend, an older woman, someone I knew I could count on for support. I went to a counselling meeting where I pretended to weigh up all my options when of course there was only one option. For me. There was only one option. Not for you. Or for anybody else because I can't speak for anyone else.

Exuberance among the Cork camogie players after their defeat of Galway to win the O'Duffy Cup in the Liberty Insurance Senior Camogie Championship Final at Croke Park in Dublin.   Photograph: Ryan Byrne/Inpho

But for me. This was the right thing to do.

I knew what had to happen next. Meeting the man in a cafe to explain how much going to England would cost, including the flights and a night in a hotel. We divvied up the damage between us. This is not a sad story. I was lucky. Think of the women scrabbling the money together on their own. Taking loans out. Afraid to tell the person who was 50 per cent responsible. Or when they do tell them, being told to sort it out themselves. Borrowing money, pretending it's for something else.

In my case he was a civilised, respectable, accountable person. He didn't want a baby either. He wasn't ready emotionally or psychologically or financially for a baby either. We agreed on that. He gave me the cash, all those notes, and I took the thick wad over the table in Bewley's in Westmoreland Street as though it were an illegal transaction. And in a way it was. The Eighth Amendment makes "criminals" of women in Ireland and packs us off to commit our "crimes" in other countries.

I didn't want to go on my own and my friend said she would come with me. I booked the clinic. There was no faltering. No indecision. I went to sleep that night relieved and unburdened. It was over. My life could carry on the way it was before. I was going to try to be more careful in future.

When I did get pregnant years later I knew I was ready. I knew what was right for me at that time was to carry on with the pregnancy to a hopefully happy conclusion. But having a baby that first time would not have been best for me. I have not had one scrap of regret or shame about what I did.

Nobody, and I mean nobody, wakes up one day and thinks: "Great, I can't wait. This is the day I have an abortion!" But it is a choice many of us make, and it's the right choice for many of us. People take the pill and the morning-after pill and they use condoms in order to exercise their reproductive rights, in order to control whether or not they get pregnant or make a woman pregnant.

When I became pregnant I had to make a decision about having a child or not having a child at that time. Individuals and couples make these decisions every day. It is our right as human beings in the world. Why am I writing this? Because I want to be a part, however small, of the campaign to change abortion legislation in this country. Because if my daughters ever come to me and say they are pregnant when they don't want to be, I don't want them to have to get a boat or a train or a plane. I want to mind them at home where I can put my arms around them and give them a hot water bottle. I want to support and love and care for them every step of the way. I want to respect their choice. I want them to have a choice. Because most countries in Europe give women that choice. Just not the one in which I live.

I know there are some women who regret their decisions to have abortions and I understand that must be a terrible pain to carry in their lives. But I also know it has been the right choice for thousands upon thousands of women in Ireland who I hope will not be silenced any longer. Who will, when the time comes, say "me too" even though that's one of the most difficult "me toos" an Irishwoman can utter. Who, as the campaign to repeal the Eighth Amendment gathers pace, will tell their families and close friends about how their terminations were a relief and how they would do it again given the same circumstances. They can do so anonymously as women have been doing on shareyourabortionstory.tumblr.com. To read these stories is to see that the women who have abortions are every kind of Irishwoman.

Everywoman. The employed and the unemployed. Women who have children and women who don't. Teachers and doctors. TDs and factory workers. Teenagers and thirty-somethings. Writers and TV presenters. Students and immigrants. Authors and barristers. They are our mothers and sisters. Our daughters and wives. They are not criminals. We are not criminals.

I know not everyone who reads this will agree. I also know my mother is right when she says I might lose

or alienate readers now that I have "come out" about my abortion. But sometimes in life you have to step up. In my life this is one of those times.

SEPTEMBER 15TH 2015

'It will not work out!' One family's arduous, terrifying journey from Damascus to Bavaria

Michael Jansen

"The journey began on 9/11 and ended on 11/9," said Jamil with a wry smile. A smuggler driver, contacted weeks earlier, rang on September 10th last year and asked, "Are you ready?"

"When?" Jamil demanded.

"Tomorrow."

They prepared their bags and said goodbye to their father and friends near St Thomas's Gate in Damascus's Old City. Jamil (32), his mother Leila (51) and sisters Lora (27) and Carla (21), hefted 25kg backpacks into the minibus and joined another nine Palestinians, several of whom had also fled the Yarmouk camp south of Damascus, which was overrun by al-Qaeda-linked Jabhat al-Nusra fighters in December 2012.

When the minibus paused at the first Syrian army checkpoint at Harasta, they claimed they were going to visit relatives in the Palestinian camp near Aleppo, even though those on duty knew "we were fleeing", says Jamil.

At Salamiya, the men had to present military cards showing they were not draft dodgers. Small bribes were paid in Syrian lira and cigarettes as they progressed from checkpoint to checkpoint.

Jamil explains: "When we reached Aleppo, we said we were going to Ain Arab [Kobani, on the Turkish

Distressed children are caught in the mêlée as Macedonian special forces police near the southern city of Gevgelija try to prevent refugees who have travelled through Greece enter the country for onward passage to Germany.
Photograph: Georgi Licovski/European Picture Agency

border]." As they drove through a wide belt of dead land between the army and Islamic State (IS), the three women put on black cloaks, headcoverings and double veils.

At al-Mahdoumeh (a word that means "destroyed"), a giant man in Afghan dress instructed them to call it Maamourah ("rebuilt").

At Jarabulus, after they changed to a second minibus for the journey to the border, they were left on the roadside until the driver checked out the situation.

"He came back and said the US was bombing so he took us to his place where his wife offered us food. It was an old house with a toilet outside. We had to hurry into the house when we heard the roar of a passing motorbike." They thought it might carry IS spies.

"If there was nothing the next day they would take us back to Damascus," says Jamil. They slept the night at the village.

Early in the morning another minibus was to take them to the border. Driving through IS territory, they noticed that traffic roundabouts, schools and even the court were "all black and white" – the colours adopted by IS and Nusra.

"A school was named after Osama bin Laden," Jamil says. "There were only men in the streets."

They passed through Nusra and government-held territory to an IS-controlled area where severed heads had been planted on stakes at a checkpoint. "Thank God, my mother and sisters could not see through their veils," says Jamil.

Outside IS territory, the women lifted the veils but kept on head coverings and cloaks. After Bab al-Salameh, a red-painted urban bus landed them in an olive grove near the Turkish border where there were sand berms, coils of razor wire, Turkish sentries every 100m and troops patrolling in Cobra armoured vehicles.

"They took us to another place and told us to run... We scaled the sand mounds, crept through a hole

As the crisis worsened, Hungary tried to seal its border with Serbia by threading razor wire along its frontier and patrolling it with helicopters, soldiers, mounted police and dogs. Seeking to evade detection, many Syrian refugees simply lifted the wire and crawled under.   Photograph: Bernadett Szabo/Reuters

in the wire and entered a trench where Carla was trapped by her backpack.

A Turkish soldier pushed the barrel of his rifle into Jamil's chest and ordered them to go back. "We waited another three or four hours to find a new place."

As the sun set, they crossed the border at Bab al-Salameh, running through trenches until they reached a Turkish village. Another minibus took them to Kilis where they caught a public bus to Ankara and another to Izmir where they stayed in a hotel in the Basmaneh quarter, a smugglers' base. The family shifted from Izmir to Bodrum to Didim and back at the pleasure of a smuggler boss they never saw.

"We only heard his voice," says Jamil. The family dealt with Syrian intermediaries.

Life jackets were bought but discarded so they could wear tyre tubes. Two backpacks were left with a clerk

at the hotel. They waited at a place "in the middle of nowhere", near the shore. "The waves were too high that night so we stayed there." In the morning they were told to walk in a line to the coast where there awaited a rubber boat, 6m-long and 2m-wide – the cheapest option.

"It could hold 27 people but we were 42. When we started we could see our destination" – the Greek island of Farmakonisi. "The engine stopped, water poured into the boat, some men jumped overboard, others bailed."

The Turkish coast guard rescued them and took them ashore where they were fingerprinted. They gave false names to the police and were told to go. Their identity documents were not checked; smugglers and police colluded.

A second rubber boat also sank after two minutes,

with 45 people on board. The captain shouted, "It will not work out, not work out!" before he and another man plunged into the water. Jamil and his family reached shore and walked for more than an hour before they found a supermarket and called a taxi.

A third rubber boat, was larger and equipped with a Yamaha engine.

"After 40 minutes we reached the territorial waters of Greece. We all shouted, 'Allahu Akhbar! We are in Greece now!' We proceeded towards the island by the light of a red-orange moon. Passengers slashed the rubber boat so it could not return them to Turkey and the Greek coast guard picked us up from the water some distance from the shore."

Jamil adds: "My mother is afraid of water and had a life vest and a ring to keep her afloat. She held above her head a plastic bag holding shawls to keep her children warm once we arrived."

At a military base on the island there was a German officer who called for German speakers among the Greeks. Jamil kept still as he was not fluent in German. The refugees slept in a "stinking" barracks without food or water and in the morning went to Leros, where they stayed the day, presented their identity papers and recuperated.

At the police station they were given an "expulsion order", which allowed them to spend just six months in Greece, Jamil says. This hung over their heads like the sword of Damocles while they were in that country.

The new arrivals were put on one ferry then another that carried them from Leros via another island to Pireaus, from where they travelled to Athens. They lodged in a hotel in the Acharnon neighbourhood, another smugglers' haunt. Jamil says the family intended to stay there until they could find a reliable smuggler and, hopefully, a reasonably safe route to Germany. It was a tense and difficult time: they feared their money would run out and they would not succeed in their quest before they would be deported. During their stay, they visited the Acropolis and met friends and relatives also seeking asylum in Europe. They encountered few Greeks – some cautious,

some friendly – as the area where they stayed "was full of foreigners from India, Pakistan, China, Sudan, and other countries who were running their own businesses there," Jamil says.

Ultimately, they decided on returning to the sea route for the first part of the journey, even though their experiences with the Mediterranean had been traumatic.

"The reason we chose to take the ferry to Venice is that the land routes through the Balkans were shut by both Macedonia and Albania, who detained and imprisoned many people we know. So we could not risk it and decided to wait and find a safer way out."

They set off from Athens to Patras where they took a ferry to Venice, spent the night there and then boarded a public bus to the German border, crossing without being checked by immigration.

They were collected by a minibus with Bulgarian plates but, after travelling on to Munich, the vehicle was intercepted by German police and taken to a police station near Nuremberg. But their journey's end was near. After two weeks in the asylum processing system, they were taken to a village in Bavaria where they were given a well-furnished two-bedroom flat.

The journey had cost $30,000 – the family's entire savings – including $11,000 meant to fund Jamil's expenses at a British university where he had a scholarship for graduate study.

Part II of Michael Jansen's report was published on September 16th

Jamil and his family arrived in Munich at night, jaded in body and confused in spirit.

"We had mixed feelings," he says. "We could not believe we reached our destination. We had been on our way for two months.

"We celebrated when we reached Turkey from Syria and Greece from Turkey. But when we reached Germany we were happy but not really happy. We understood we were entering another stage in our lives. We celebrated but it was not a pure celebration."

The image that shocked and galvanised public opinion: the body of three-year-old Aylan Kurdi lies washed up on Ali Hoca Point beach near Bodrum in Turkey. Aylan came from Kobani, a town in northern Syria close to the border with Turkey but no longer under the control of the Syrian authorities in Damascus. Instead, Kobani has been the subject of intense fighting between so-called Islamic State insurgents, the Free Syrian Army and Kurdish forces known as People's Protection Units.

It was from this fighting that Aylan's family fled – father Abdullah, mother Rehan, five-year-old brother Galip and Aylan – into Turkey, hoping to get eventually to relatives in Canada . They paid smugglers for an inflatable boat to take them from Bodrum to the Greek island of Kos but it sank and Rehan and her two boys drowned.
Photograph: Nilufer Demir/Reuters

Jamil (32), his mother Laila (51), and sisters Lora (27) and Carla (21), spent two months travellingtravelled by land and sea from Damascus to Bavaria – negotiating sinkings and smugglers, fear and exhaustion. They slept the night in Munich and were collected the next morning by a driver in a minivan with Bulgarian number plates and proceeded towards Berlin.

"He was a regular guy," said Jamil (32). The family had freed themselves from the grip of smugglers but the minivan they hired had plates from a country known for smuggling networks.

Near Nuremberg a police car directed them to the side of the road, the patrolman checked their papers and led them to a station where they were finger-printed and sent on to Zirndorf to have chest X-rays and blood tests.

From there they were taken by the authorities to a reception centre at Fürth. The family was assigned a cubicle enclosed with blankets in a large exhibition hall already hosting Albanians, Kosovars, Serbians, Ukrainians, some Syrians and Palestinians from home ground in the UN-run camp in the Yarmouk district of Damascus.

After 15 days, the family was taken to a Nuremberg flat shared with two other families, one from Serbia and the other from Ukraine. Each family of four had a room with three beds. Communication with the Serbs was possible because the boys understood a little English, but not with the Ukrainians, who knew none.

After six days, Jamil's family was moved to the apartment they now occupy. "It was a big relief to be private, in our own flat," he says. Their neighbours are Ukrainians, Russians, Azeris and a Syrian who is in Turkey trying to bring his family to Germany. Communication is limited to friendly nods and hellos.

I had not seen Jamil since the spring of 2014 in Damascus and found him thinner, the bones of his face prominent, when he met me at the railway station in a small town.

We took a taxi to his family's new home in a classy "dorp" or hamlet with handsome houses painted in pastel pink, green and yellow and set in flower gardens.

We slipped off our shoes when we entered the flat, as is the custom in Arab – and many German – homes. From a small shelf in the dining room hung the snakelike tube of a "shisha" (waterpipe) mended with scotch tape. The glass bowl and apparatus stood by the dining table. I settled into one of the two bedrooms.

In proud possession of German refugee passports allowing them to travel within the European Union without visas, Leila and Lora had gone to the Netherlands to visit relatives whom they had not seen for years. Syrian refugee documents get them nowhere.

Carla had cooked a dish of macaroni-cheese layered with meat and prepared spiced plates of hummus, for a taste of home. "You know, Carla and my mother cooked when [the al-Qaeda linked Jabhat] al-Nusra and the Free Army took over Yarmouk from the Palestinian defenders [December 16th, 2012]. There was celebratory shooting but they fried potatoes." The next day Leila and Carla walked out of Yarmouk in a vast stream of humanity fleeing the war.

"Lora and I found them by accident on the way and took them to a hotel at St Thomas Gate [in the Old City]," says Jamil. "My father [Ahmad] stayed for another two months." After he left, their house was looted and destroyed. Possessions they rescued are now in Germany, sent on in huge suitcases via Beirut by Ahmad, who plans to apply for family reunion.

Jamil received his German refugee passport a week ago – his German is fluent; his scholarship awarded for a British university has followed him to Germany and he will begin a master's course in Berlin next month. His mother and sisters will sit the first German exam next week and begin the integration course. Lora, a Damascus-trained architect, has been offered a job at an architect's office.

Having lost three years at university due to the war, Carla is looking for a course in economics. They plan to follow Jamil to Berlin once he finds accommodation. "The university has offered me a buddy to help me settle in," he said proudly.

Europe is a truly foreign land for Leila, who did not want to leave Syria and is likely to find adjusting to a new life difficult. People she meets in the street make her feel uncomfortable over the headscarf she wears.

Her roots are deep in Damascus but she uprooted herself, faced death, injury and trauma on the journey from Syria to Germany to give her children security and a future.

Over the past few months, Jamil has volunteered as an Arabic-German translator at a refugee centre located at a school gymnasium in the nearby town.

When we visited, there were several Syrian couples with small children as well as Palestinians from the violent Ain al-Hilweh camp in Lebanon.

They were set to move to flats on the weekend and 100 Syrian and Iraqi men were due to arrive. Camp beds had been set up for them.

Refugees come and go.

SEPTEMBER 21ST 2015

Dublin show their true grit as Kerry forwards fail to spark

Seán Moran

Dublin 0-12 Kerry 0-9

Croke Park surfed the blue wave, as Dublin celebrated an All-Ireland victory as sweet as it was unsightly. Undermined by the torrential rain, which together with a nervousness that appeared to afflict both teams led to a high error count, it was the lowest scoring in 12 years with few players able to give of their best.

Although Dublin were clearly the better team they didn't manage to translate that onto the scoreboard and ended up under the additional downpour of dropping ball, as Kerry frantically threw everything at securing the late goal that might have turned the match on its head.

Video review suggests that Rory O'Carroll was lucky not to concede a penalty in the 70th minute when appearing to pull down Kieran Donaghy, as a ball dropped into the Dublin square.

The win was sweet because it was the first time Dublin have beaten Kerry in three successive championship encounters (after 2011 and '13) and two successive final contests.

Furthermore Jim Gavin's team have been living on the edge since losing their 2013 crown to Donegal last year and they went into the final under the shadow of suggestions that they'd lost their nerve and would struggle. They must have been among the most questioned bookies' favourites going into a final.

In the end the disappointment was far more profound for Kerry, who never performed - as acknowledged by manager Eamonn Fitzmaurice. Their highly regarded attack never got traction (literally, on the ice-rink surface) and were well contained by Dublin's defence. More disastrously - especially on a day when Stephen Cluxton's kick-out yips intensified - their centerfield of David Moran and Anthony Maher, by consensus the best in the country, malfunctioned and was outplayed by Dublin's less heralded unit of Denis Bastic, Michael Darragh Macauley and especially newcomer Brian Fenton, whose movement and hard work were invaluable on such an awful afternoon.

Fifteen seconds into his first All-Ireland final he kicked a point and hit the post with a goal attempt in the 47th minute.

In fact although Cluxton had a nightmare with kick-outs - pressurised by Kerry and unable to take his customary quick re-starts - Dublin's statistics were better than Kerry's with just seven out of 19 lost compared with 10 from 24.

This was an impressively gritty performance from Dublin because they must have known as the chances went a-begging in the second half - 10 wides - that they were leaving themselves very vulnerable going into the last 10 minutes but they continually pressed,

Dean Rock of Dublin and Stephen O'Brien of Kerry tussle for the ball during the GAA football All-Ireland Senior Championship Final at Croke Park in Dublin which Dublin won.   Photograph: Donall Farmer/Inpho.

undaunted by the growing apprehension beginning to grip the blue hordes.

They worked hard though. Diarmuid Connolly, Paul Flynn and Ciarán Kilkenny were well on top of the Kerry half backs and maintained the pressure regardless of the setbacks.

Their composure shone through in the two last points, stretching the lead to three and four points. The first saw Paul Flynn, industrious and reliable after a difficult season, start and finish the move with a great ball to Fenton and super support work to complete the 1-2 and score.

The second represented a four-point turnaround.

Kieran Donaghy had been introduced in the 50th minute and the dropped Kerry captain caused difficulty for Dublin even if his presence as usual appeared to encourage Kerry to treat him as a new Plan A rather than an optional Plan B.

Aside from the penalty claim, Donaghy set up Killian Young, breaking from the back, for a one-on-one goal chance in the 67th minute but the wing back

slipped and lost the ball. James McCarthy intervened to clear and within seconds Alan Brogan, just in as a replacement, was advancing down the left wing weighing up options left and right like a quarter-back. Having held on in the face of a retreating defence he decided to go for the point himself and flighted over a vital score - a four-point turnaround in less than a minute.

Dublin's defence was the bulwark of the victory. The spine of O'Carroll and Cian O'Sullivan, who overcame his hamstring injury, was secure although Paul Geaney started well and kicked two from play in the first 26 minutes. O'Carroll though commanded his square well.

O'Sullivan organised the backs with the usual authority although Kerry didn't test his mobility until bringing on Darran O'Sullivan in the second half, which prompted a switch with Jack McCaffrey.

James O'Donoghue kicked three points but was fading when replaced in the 61st minute although with the team needing a goal, his presence might

256

have been useful particularly as Colm Cooper was struggling.

Philip McMahon marked Cooper so comprehensively that he actually out-scored his much decorated opponent with a first-half point.

That was the last score before the break and concluded the most significant scoring sequence in the match, as the winners went from 0-4 each to an interval lead of 0-8 to 0-4: other scores from Bernard Brogan, snapping up a loose ball and firing over, Jack McCaffrey starting and finishing a move from his own defence and Paddy Andrews, again the most threatening of the full forwards, finishing a fine move by Bastic and Dean Rock with a run past Fionn Fitzgerald and point.

If they nearly won it in the second quarter, they nearly lost it in the third. The best goal chances came when Andrews caught, turned and fired just inches outside the post and then Fenton.

Kevin McManamon was on at the interval and ran hard at Kerry albeit without the usual return.

But the pressure told in the end, as history beckoned and Dublin followed.

Index